THE RESISTANCE, 1940

THE RESISTANCE, 1940

An Anthology of Writings from the French Underground

Edited and Translated by CHARLES POTTER

Louisiana State University Press
Baton Rouge

Published by Louisiana State University Press

Manufactured in the United States of America
LSU Press Paperback Original
First printing

DESIGNER: Mandy McDonald Scallan
TYPEFACE: Whitman
PRINTER AND BINDER: *McNaughton & Gunn, Inc.*

Library of Congress Cataloging-in-Publication Data

Names: Potter, Charles, 1944– editor of compilation.
Title: The Resistance, 1940 : an anthology of writings from the French underground / edited and translated by Charles Potter.
Other titles: Anthology of writings from the French underground
Description: Baton Rouge, LA : Louisiana State University Press, [2016] | Includes bibliographical references and index.
Identifiers: LCCN 2016026948| ISBN 978-0-8071-6392-4 (pbk. : alk. paper) | ISBN 978-0-8071-6393-1 (pdf) | ISBN 978-0-8071-6394-8 (epub) | ISBN 978-0-8071-6395-5 (mobi)
Subjects: LCSH: World War, 1939–1945—Underground movements—France—Biography. | Guerrillas—France—Biography. | World War, 1939–1945—Personal narratives, French.
Classification: LCC D802.F8 R3895 2016 | DDC 940.53/440922—dc23
LC record available at https://lccn.loc.gov/2016026948

The paper in this book meets the guidelines for permanence and durability of the Committee on Production Guidelines for Book Longevity of the Council on Library Resources. ♾

CONTENTS

ACKNOWLEDGMENTS

I wish to thank the many people who helped me to find these documents and to come to understand them better: Johnny Andarelli, a resister at age fourteen; Odile Barthélemy, of Editions Barthélemy in Avignon; Martine Bertea, Centre national de la recherche scientifique; Serge Blovac, son of the last blacksmith of Bonnieux, who was also a resister; Rachel Brooke at the Georges Borchardt Agency; Marion Colas at the Presses universitaires de France; Françoise d'Avout at Editions Gallimard; resisters Pierre Desorgues and Jacques Dodeman; Rand Dotson, at Louisiana State University Press; scholar and bookseller Marc Dumas; Jean-Patrick and Pierre-Michel Garcin; Jean-Marie Guillon, professor emeritus of history at the University of Aix-en-Provence; Stan Ivester and Catherine Kadair, for their patient and insightful editing of the text; Odile Riviere, curator at the excellent and ever-helpful Musée Jean Garcin, 39–45 L'Appel de la Liberté, Fontaine de Vaucluse; and Mireille Sidoine-Ardouy, the youngest resister of them all. My special thanks also go to acquisitions editor Alisa Plant, whose interest in the book was inspiring; to poet and scholar Peter Wilson; and certainly not least of all of these, to my wife and *editrix extraordinaire*, Helene Potter.

I also wish to thank the Institute for American Universities in Aix-en-Provence for giving me the opportunity to teach a course on history and media that led me to this subject in the first place. My starting thesis there was that human history begins with, and still stands or falls on, our ability to tell stories. My ultimate thanks, too, must go to my students, who listened to what I was discovering with enthusiasm. For them, here are four more great stories, in the words of the people who lived them.

THE RESISTANCE, 1940

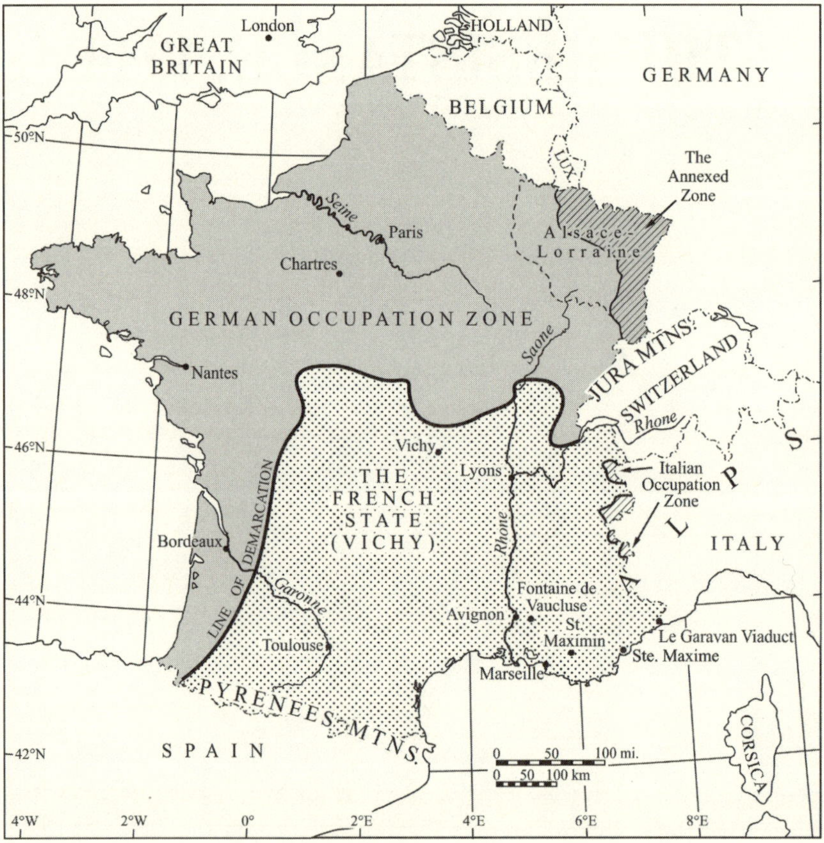

France in late 1940. (*Map by Mary Lee Eggart*)

Introduction

The French Resistance. The mere mention of it conjures up a clear if somber image: men and women in no-nonsense clothes, a raincoat and a dark fedora for him, plus perhaps a small pasteboard suitcase. For her a plain gingham dress and sober footwear. A sense of imminent danger. A lot goes unsaid. But something clearly went on, if in secret, and the legend has been intriguing enough to have spawned considerable scholarly debate, a vast literature, and quite a few films. One British television series that made a standing joke out of little more than exaggerating the stereotypes ran to eighty-five episodes over ten years. The Resistance has even made its way into popular American culture in vehicles as diverse as a *South Park* Christmas-special movie and several episodes of *Star Trek: Deep Space Nine*. The French have a made-for-TV series, *Un Village français*, that is now in its fifth season and is highly popular, with a demographic as wide as the country itself.

Equally as persistent, and about as widespread, is a notion that there were really only a few people who resisted the German occupation in 1940s France, and that many who said they were members of the Resistance in 1945 really were not. This argument has it that, at best, most had become resisters only after 1943 or 1944, when it was clear that the Germans would be defeated and that it no longer made sense to support the collaborationist regime in Vichy. On one hand we have the so-called Gaullist myth, that in their hearts the French people did not really collaborate, and that actual resistance was pervasive; on the other hand is the belief that this is largely feel-good hype.

Scholars have examined this all quite thoroughly, and it appears that there is truth on both sides of the debate. Some very distinguished Frenchmen served Vichy well before acquiring bona fide Resistance credentials. We need not get sidetracked with case histories, but Henri Frenay, whose early manifesto figures in this collection, is definitely one Frenchman who left Vichy early. Some worked for Vichy and the Resistance simultaneously. Others lied about having a role in the movement at all. The postwar authorities in France researched claims carefully, and I see no reason not to think that *most* of the 200,000 holders of the coveted "green card," the *carte du combattant volontaire de la Résistance*, truly earned the distinction. Moreover, as many of them attested, these men and women were often aided by acts of resistance on the part of others, ordinary citizens whose bravery often went unrecognized. And a number of very real resisters never asked for certification at all.

The most rewarding work on this subject seems to me that which seeks to assess the sentiments and goals of French men and women who lived through the period, carefully weighing the views of people who claim to have resisted as well as those who did not. I am thinking of work in English like H. R. Kedward's *Resistance in Vichy France: A Study of Ideas and Motivations* and Matthew Cobb's *Resistance.* Olivier Wieviorka's *Histoire de la Résistance* is the most recent contribution to a tradition of excellent studies of the subject in French, while Robert Gildea's *Fighters in the Shadows: A New History of the French Resistance* has just appeared as this collection goes to press. The present volume does not seek to replace this kind of analysis of motivations, but to supply anglophone students of the subject with documents that will help them to form opinions on their own. The texts presented here include a short book by a man who was arguably the first and incontestably France's most famous *résistant* (we will henceforth use the English word *resister*), and a scholarly article by a woman who was part of the Resistance from the very first hour: these two are Jean Moulin and Germaine Tillion. Both have been honored by the French people with a final resting place in their nation's Panthéon, an honorary burial site in Paris. Then there are two texts by soldiers who had served in the defeated French Army, one a call to resistance that was first drafted in the late summer of 1940, the other an excerpt from a memoir that was written years later, but which is remarkably clear on the progression of acts of engagement that led the writer to become a resister within a year of the Armistice: these are Henri Frenay and Jean Garcin.

The proportion of three men to one woman may actually be generous to women in the statistics of participation in the Resistance. The percentage of those deported for acts of resistance who were women can be fairly accurately calculated at 15 percent, according to the Centre d'histoire de la résistance et de la deportation in Lyon. It is impossible to know what their exact numbers were on the ground. Consequently, no claim for being comprehensive is being made here; there are many relevant documents available. One woman from the North, one man from the center, and one from the South, and a prefect who would unify them all: my goal has been to make available eyewitness accounts of how people decided to begin to break with the law of the land, and the rule of the military occupier, to adopt a clandestine existence, and to join with like-minded people in resistance. The ones included here all recommend themselves by their candor, as well as by their proven stature in the eyes of the French.

There can be no doubt that, to appreciate the range of political opinion in France in 1940, students might want to see a Communist among our authors. In the politics they represent, the four texts presented here do span a wide range of views, from Socialist to the traditional right. The French government at the time of its collapse and surrender to Germany was the last cabinet in what is known as the Third Republic. The extreme diversity of political views in France was already seen in the 1930s, and in subsequent studies such as William Shirer's magisterial *The Collapse of the Third Republic*, as being a weakness in itself.[1] As one former resister recently said to me, there were easily as many political parties in France as there were kinds of cheese. So we obviously cannot hope to offer a text for each one in the scope of a collection such as this. But the absence of a piece by a Communist is remarkable. Suffice it to say that I have not yet found a text from a self-declared Communist that meets the qualities found in the present foursome: a personal statement of commitment to engage in active struggle against the foreign power that occupied France, and/or resistance to the collaborationist French state known as Vichy. Of course negative information doesn't prove that such a text does not exist.

Some discussion of this absence seems warranted, however. The contribution of a variety of men and women who defined themselves as Communists to the Resistance was enormous. Many Communists, a distinguished proportion of the total number, whatever it might have been, were active in the Resistance from 1942 until the Liberation, and the sincerity of their commitment is not contested here. Communists both inside and outside the French Communist Party, or PCF,[2] had been staunch anti-fascists from the late 1920s onward. Statements of opposition to Hitler from French Communists could easily be found from *before* the war in France. The pact between the German Reich and the Soviets signed by von Ribbentrop and Molotov on August 23, 1939, caused great consternation and a reassessment in Communist thinking regarding

1. The Third Republic extended from 1870 until June 1940, when the collaborationist regime in Vichy abrogated its constitution. Anyone unfamiliar with the events of 1930s France, in particular the attempted coup by right-wing fascist and royalist groups in February 1934 and the election in 1936 of a left-wing coalition called the Front populaire (Popular Front), could do no better than consult Shirer's book.

2. Parti communiste français. (See glossary.)

opposition to Germany, at least within the PCF, which decided to continue to align itself with Moscow. Its newspaper, *l'Humanité*, was shut down on August 27. The party itself would be dissolved by official fiat one month later. French Communists of all stripes spent the nine months of the so-called Phoney War (*la drôle de guerre*)[3] somewhat in disarray. The party chiefs scattered—Maurice Thorez ultimately to Moscow, Jacques Duclos to Brussels. And then, irony of ironies, with the German invasion, they became quasi-legitimate again. Still largely underground, they even petitioned the German authorities to allow their press to reopen. And they began to engage in labor disputes in what was now occupied France.

We might have elected to include the article "Les Communistes accusent" from June 19, 1940, in the party's paper, *l'Humanité* (which by then had reopened its doors), or the "Appel du 10 juillet" (1940) by party chiefs Thorez and Duclos, but neither corresponds to the personal statements of engagement that we are looking at here. The earliest of our texts, Jean Moulin's short book *First Fight*, doesn't yet talk about organizing for clandestine struggle against the occupier, but it does in fact describe his refusal to obey his own government's call to leave his post. This is the duly elected Third Republic government under Paul Reynaud, whose order to fall back to the South he chooses to ignore. And when the Germans ask him to do something he deems unprofessional and against his convictions, he realizes that he must refuse them as well. When they begin to coerce him physically, he decides to resist them. This is not a recruitment document, but it is one man's description of what it took for him to become a refractory individual in society. It occurred to me that a text from a Communist victim of early repression such as Guy Môquet's letter to his parents might fit the bill here. Môquet's letter is a personal statement indeed, and it does demonstrate a desire to die for some purpose, although what this purpose is remains unstated.

The text of Môquet's letter is widely circulated in France today. It became an issue in public education in 2007 when then-president Nicolas Sarkozy proposed that it be read in secondary schools nationwide. The response of teachers was divided, and the practice has not become universal, although it continues to be debated. American students should be made aware of this letter if only because of the great sacrifice that seventeen-year-old Guy Môquet was forced to make, and the thoughtfulness of his response. Here is his letter in its entirety:

3. September 3, 1939–May 10, 1940. (See glossary.)

> My dear sweet mother, my darling little brother, my little father whom I love so much, I am about to die! What I ask of you, and of you in particular, little mother, is that you be brave. I am, and I want to be, just as brave as those people who have gone to their death before me. Naturally, I would have preferred to live. But what I wish for now with all my heart is that my death might serve some purpose. I didn't have time to kiss Jean. I was able to kiss my two brothers Roger and Rino.[4] As for my real brother, alas, I was not able to! I hope that all of my belongings will be sent home to you, they might be useful for Serge,[5] who, I imagine, will be proud to wear them one day. As for you, little father, if I caused you and Mother a lot of worry, I salute you for the last time. Know that I have done my best to live my life following the path that you pointed out to me.
>
> A final farewell to all of my friends, and to my brother whom I love very much. I hope that he will study hard in order to grow into a man. Seventeen and a half years, my life was short, but I have no regrets, except that I must leave you all. I am going to die along with Tintin and Michels.[6] Mother, what I am asking of you, what I want you to promise me, is that you will be brave and overcome your sadness.
>
> I can say no more. I am leaving you all, all of you, you Mother, Serge, Father. I embrace you with all of my young heart. Courage!
>
> Your Guy, who loves you.

"But what I wish for now with all my heart is that my death might serve some purpose." He doesn't mention his country or the foreign occupier. He also says that he believes he has lived his life as his father had laid it out for him to do. He does not say what this means, however. All of this may constitute an "approche de la Résistance," as the Fondation de la Résistance (www.fondationresistance.org) would have it,[7] but in truth it does not demonstrate or advocate resistance so much as a desire to meet his death with courage and

4. Roger Semat and Rino Scolari, Môquet's comrades-in-arms.

5. Serge was Môquet's real brother.

6. Tintin was Jean-Pierre Timbaud, a friend, and Charles Michels was a Communist leader in Paris.

7. One of a number of French organizations devoted to the study and preservation of the memory of the Resistance. A list of online history sites is included in the bibliography.

dignity. And this is already October 1941, four months after the Germans had turned on their former Soviet ally.

Independent-minded Communists existed in considerable numbers in France in 1940–41, and some of these men and women joined early clandestine resistance organizations that we associate with other leftist positions, notably Libération-Sud and Libération-Nord, which together were commonly considered to have been a Socialist movement. Still others organized under the names Franc-Tireur and Francs-Tireurs et Partisans. The further designation as Main d'oeuvre immigrée (MOI) actually identifies groups that were organized by the PCF prior to the war as immigrant labor groups, who generally were union members, recognized by the Confédération générale du travail (CGT) but who were not inducted as members of the French Communist Party.[8] These were people who were deeply committed to social and political struggle, were immersed in theoretical rationales for it, and had sometimes already participated in armed struggle against fascism (the *et Partisans* suffix expressed solidarity with the Republican side in the recent Spanish Civil War). They were familiar with violent repression and a consequent need to organize into clandestine groups that they called "cells." (Germaine Tillion discusses some of this terminology in the second document in the present collection.)

Repression of the PCF starting in September 1939, like the violent repression of the German Communist Party (KPD) that had been going on for some years in Germany, could only have strengthened these tendencies. In short, Communists didn't need to talk themselves through taking up a struggle. There are texts that put forward the position of some of these groups, but they usually aim to delineate a doctrinal position and do not have the quality of a personal statement. Where they do call for immediate action, they appear to be expressing a commitment to armed struggle that was present long before the invasion of France, with a lineage that extends back to the Spanish Civil War and to the Bolshevik Revolution beyond that. A text written by a Communist during the early years of the German occupation of France that expresses an early personal awakening may exist, but if one is found it may simply be the exception that proves the rule. The PCF did begin to create a number of special action cells (*organisations spéciales*) beginning in October 1941, and it was indeed one of these that was responsible for the assassination of Lieut. Col. Karl Hotz in Nantes on October 20, 1941, which led to the execution of Môquet and his twenty-six hostage comrades two days later in Châteaubriant.

8. All of these organizations can be found in the glossary.

(Twenty-one others were executed in Nantes and Paris in reprisal for this same assassination.)

The situation for the PCF had already begun to change in late April of that year when the Komintern, in contact with elements of the Communist Party through its office in Belgium, enjoined its French adherents to form a National Front (FN) to struggle for national independence. This was before Operation Barbarossa put an end to the pact between Nazi Germany and the USSR. But, in keeping with their longstanding sense of particularity in the fight for the proletariat against imperialism, these party policymakers actually saw the goal of such a front as being to take France out of the war between England and Germany, to resume the struggle for a France that was guided by the working class with the PCF at its head, and certainly not to join the British or de Gaulle against Hitler. After the German invasion of the Soviet Union on June 22, 1941, this began to change, as Germany became the preeminent enemy of the People's Revolution. But it would not be until over a year later, in a manifesto of April 1943, that the PCF's Front National officially proclaimed a policy of collaboration with all resistance organizations, including with the Free French office in London. And that declaration is far from being the kind of *cri de guerre* that we see in the tract by Henri Frenay presented for the first time in English in this collection.

What I am offering here is a text by a distinguished civil servant from the Parti Radical (center left); one from a woman who was admittedly not very political to begin with, a university-trained intellectual who moved equally well among colonial military and Parisian leftist circles (center); one from a military officer who supported Vichy but not the Nazis (right); and one from a noncommissioned military man of solid Socialist upbringing (left) who actually began by viewing Vichy as the principal target of his resistance activity. The two military men are diametrically opposed regarding their view of the French Republic, but they had apparently both read *Mein Kampf* and were staunchly opposed to Hitlerism.[9] The other two authors make no mention of having formed an opinion on German National Socialism before the invasion of France, but they immediately identified the foreign occupier as their enemy. So, even if we do not have a Communist in the lot, the documents give the reader a considerable range of starting points of view.

This collection is intended as support for study of the Second World War in France, and in particular study of the Resistance. It does not attempt to

9. *Mein Kampf* was Adolf Hitler's personal statement of his political engagement. (See glossary.)

explain the entire range of events in that country, nor to assess outcomes, though it will undoubtedly aid in attempting either. Notes on the texts aim to help the reader identify people and places that might be unfamiliar, and I hope they are at once adequate and unobtrusive. I have also created a glossary that includes parties, people, and places as well as foreign words mentioned in the introductions and in the texts themselves. I am presenting documents here that show how the French experienced the Collapse of the Third Republic, the country's military occupation by Nazi Germany, and the subsequent formation and growth of the Resistance in the interior. The run-up to World War II in France was characterized by intense inter-party conflict, along with the sentiment by people mainly on the right—who would become the leaders of occupied France—that political parties were ineffectual, counterproductive, should be gotten rid of, and that the country should be governed from the top down by an authoritarian figure or regime. (There were even those at the time who wanted a return to monarchy.) These documents speak repeatedly to this point, and to others. There was also fear engendered by the Bolshevik Revolution in Russia and by the presence of a wide spectrum of Communist and Socialist parties gaining strength in the country on the left. There was similar fear on both the left and the right engendered by the fascism that had emerged in Italy and Germany in the 1920s and 1930s and that had taken control of Spain so violently between 1936 and 1939. This much is assumed to be the understanding shared by all. But even students who have already developed a nuanced view of this period are likely to be surprised and intrigued by the material presented here.

Human history appears to begin at least with war itself. In any case, if we did not have war, we would certainly have far less history to tell. "Of arms and the man I sing," over and over again? Yes, surely, to some degree. But the Resistance is also a complex and compelling tale after all of these years in part because it is almost entirely about what ordinary people did, in great adversity, and with great courage. Even a scholarly article such as the piece by Germaine Tillion is basically still about just such people—colleagues, and often friends, coming together in small groups, two or three people talking and agreeing to take a deadly risk together. Yet these stories take place in day-to-day environments, and on a familiar, human scale. So, war stories, yes. But the four texts that follow also show quite convincingly that, while war may be inevitable, it is also possible to resist.

FIRST FIGHT

Editor's Introduction

To many Americans, even ones who know France quite well, the name Jean Moulin means nothing at all. Ironically, perhaps, it seems to some ears like a made-up name, like "Joe Smith," or a purposefully bland pseudonym for use in a clandestine organization, like the old Communist Party. Or the French Resistance. Moulin's is a real name, however, and one we all should know, for reasons that will become clear from reading his unusual little book.

American attitudes towards France have changed over the years. Or, more correctly, the American attitude toward France is constantly changing. We love her and we distrust her. Lafayette and Rochambeau secured her an eternal place of honor in our national hall of fame. But between then and the "freedom fries" episode, passing through de Gaulle's expulsion of US forces from France in 1966 and her withdrawal from NATO, there have certainly been moments when we wondered if France loved us in return. During World War II we tended to view France as a friend in bondage, and generally American sympathy for France ran high. But one recent study of France under the Occupation suggests that already at the time of Normandy many American soldiers felt that the French Army had collapsed remarkably fast in June 1940 (see Richard Vinen, *The Unfree French*). This perception has not faded, as the characterization of the French as "surrender monkeys" on a recent US television cartoon series notably reveals.

Jean Moulin certainly did not surrender. His behavior, when the German Army rolled into Chartres, is a striking example of how some French people behaved—extremely bravely, despite overwhelming odds—people who did not by any means roll over, who in fact resisted their own government's abdication as well as the invader from the very start. Moulin was exceptional, no doubt, but his version of the events of June 1940 also suggests that the French soldiers of that time did not want to withdraw as quickly as they were ordered to do, and suggests that their fighting spirit and their confidence in their equipment, at least as far as he perceived these factors, were high. American perceptions of what happened during those six weeks when France collapsed should certainly change, if we can believe his story.

As his *Journal*, which forms the heart of his book, also makes clear, Moulin thought that the French government of this period behaved in a highly irresponsible manner when the German Army entered France in mid-May 1940. He stops well short of accusing the military high command of any dishonor. The mid-level commanders and ordinary soldiers are portrayed highly sympathetically. Moulin was at this time a prefect, which means that he was a part of the government himself, an appointee of the Ministry of the Interior sent to represent the government in a city of twenty-seven thousand, the principal locality in the French administrative department of the Eure-et-Loir.[1] As such, he had a staff under his direction, many of whom were, like him, career civil servants working for the national government. These people were all clearly told to leave their offices and homes and flee south with the rest of the government on June 14, 1940 (pages 1–2 of the *Journal*).

Moulin appears to have understood the order. Within one page of the beginning of his text he refers to individuals in the government who were *affectés spéciaux*. This is one of the harder phrases to translate in the book since it involves a special category, which is to say one that does not have a preexisting definition, and one that has no real equivalent in American administrative language. The affectés spéciaux were French men who had been deferred from the military draft in order to serve in vital government services as diverse as secretary to the prefect or manager of public works. Moulin complied to the extent that he conveyed the order—the last he would receive from Paris—to his subordinates, and he did not obstruct those of his staff who wished to go, but he asked anyone who was willing to remain, in addition to the locals who had not fled, to help his city face the crisis. This meant helping many old people who were left behind when the townspeople fled, as well as the many thousands of people from Paris, northern France, and beyond, who were on French highway RN 10 fleeing the German advance in what would later be called *l'Exode*.

The picture Moulin paints of what this exodus felt like on the street is unusual in itself. In addition to being an eyewitness account by a trained civil administrator, Moulin's *Journal* was written within a year of the events themselves, and well before the outcome of the war was known. The book

1. Prefects are officials appointed by the Ministry of the Interior in Paris to oversee activities for the national government in every region of France. They wear a uniform that identifies them as an officer of the National Police and have offices in a building called the Prefecture. Prefects and their highest-level staff are trained by the École nationale d'administration (ENA).

was edited and published after the war was over, receiving, among other important touches, the title *Premier Combat.* In this text, the prefect tells how he managed to get people in Chartres to volunteer for the many tasks that needed to be performed under bombardment and while the French Army was in full retreat all around. Setting up reception centers for transients, staffing the hospital while the city was under air attack, putting out fires, policing the streets, and finding and helping people who had taken shelter in cellars all over town were at the top of the list. Among the many businesses that soon closed were the city's bakeries. Moulin tells how he and others together found bakers to reopen two facilities and to turn out sustenance for the remaining Chartrains, as well as for the countless refugees who found themselves in the city when their gasoline, or their feet, gave out. There were fifth-columnists at work, and one of them tried to thwart some of these efforts. Moulin's description of the Collapse of France as seen from its heartland is astonishing in clarity and portent.

Then comes the hair-raising account of how the German Kommandantur took notice of this unusual prefect and attempted to bend him to their will. Moulin's account gives a very early glimpse into the methods of the German Army in the handling and coercion of prisoners. It can be judged as fairly revealing how the Abwehr (German Army Intelligence) went about the business of gathering information in the early months of the war. The methods described here are brutal, but they are distinct from those employed later, when police informed by Nazi Party ideology would take over this important work from the army. Above all, this is a compelling account of a human spirit standing up for the honor of his country and for his own integrity against incalculable power and brutality, and it deserves a place in the literature of World War II alongside works by Agnés Humbert and Arthur Koestler (see bibliography).

A brief appendix was added to Moulin's *Journal* when his sister brought the manuscript forward for publication. This was after the war, when the combined texts were published under the title *Premier Combat* by the fledgling publishing house Les Éditions de Minuit, in 1946. The company had been founded during the darkest days of the war to publish resistant literature, starting with Vercors's novella *Le Silence de la mer.* I see little reason to remove this appendix now, even though the issues of who selected its various parts and what exactly that person's agenda was might lead some to question the validity of the text as a whole. I think the book, as published, is a significant document that English-speaking students and the general public should have.

It was written by a man who was on his way to becoming, for many, the greatest resister of the war.

Five months after the events described in *First Fight,* Moulin was dismissed from his prefectural position by the new Vichy government. He returned to his hometown on half-pay, proceeded to officially protest his status, and wrote this eyewitness account of what happened to him in June 1940. He also began very methodically to network with other French men and women who were determined not to accept the Armistice. The rest of Moulin's story—his clandestine trip to London to meet de Gaulle, his parachuting back into France during the last night of 1941, and the campaign to form a unified resistance—has tempted not only a few filmmakers but a growing number of authors writing in French and in English. Moulin died in captivity after being arrested in June 1943, the exact how and when of his death alone being a mystery that has occupied several popular and scholarly works much longer than the text we deliver here. Reading this book will certainly help their readers understand just whom these historians and storytellers are talking about.

As odd as it seems, French people themselves have rarely read this short book. This is not because they reject its authenticity, as far as I can tell. It is in print, but it is not widely available, requiring a special order in every bookstore where I have asked for it. What seems even more surprising, given Moulin's popularity, is that many French people don't seem to know that it even exists. They almost all know who Moulin was, of course, and many have read a considerable amount *about* the man. Today Jean Moulin is the most popular name for new high schools in France, and it is still popping up on street signs and auditoriums all across the country. This book tells an important part of how he came to earn such admiration—in his own voice. Moulin's name is one that Americans will also inevitably learn if they keep on visiting France, as they have in ever greater numbers since World War II. They are sure to be rewarded by trying to find out more about this man, about who he was and why he has become so popular in his homeland.

But there are at least two even more compelling reasons why Americans, and others everywhere, ought to read Moulin's book. First and foremost, it is a gripping account by a plain and upright civil servant, the kind most likely to give government a good name, who refuses to shirk his responsibility to the people he has been appointed to oversee. Moulin is a role model we could all consider emulating. Second, the book makes a brilliant and accessible contribution to the literature of civil disobedience. Moulin's defection—by remaining at his post during the Collapse—is already an impressive feat. What follows becomes truly heroic. He had much to deal with in Chartres during the summer and early autumn of 1940, including writing and filing an official report covering these same events that is included in the appendices of Laure Moulin's biography of her brother. By the spring of 1941, he and his fellow French men and women had an iron-fisted German occupation in place in over half the country. In the South, the so-called French State, *l'État français*, that many at the time still called the Free Zone and which the world today knows as Vichy France, the true scope of the betrayal of France's traditional republican values was just becoming known. Add to these good reasons the fact that the book is well written. It has the precision of language of a trained public servant. And it is a piece of first-rate battlefront journalism. It deserves to be better known than it is, both here and in France.

+ + +

Anyone looking to really get to know the complex character that was Jean Moulin, whose clandestine name was first Rex, then Max, can turn to a number of fine biographies. The French-language biography of record is *Jean Moulin: L'Inconnu du Panthéon* (1989–93) by Daniel Cordier, the first three volumes in a proposed six-volume treatment of the subject. These were followed by *Jean Moulin: La République des catacombes* (1999), also by Cordier, who was Moulin's personal secretary from 1942 to 1943. Patrick Marnham's *The Death of Jean Moulin: Biography of a Ghost* (2000) covers his entire life well and then takes on the final days in detail, as the title indicates. These are in addition to many others, including the Laure Moulin book, *Jean Moulin*, mentioned earlier. I undertook the translation below thinking of my students at the Institute for American Universities in Aix-en-Provence, but I hope that *First Fight* will encourage English-speaking audiences everywhere to find out more about the man. A number of mysteries, and considerable controversy, are connected with Moulin's wartime record, in particular with the circumstances of his death. It is undisputed that he was a key player in organizing resistance to the German occupation, starting in early 1941 and culminating in the convening, in occupied Paris, of a Conseil national de la Résistance (CNR) in May 1943. Moulin's own involvement in the fight ended with his capture the following June and his death, following brutal torture, some time after that. Beyond this, everything about his demise appears subject to dispute.

Recent studies of Moulin's life are distinguished by how they answer several key questions: Was he indeed a staunch supporter of de Gaulle, as tradition would have it, or was he working for the Soviets or even, as some have suggested, for the Americans? Was he betrayed by one of the men around him, or was his arrest merely the result of being in the right place at the wrong time? How deep was his commitment to leftist ideologies? For the purposes of providing a companion guide to the non-French reader of this translation of *First Fight*, the only book ever published in Moulin's own name, we offer the following brief survey of his life and political career. In order to understand both, some discussion of French governments and events in Spain and Germany during the years leading up to World War II will also be necessary.

Jean Moulin was born in the South of France, in Béziers (Hérault) on June 20, 1899. He grew up in a family with a strong attachment to what the French call Republican values, which is to say a firm belief in democratic government and an unswerving respect for the Declaration of the Rights of Man and of the Citizen (of August 26, 1789). His grandfather had even been briefly imprisoned for having annoyed a conservative and monarchist administration in 1877. Moulin *père* was the first in the family to attempt to raise himself up through education: upon his graduation with honors from high school in 1875, in Avignon, he caused a minor disturbance by getting his classmates to cheer for a lone Republican lawmaker among the guests of honor at the event. The family was from Saint Andiol (Bouches-du-Rhône), a small town on the RN 7 between Avignon and Aix-en-Provence, very near the spot where Moulin would parachute into the country at the start of 1942 to begin the mission that would end with his capture and death in 1943.

Jean Moulin graduated from high school in Béziers in 1917, and he enrolled in the law school of the University of Montpellier. He soon began to work as an assistant in the office of the local prefectural representative in the department of the Hérault. In 1918 he was called up for military service, given an accelerated training in an engineering-corps unit, and sent to northern France to join the ranks in November. But by this time World War I was to all extents and purposes over; the Armistice was signed on November 11, and it was too late for Moulin to fight. In November 1919 he returned to Béziers and went directly back into work at the Prefecture. He received his law license in 1921. During these years, while he was both a student and a junior-level employee at the Prefecture, he also found time to become active in student politics and became a member of the Jeunesses laïques et républicaines. In 1922 he began to work as a full-fledged prefectural employee, as the chief of staff to the prefect in Chambéry (Savoy), and in 1925 he was appointed subprefect in nearby Albertville, where he would serve for five years. These are impressive responsibilities for a man of his young age, and the immediate impression one draws from his record during this time is that Moulin was a team player and certainly not a refractory extremist of any one stripe or another.

Moulin married Marguerite Cerruty in 1926, but the union did not work out and the couple divorced two years later. Moulin would subsequently have affairs with a number of women, and his relations with two in particular come in for close scrutiny—and some opprobrium—from one biographer, Pierre Péan. Neither of these is Mademoiselle Cerruty, who has little bearing on the Moulin of *First Fight*. Moulin was thirty-one when he moved to Brittany and became a subprefect in Châteaulin. The posting itself was not a great improvement or a step up, but it was a lot closer to Paris, and at this time Moulin began to frequent a local *beau monde* of literary and artistic figures, including the poet Max Jacob, who was in nearby Quimper. Moulin also began to make some reputation for himself as a cartoonist. He drew political cartoons for the magazine *Le Rire*, and did illustrations for some books as well. (He signed with the pseudonym "Romanin," the name of a château near Saint Andiol.) It is not clear exactly how he first met and became friends with Pierre Cot, but it was probably in Savoy, where Cot was elected as a deputy from the Parti Républicain-socialiste in 1928. Five years Moulin's senior, Cot was on his way to becoming a major figure in 1930s French politics. In 1932 he invited Moulin to be his assistant chief of staff at the Ministry of Foreign Affairs. Moulin took the job and at the same time remained as subprefect in Châteaulin. He again shifted subprefectures in 1933, moving to Thonon-les-Bains, back in Savoy, and he advanced to chief of staff when Cot took on the portfolio of minister of air in the fall of that year.

Jean Moulin's connection with Pierre Cot is one of the more controversial parts of the young prefect's story, although this may have more to do with what Cot became after the war than with what happened in 1936. By the early 1930s, Cot was a Radical Socialist.[2] He was first invited to head up the

2. A mainstream left-of-center party at the time, the Radical Socialist Party embraced French Republicans with a wide range of political outlooks. In the 1930s, it was the party of Edouard Herriot and Pierre Cot on the one hand and of future Vichy police chief René Bousquet on the other.

Air Ministry in 1933 by the *président du conseil,* Edouard Daladier, himself a member of the Parti Radical.[3] Moulin's first service as Cot's chief of staff at the Air Ministry began in January 1933. Cot served until the turbulence of February to June 1934 forced Daladier out. In May of 1936 a leftist coalition government called the Front populaire came to power in France, led by Léon Blum. Daladier returned, now as minister of defense, and Cot was restored to the Air Ministry position. Moulin was back as his chief of staff.

Two months after this government came in, civil war broke out in Spain. Officers of the Spanish Army turned against the Republic after a similar duly elected leftist coalition came to power in Madrid. During the first two years of this conflict, the French Air Ministry under Cot, and aided by Moulin, was involved in clandestine intermittent efforts to send aircraft and munitions to the Republicans in Spain. This was approved by Blum, but it was also possibly illegal. Whether or not this, or any other transgression of Cot's actually contributed to the French Air Force's state of disarray in May 1940 has been hotly debated ever since. Moulin's connection with the Air Ministry ceased in 1938 when Cot was replaced as minister by Guy LaChambre.

In January 1937, Moulin, then thirty-eight, had been named as prefect of the Aveyron, in Rodez. At that time he was the youngest man in France ever to accede to the rank.[4] In recent years the French have become suspicious of holding dual and even triple responsibilities in government, the much-criticized *cumul d'emplois,* but in the 1930s this practice was an accepted fact of political life. During these years, Moulin was close to the highest level of government in France. He and Cot were friends and by all accounts shared an interest in winter sports. Between January 1936 and December 1938, Moulin, a good-looking single man in his mid-thirties with a promising career in

3. Daladier would be ousted, then serve a second term, in 1934, and a third from 1938 to 1940. "The Bull of the Vaucluse," as he was known, Daladier was the "other person" standing next to Chamberlain, opposite Hitler and Mussolini at Munich in 1938. He deserves to be better known in the English-speaking world as well. It is generally believed in France that Daladier did not want to sign the accord, and that he was only persuaded to do so by considerable effort on the part of Chamberlain.

4. Jean Moulin would hold this distinction until 1941 when René Bousquet was named prefect of the Marne, also at age thirty-one. This rising star of the French political scene would shortly become the head of all French police under the Vichy government, and subsequently be perhaps the greatest collaborator to escape justice following the war. He was shot dead on the street in 1993, a few weeks before his trial was to begin.

government well underway, was introduced to many interesting and attractive women, and it was during this period that he met the two women who, besides his sister and mother, were important in his life at the time when the events of *First Fight* occurred. These were Antoinette Sachs, a painter and the mistress of a well-known artist when she began an affair with Moulin, and Gilberte Lloyd, née Riedlinger, a divorcée like Moulin and, according to some, the most beautiful woman in Paris. Among his biographers, Pierre Péan is perhaps the most informative about the women in Moulin's life. Daniel Cordier says little about either of them. (Moulin's sister Laure seems to have been aware of Sachs, whose name she spells "Saxe.")

In 1938, Hitler began to make his territorial intentions sharply clearer, in particular with regard to the Sudetenland, a region of the recently formed multiethnic state of Czechoslovakia. This part of the country was populated by ethnic Germans, and now Hitler wanted it brought into the Reich. Czechoslovakia's sovereignty had been underwritten by France and Great Britain in 1919. The debate over Hitler's demand was intense and full of portent, but in the end both countries chose to appease the Führer, and in September, Prime Minister Neville Chamberlain and President Edouard Daladier both signed what became known as the Munich Accords, ceding the Sudeten region to Germany. In Paris, opinion was very hotly divided over this matter, although when it came time for the Chamber to vote, only two right-wing nationalists joined the 73 Communist delegates in voting against the accords. The final vote was 535 to 75. However overwhelming this vote may seem, in Paris sentiment became sharply polarized into pro- and anti-*Munichois* factions, effectively paralyzing the government for many months to come. (As an example, Cot, as a *député*, voted in favor of the accords, although he viewed Czechoslovakia as a key in France's Central European strategy, and he immediately thereafter vociferously opposed them.)

In September 1939, Germany invaded Poland, and France and Great Britain declared war on Germany. There could no longer be any other course of action. Both countries were bound by treaties with Poland, which they clearly took more seriously than the ones they both had signed with Czechoslovakia. But they did not really go to war. At first no one moved, and few shots were fired. This is the period referred to as the "Phoney War." Moulin was only a prefect, not a position that implicated him in the nation's foreign policy. As an indication of his sense of what was going on at the time, he had been persistently seeking official release from his prefectural duties so that he could rejoin his military unit, but his request was repeatedly denied. During these two years, he did succeed in getting his military assignment in the reserves transferred from an engineering company to the Armée de l'air. And he rose from the rank of corporal to sergeant in December 1938.

By February 1939 Moulin had moved to the post of prefect of the department of the Eure-et-Loir. Again, this was not really a step up—both it and the Aveyron were considered class-three appointments—but Chartres was only a one-hour drive to Paris. Moulin was once again closer to the people who mattered professionally—Cot was still a député, though his star had fallen considerably—and to those who perhaps mattered to him sentimentally as well. France went about business, certainly not "as usual"; Daladier stepped down in favor of Paul Reynaud, who was reputedly more disposed to fight, and the country was overrun by thousands of refugees from Germany, Austria, and Poland, and from Spain, where the Republic finally collapsed in January 1939, putting a large number of leftists and anarchists, many of them armed and hardened by war, onto the roads over the Pyrenees into France. Rounding them up in camps across the South, and attempting to control the huge influx of desperate refugees from the Reich—now technically, one could also say absurdly, considered to be belligerent nationals—kept the French government, and certainly law enforcement, busy from September 1939 until the following spring. On May 10, 1940, the Germans entered Belgium, and World War II on the western front really began.

What Moulin might have thought about all these matters is not clearly documented. Chartres is the center of an agricultural region of 250,000 souls led by a number of large wheat farmers, and in 1940 his attention was certainly directed at these people. He no longer had any official connection with the Air Ministry, although Chartres had an important military air base. The war was not really his brief. Another reason why we do not know some things about what Moulin and his colleagues wrote to each other at this time is that, as war drew closer, French authorities began destroying documents that might be compromising, should the Germans break through. It is reported that the first inkling the inhabitants of Paris got of their government's imminent collapse was on May 15, when they perceived a huge bonfire on the lawn of the Foreign Ministry at the Quai d'Orsay. This activity soon went on across much of the country. Many documents at the Prefecture in Chartres were destroyed by Moulin as the Germans approached the city. Moulin wrote in the manuscript of his *Journal* that he was still desperately engaged in burning documents in Chartres as late as June 16. (The passage was cut in the version published in

1946 that we have used as the basis of our translation.) Moulin's principal biographer, Daniel Cordier, uses the public record of his close associate Maurice Viollette, the mayor of the neighboring town of Dreux (who appears early in *First Fight*), to elucidate what some of Moulin's preoccupations might have been at this time.

First Fight begins on June 14, the day Paris fell. Moulin tells in detail what happened to him over the course of the next week. There are two brief entries at the very end, one on June 22 and one on November 14 when Moulin had been dismissed by his superiors, now in Vichy, for reasons that are alluded to in the appendix but that are not really made clear anywhere in the book. Without giving away anything of the gripping finale of *First Fight*, we can say that Moulin survived and continued as prefect of the Eure-et-Loir following the events described here, although his relationship with Vichy, the French government that immediately replaced the collapsed Third Republic, was not good. Vichy was aware of the extreme valor of the young prefect during the Collapse, and it had received letters in praise of his conduct from military and local business sources, but even these could not erase the stain of Moulin's association with the Third Republic in general, and with Pierre Cot and the Popular Front in particular. For Frenchmen like Moulin, for whom there was never a moment of surrender, there was likewise never really an hour when Vichy was seen as the legitimate French state either, and we can safely conjecture that the distrust was mutual.

Exactly when and how Moulin crossed over from being a disobedient civil servant to a resister is impossible to say, although it appears certain that he was not alone in rejecting Vichy from the moment it dissolved the Third Republic. What seems to define Moulin's thinking during his entire adult life is his loyalty to the Republic, and this moment had to come as a deep shock to him as it did to many. Immediately upon being dismissed from his functions, or perhaps even before November 2, Moulin appears to have started locating people of like spirit around him in the occupied North of France and in the so-called Free France, the southern zone governed from Vichy. Many of these men did not actually hear Charles de Gaulle's famous appeal of June 18 live over the BBC, but they heard about it very soon thereafter. As he continued as prefect of Chartres following the events in *First Fight*, Moulin would have had privileged access to information about sedition in the weeks that followed the Collapse: he read police reports warning of troublemakers, and these included notices about people working for the renegade ex-general in London. At this time "Gaullism" became the first synonym of resistance. (The word "Resistance" itself was quick to emerge as the defining term. That word was chosen by Boris Vildé of the Groupe du musée de l'Homme as the name for their newsletter, which first appeared in the month following Moulin's dismissal.) Soon it would also become known as "terrorism."

From what Cordier says about Moulin during these months, which is based on interviews and published statements by the people around him who knew him best, it is clear that by July–August 1940 what would soon come to be called the Resistance was taking shape. Official statements from Vichy on acts of resistance and "Gaullist activities" begin to appear at this time. A close friend interviewed after the war reported that Moulin was contemplating resigning by September, but that he was persuaded not to do so as this would attract attention and make him a marked man. No loyal prefect in his right mind would ever consider doing such a thing under normal circumstances. These times called for extreme discretion. More significantly, he did take the trouble during his last months in office to have false identification made for himself. This included a fake identity card under the name of "Joseph Jean Mercier," which Moulin presented in order to get a passport that he then used to leave the country scarcely one year later. In November, the government chose to apply a law adopted by Vichy on July 17, 1940, allowing for the immediate dismissal of government employees who were Communists, including other civil servants, such as prefects, who refused to dismiss subordinates and even locally elected officials, including mayors, who were from the left in general. Moulin, the staunch Republican, was just such a prefect. He went home under protest. Sometime following his dismissal from government service in November 1940 he wrote the text that later appeared as the central document of *Premier Combat.* His sister, Laure, said that he wrote it "in Montpellier in the spring" of 1941. (He had already filed his official prefect's report on these events on July 12, 1940.) He also traveled extensively in northern and southern France during the first months of 1941, contacting people he identified as being potential resisters, networking, and preparing himself to meet with the Free French who were gathering in London around Charles de Gaulle. His old friend Pierre Cot had already been through London, reportedly to offer his services to the Free French, but he was passed over and soon moved on to New York, where he spent most of the war, drifting further and further to the left all the while.

The story of Moulin's life after his dismissal, though short, is charged with adventure, political maneuvering, and macabre drama. Moulin spent most of 1941 traveling around France, which was now divided into the northern, occupied zone, and the southern zone governed by French authorities located in

Vichy. Moulin's base of operations was the family home in St. Andiol, although he made frequent visits to Montpellier to be with his mother and sister. He also began to set up other addresses and to elaborate alternate identities for himself that he would use in the months to come. He was simultaneously following up leads, meeting people, networking, assessing sentiments and capabilities regarding the possibility of resisting the German invader from within. Many French men and women simply did not think this was possible. Moulin's sister Laure said that she was one of these. Others, even some who became great resisters, felt at first that it was their patriotic duty to support Vichy.

Moulin moved cautiously among his friends and fellow citizens and carefully collected information. He appears to have had an innate grasp of clandestine activity. From his initial choice of a pseudonym using his own initials, an invented identity from a locality where the public records were known to him to have been destroyed, to his setting up addresses for himself in buildings with separate entryways on two streets, he appears to have been something of a natural. He explained what he was doing by saying that he intended to go to London to try to coordinate activity inside the country with the Free French forces gathering around de Gaulle. Moulin wrote this *Journal*, apparently quite quickly and "with few cross-outs," in spring 1941 and entrusted the manuscript to his sister. In September, less than a year following his dismissal from the Prefecture in Chartres, he left France via Spain and Portugal with the passport he had obtained in the name of Joseph Jean Mercier. He met de Gaulle in London and managed to impress the general and the men around him well enough to get himself sent back to France with a letter designating him as the official liaison between the Free French forces and the nascent Resistance in the southern zone.

Moulin parachuted back into France on the last night of 1941, almost into his old backyard. The men of the Vaucluse who in 1943 would later run well-lit drop zones and landing strips all over Provence were already there that night, albeit only as lookouts. Armed with de Gaulle's letter, which he kept with him on microfilm, Moulin now began in earnest to try to bring an expanding, though by its very nature extremely secretive and ideologically divided, constellation of resistance movements into contact with each other. His code name was now "Rex." Simply put, de Gaulle's strategy regarding the Resistance at this time was for it not to engage or provoke the enemy directly but to prepare for the day when an invasion would be launched and be ready to help it. Moulin tried to create agreement around this program and undertook the task of distributing funds and supplies to the various groups that were mobilizing throughout the South.

The first giant step Moulin succeeded in taking was convening the short-lived Comité de coordination in November 1942, followed by the creation of the Mouvements unis de la Résistance (MUR) in January 1943. The direct-action wing of the movement was known as the Armée secrète (AS), which would at first be led by Henri Frenay, the head of a powerful right-of-center group called Combat. Much is made of the rivalry of Moulin and Frenay, but I think the evidence is that they had each other's respect and confidence, at least at first. In February–March 1943 Moulin returned to London, where he was decorated by de Gaulle with the Cross of the Liberation and made a government minister. He returned to France with a mandate to unite the Resistance movements in the South (the MUR) with those in what had been the northern zone—in short, in the entire country. By this time the war was by no means over, but the tide had turned. The Allies were now on the Italian peninsula, and plans to invade France were underway. There was a growing perception that the French Resistance was real, and there was a corresponding willingness in London to provide increased supplies and real money to help it grow. Moulin was the gatekeeper for much of this support. Accounts of what the various groups received from him were meticulously kept and are a matter of public record. The actual money and supplies were filtered into France via drop zones and landing sites all across the country. This access to growing financial assistance naturally gave Moulin a considerable amount of power back home. With his mandate to operate in the North in addition to the South, Moulin's code name would be changed to "Max."

Back in France, Moulin went to work right away, and two months later he successfully convened a Conseil national de la Résistance. He chaired the first meeting of the group in Paris on May 27, 1943. At about this same time there was a calamitous leak of information somewhere in France.[5] The Germans began to arrest Resistance members throughout the country, notably the man who was now the designated commander of the united Armée secrète of the North and the South, General Charles Delestraint, who was captured on a subway platform in Paris. Moulin immediately convened a meeting with the intention of deciding on someone to fill this key post. It was to be held at a doctor's office in a suburb of Lyon on June 21, but the Gestapo showed up and arrested all of the participants, including Moulin. This event alone has

5. Jean Garcin thinks the source of the leak was a man named Multon, who was arrested in Marseilles. Garcin was one of the local hands engaged to serve as lookouts on the night Rex parachuted into the Alpilles. See Garcin, *We Were Terrorists*, in this collection.

generated volumes of commentary and speculation in addition to having been portrayed several times on film and television. The police knew the name of the man they were seeking was Max, but they did not know which of the men he was, nor that Max was Jean Moulin. If they had, they could of course have identified him by the scar on his neck that he had received while in their custody back in Chartres. They proceeded to torture the entire lot, and they may have figured out which one of them was Max, but even this is not certain. It does seem unlikely that he himself divulged any information to his interrogators.

Moulin was sighted three times during the days that followed, by some accounts his head badly beaten. He was among a group of men transferred to Gestapo headquarters in Paris, where reportedly his chief captor, the infamous SS Obersturmführer Klaus Barbie, was reprimanded for having beaten his prisoner so badly that the man could no longer be questioned. At some point after this, Moulin was placed in a train headed for prison in Germany. *Nacht und Nebel* (Night and Fog) were at the end of so many of these stories. Moulin's death was attested by a German officer on the arrival of his body in Frankfurt. The place of death was given as Metz, the border city on the railway line. Metz was then in the portion of France that was designated an "annexed zone," though it is again a part of France today. So even that designation is a bit shaky. The presumed date of death is July 8, 1943.

An urn filled with ashes "Presumed to be those of Jean Moulin," originally buried in the Père Lachaise Cemetery, was formally interred at the Panthéon in Paris on December 19, 1964. Most of the surviving members of the Resistance were present, as was General de Gaulle in full military uniform. A remarkable speech was given by Minister of Culture André Malraux: "Today, young people, I hope that you will think of this man as you might have, reaching out to touch his beaten face on that last day, to touch his lips that never talked; on that day, his was the face of France!"

\+ + +

By "young people" Malraux certainly meant the France that came after, the France that had not lived through the war. *First Fight* might best be considered Jean Moulin's own attempt to speak to those people directly. Patrick Marnham, in his often excellent commentary in *The Death of Jean Moulin*, says that Moulin wrote *Premier Combat* "mainly for his sister," but surely that cannot be. Moulin had seen Laure many times over months between when the events transpired and when he wrote it, and his scar was in plain sight. He would surely have told her this entire story long before the spring of 1941. The question "For whom did Moulin write this account?" is a good one, however, and one of the first that a reader will ask as the story gets underway. We know that Moulin had already written a different version of it in the standard administrative style in his official report, dated July 12, 1940, shortly after he returned to work as prefect of the Eure-et-Loir. So he was not simply trying to ensure that the events were documented. Moreover, it must have occurred to Moulin fairly early on that if this text became public, he would become a clear target for Vichy's and the Germans' anger.

It was now almost a year after the events had transpired. As a prefect on half-pay, Moulin faced an administrative battle to protest his having been suspended from his duties as a matter of routine professionalism, ironically in order to appear *less* refractory. I find it hard to imagine this very purpose-driven young man, faced with what was ever more clearly a *coup d'état* against his beloved Republic and occupation by a brutal enemy about whom he could have no illusions, taking time out to write this journal as a memento for any single individual. As long as we are novelizing, we might as well consider the possibility that he wrote it for Gilberte Riedlinger Lloyd, the "most beautiful woman in Paris," or for Antoinette Sachs, who was working fairly closely with Moulin in the South of France at the time he was writing this journalized version of the events of nearly a year prior. But he did not give it to either of them. And both of them would very likely have heard this story already, too, so we really are left wondering why in this period of crisis he took the time, however brief, to compose these pages.

There may not be a simple answer to this question. Perhaps it was in part for these close friends, but I believe he had to be thinking of a wider audience—the people of his former department, perhaps, or of all the departments in which he had served. It is, after all, a testimonial about public service, his public service, and a powerful statement about moral commitment to duty, and it is not just the appendix that skews his tale in that direction. It would be quite natural for him to be writing it broadly for people his own age. Moulin was now forty-two years old, and he came from the first generation that had not participated in World War I. He probably would not be trying to reach out to much older people particularly. The older men in France, many of whom had been in World War I, were among Marshal Pétain's staunchest supporters. To suggest something more in character, perhaps Moulin, who had already exhibited artistic tendencies, put out of his job by a gang of anti-Republican right-wing usurpers, decided to try his hand at crafting a parable on civic duty for his fellow citizens.[6] At times his *Journal* does seem to be a first draft, and as Marnham does say, that works well considering it is supposed to be a real-time journal; but might that not also be due in part to the circumstances: that he wrote it when he was on the move, busy with bigger things, and quite understandably didn't really think about getting it ready to go into print? But Marnham is certainly right when he says that the book is "among the most vivid and convincing eyewitness narratives of the Fall of France."

Even if one were to read the text casually, not really looking for literary subtleties, it would be difficult not to ask oneself for whom the book is intended. And it would be difficult not to notice the ease of the author's expression. He seems to be a likable man, a peer rather than a prefect, neither a stiff bureaucrat nor yet a politician wild with anger. There is a clarity to Moulin's descriptions of events, coupled with an understated intensity, and both are certainly appropriate to the subject matter but somehow still manage to astonish. Once the reader begins to think about how the text is written, a flood of thoughts ensues. This is because it seems so perfectly aimed at a modern public highly attuned to Moulin's take-charge-and-get-it-done attitude, and the reader sympathizes with his sense of fully engaged civic responsibility and with the righteousness of his struggle. His story is meant to rouse and motivate, to comfort and legitimize. To this end, he has adopted what seems to be an appropriately modern colloquial literary style.

As a prefect, Moulin also had to be a speechwriter, and he had a reputation as a good one. He knew how to wield rhetoric, how to adopt different voices, how to reach his fellow citizens' minds. In *First Fight*, Moulin draws his readers right into the action along with him. From the opening words, "*Coup de téléphone*," with no other lead-in, we are invited to hear the story jangle to life, and it begins to spring forward. He uses the effect again in the entry after the next one, at 5:00 a.m.: "Order from the Government requiring all 'specially appointed' individuals to be withdrawn immediately"—and again whenever he wants to snap the scene to a new location (for example, 3:00 p.m. on June 15). He also uses an elliptical, telegraphic style along with the historic present tense, making it seem as if he is describing events as they are happening. At 3:30 p.m. on June 14 he declares: "Paris has fallen!" There is certainly nothing

6. In her 1947 introduction to his book, his sister, Laure, calls him "a born artist and a man of action."

inappropriate about the anguish Moulin expresses here, but he seems to be addressing a broader audience than just his ministerial superiors. It would be an odd way to put it to his sister, too, a year after the event. It is a literary conceit. In fact, the entire book reads like a very tight script, from the downbeat to the unintentionally ironic speech by the Feldkommandant that closes the *Journal* 114 pages later.

It is certainly no accident where Moulin begins his story, nor that already in the second entry he evokes the matter of the affectés spéciaux—the specially deferred civil servants (such as himself) who were precisely at this moment being told that they should fall back along with the rest of the government. This establishes the setting for Moulin's insubordination, his refusal to follow the order of his ministry to close the doors of the Prefecture and go south. This is Jean Moulin versus the dysfunctional government, the drama that constitutes part one of the story in *First Fight.* (Part two will be the German Feldkommandantur's attempt to coerce Moulin to sign a bogus "*protocole*" by extreme physical and psychological abuse.) Moulin mentions in these opening paragraphs that his specially deferred subordinates all seem to be steadfast and in good spirits. He also points out two things that must be quite obvious to all: that these professional civil servants are precisely the people he as prefect most needs in order to stand and deliver and, no less important, that it is precisely these people's holding their ground that might discourage the remaining civilians from leaving in a panic. Six pages later (at around 7:00 p.m. on that same day), his staff members' spirits have collapsed and most of them are leaving, if they haven't slipped away already. This leaves Moulin with the task of rounding up a team of volunteers, then convincing and managing them as they pick up the reins in the city of Chartres, a ghost town that has become a transient camp for refugees as the German invader draws closer.

This is not scholarly history, nor is it an official report. Compare its style with the dense exposition of Marc Bloch's *Strange Defeat,* for instance, to see the difference between what Moulin has done and straight academic historiography of the time. Compare it in style with Moulin's official report, written in July 1940, which appears in the appendix of Laure Moulin's biography of her brother. In *First Fight,* Moulin employs the historical present tense throughout, along with the frequent use of ellipsis. The entries are all brief, and they are broken into very short paragraphs. It is an action piece, yet it is rich in thoughts and ideas. As a prefect, Moulin had certainly been trained to write official reports, and his official report of these goings-on is a part of the public record. It is written in the past historic, using all of those *passé simples* that no one ever uses in speech anymore, including frequent parenthetical thoughts driven by present participles that make for very long sentences reminiscent of Caesar's *Gallic War: N'ayant plus aucune nouvelle de Dreux, le 14 juin au soir, par suite de bombardements et de la mitraillade continue des routes, je retournai une derniere fois dans cette ville . . .* ("Having received no news from Dreux, on the evening of the 14th, following the bombardment and the continuous machine-gunning of the roads, I returned for one last time to this city . . ."). This is the more formal way of telling the story. Occasionally Moulin slips into it here, but then he catches himself and returns to the more modern, journalistic style: "After assuring myself that all of the measures I had called for were being carried out, and having given the subprefect, who has a special deferment, the instructions he needed for his departure, I leave Dreux." Present tense.

Although it is probably very accurate writing, *First Fight* is more a personal account than a work of history, and in terms of its written style it seems to have more in common with contemporary writing by Albert Camus than that of Irene Némirovsky.[7] In its language and its tone, Moulin's account leaves the old behind and steps resolutely into the modern world. At the time he was writing this journalized version of his story, Moulin was simultaneously engaged in changing his identity, becoming clandestine, and starting to reach out to French people of all walks of life in a struggle against his country's oppressors. I believe it is these people he is thinking of as he writes his story, these people he wishes to motivate. But the book would have to wait. In the spring of 1941 it was a liability, so he gave it to the only person he could trust entirely, and that was Laure. Years later, his sister, working with Les Éditions de Minuit, added an appendix that in some ways tips the tone of the book as a whole back in the direction of record keeping, and it became the compelling document that it is today.

+ + +

Another question that might be asked is whether the story told in the *Journal* itself is credible. By this I do not mean that there can be any doubt that Moulin himself wrote it. As I said, according to Laure, it was written by her

7. Albert Camus (1913–1960), author of *La Peste* (*The Plague*) and *L'Étranger* (*The Stranger*); Irene Nemirovsky (1903–1942), author of *David Golder* and *Suite Française.*

brother during the spring of 1941, when he was back in Provence after being stripped of his prefectural duties by Vichy. He had fully recovered from his ordeal with the Germans, his "first fight" and to some degree the Resistance's as well. The question of the text's credibility involves the way in which Moulin tells the story, whether he has intentionally distorted the account for some purpose, and whether he has told his readers everything relevant to these events. (He might be forgiven for not having really "told all" inasmuch as some of the events he was engaged in during the week in question do not bear on the two episodes in this account, his decision to remain in Chartres to cope with the exodus and his encounter with the Feldkommandantur.) Most of the events described in *First Fight* were witnessed by many people, and many of them lived to see the account appear in print. There have been no substantive claims of falsehood or fabrication in his account to this day.

One could argue that a lot of outright lies about people's records have gone unchallenged in France during the seventy years since its Collapse in June 1940, and that in any case Moulin's reputation has risen to where it is almost untouchable. Both of these assertions are true. What seems clear, however, is that the publicly visible events in Moulin's brief narrative are accurate, starting with the very first point, the critical moment when Moulin said no to the government's abandonment of its civic duty. This government was not yet the one we now call Vichy, and Moulin had no crystal ball telling him where this was all headed. He just knew what his job was, and he was determined to do it. The German Army officer's statements reported in Moulin's *Journal* may or may not be accurately reported. The German unit that entered Chartres might not have ever run into a prefect who stood his ground before, from the Belgian border all the way to the Eure-et-Loir. We couldn't tell if it was true even if we knew the officer did say it. The French record of what happened during June 1940, even when optimized after the fact, does not support the suggestion that Moulin's actions during these events were anything but exceptional.

Patrick Marnham points to two passages in the text as indications of some disingenuousness that I do not sense at all. One is the book's inversion of the itinerary the Germans took when they drove out to the farm at La Taye, and the other is Moulin's apparent failure to recognize the building where he was incarcerated for the night with a Senegalese soldier. As far as the jumbled itinerary is concerned, Moulin could not have done this intentionally for any reason I can think of. It sounds like a mistake, pure and simple. Surprisingly, perhaps, his editors did not catch it either. Or else if they did they decided that it did not matter. As far as Moulin's not recording that he did or did not recognize that he was finally delivered to an outbuilding of the hospital, I can easily believe he could have simply not noticed. It was nighttime, and he had been maltreated and forced to go here and there for hours. He says he was aware that he was not driven far in this last move, but he does not identify the building. This is not surprising given the way in which he was transported, roughly and probably not in the front seat of the car, and that his captors were probably, literally, in his face. So Moulin does not say that he recognized the gateway where he was forced to enter.

Marnham's suggestion is that Moulin knew where he was but didn't say so in order to hide his intentions in the events to follow, that knowing how close to the hospital he was, Moulin decided to slit his neck superficially—careful now!—not in order to kill himself, but to create a spectacle that might make the Germans call a halt to their attempt to extract the much-wanted signature from him. This does provide a possible motive for hiding the awareness of where he really was from his reader. But if Moulin's suicide attempt was indeed *intended* to be just that, an attempt, why would he not say so? It would provide an even better example for his reader, mitigating the taint of suicide and showing him to be incredibly wily. Had the scheme been forming in Moulin's mind from the moment he saw where he had arrived? Marnham says that Moulin's suicide bid would have been "informed by" his military training. This might be more convincing if Moulin had been trained as a medic. (He was trained in 1917 as an engineer, and then certainly very quickly in 1937 as an in-flight gunner.) Perhaps Marnham means that all French soldiers received the indoctrination necessary to behave with such pluck, but probably not. Rather, it would appear that this is all said in support of a thesis that Moulin was a duplicitous individual who was in reality a Communist mole determined to survive so that he could help seize France for Moscow. If this is indeed what was motivating Moulin in the spring of 1940, then we need some explanation either of why he changed his orientation or of how he managed to trick the entire team around de Gaulle into trusting him. (They had sent Cot on his way during the summer.) But, in the last analysis, this kind of speculation is a waste of time. The Senegalese soldier who spent that night with Moulin might throw some light on what happened in that dark room, but as far as we know the man was never identified. And, unless Moulin *spoke* to him about these matters, and we find him soon, all we will ever have to go on is the narrative in Jean Moulin's book.

I do not call it a "narrative" in order to belittle it. In studying history, we crave facts, yet what we get from even the best of witnesses are stories. There are many official documents, including vetted "accounts" of what happened in some places, at some times, in France during the years 1940–45. There are few, if any other, texts like Moulin's. Historians have an essential job to do for us, separating the wheat from the chaff and letting us know which is which. But, in the end, Moulin's entire text is another story. It is the story the way he wants to tell it, and at the time he wrote it. He may have had an agenda, if not a plot, in mind. After all, it took a certain amount of time and privacy for him to write this version of these events, and Moulin was a busy man, and his attention was highly solicited during these weeks. It was at this same time that he was setting up false cover for himself, including one as an art-gallery owner in a storefront in Nice. But he was used to a life that placed even greater restraints on his schedule than this, and he might have felt he had time on his hands since being put out to pasture in November. But still, why write a story that he had already recorded in an official report months before? Clearly he was thinking hard, if not exclusively, about the defeat of France and the Occupation. It was also precisely at this time that, in Paris, a number of the earliest resisters, members of the Groupe du musée de l'Homme, were being broken up by the Germans after having published four issues of the newsletter *Résistance*. This would have been known to Moulin, and the danger of anyone seeing this journal must have been clear to him even as he wrote it. If he did have an agenda, it is difficult to imagine it was an immediate one.

Perhaps we can infer what his purpose was by what the writer does not say, if not by what he does. Both the brevity of his account and the relative absence of dialectical rant or philosophical exegesis are indications that, in this relatively colloquial version of the events, he wanted to place emphasis on the accuracy of his description rather than on delivering any ideology. And what he is describing is by and large himself, citizen Moulin. In this account of his life as a prefect during the Collapse, some things are described in detail (his exchanges with Maurice Viollette, or with the volunteers, for example). Other things we might be interested in are not even mentioned. Pétain's June 17 speech, which was broadcast nationally at 12:30 p.m. on June 17 and which Moulin does not so much as mention, is a striking example of that. Could it be that they did not hear it at the prefecture that day when the Germans arrived? Some details he might have assumed most audiences would not be interested in. He doesn't say much about the steps he took to pay people for their work, either, although he did do this. The account he does give certainly leaves some room for speculation.

In the end, what makes this narrative most compelling is the personality of the man who is speaking. He is full of contrasts: he sounds many a positive note from the very start, straightforward and sincere, even as he informs us of the greatest disaster that could befall his country. From the very start he makes it clear that he is deeply concerned with ethics, but he also appears to be resolutely pragmatic. He is ready to work, but he considers it a part of his duty to question his own government's orders. All of this is done with the light and yet precise strokes of the artist that he apparently also was. His professional life had already obliged him to become a political organizer and an executive, and he was clearly up to that challenge. But the Collapse required him to act as an independent-minded individual, which is not the same thing at all. His description of himself in the days leading up to his confrontation with the Germans wins us over. And when we see him singled out for extortion and abuse by the enemy, we are with him completely and find his resistance irresistible. The personality reflected in these pages coincides with, and greatly enriches, what we learn elsewhere about Rex/Max, in the story of the two years to come. This should be of considerable interest to students of this dark period. Moulin's optimism in the face of adversity, his capabilities as an organizer, his resoluteness under torture, none of which Jean Moulin the prefect could possibly have known he would possess, are all right there. All of this makes it extremely difficult to deny the authenticity of the man we hear finding his authorial voice in *First Fight*.

First Fight

JEAN MOULIN

Preface

Max, good and true companion among those who believed only in France, managed in the end to die heroically for her.

The key role that he played in our fight will never be told by Jean Moulin himself, but it is not without intense emotions that the reader will discover this Journal that he wrote about the events in 1940 that first led him to say *No* to the enemy.

The strength of character, the clear-sightedness and the energy that he demonstrated at that time never flagged.

May his name be remembered as indeed his legacy remains alive!

Ch. de GAULLE
June 1, 1946

Foreword

It is not without emotion that I offer to the public these pages in which my brother described the dark days of June 1940 in Chartres, and his heroic resistance to the Nazi savages.

He wrote them in Montpellier, during the spring of 1941, during one of his clandestine visits to his family. His recollections, which ranged back over many months, had remained astonishingly vivid.

I recall my brother, hunched over these pages, recounting almost without any cross-outs the hour-by-hour unfolding of events in his struggle and his suffering.

Until then I had only known through others, or by fleeting allusions, to what heights of patriotism he had risen in the days of the Nazi onslaught.

Translation of Jean Moulin, *Premier Combat* (1940; Paris: Les Éditions de Minuit, 1983).

He scarcely liked to boast, and although he was quite bold in other ways, he was extremely reserved where his feelings were concerned, even towards his nearest and dearest. One can only imagine the repugnance he felt in relating the events of the 17th of June.

Having finished the task, he gave the pages to me to read, and entrusted them to me for safe-keeping. We spoke little about these matters, but our thoughts and our hearts were closer than ever. Before undertaking his first trip to London, which he did entirely on his own, he wanted to leave behind this testimonial to the treachery, the barbarity and the sadism of the Germans to be added later to the historical record. In publishing it I am carrying out his wish.

One will find in these pages some assessments that may appear quite severe. One must try to put oneself in the mood of June 1940, in the state of mind of a patriot who was making superhuman efforts to resist his country's collapse, of a leader ready to be killed at his post and who would not allow any shirking of duty. If he had survived, he might have revised some of these judgments. No one should try to cite them as evidence to judge anyone.

He considered taking this journal with him to London, but that would have run the risk of compromising a trip whose outcome was vital to the future of the Resistance.

I carried the manuscript with me to Provence, along with some other compromising papers, to "La Lèque," a remote farmhouse in the Alpilles whose location was dear to my brother. It was there, upon his return from London, on December 31st, 1941, that he parachuted back into the country.

After the Liberation, I went to dig out the papers. Except for rust where the staples were, and some stains and moldiness, the pages were intact.

Why did I wait so long to publish this journal? It is because, in the doubt that swirled around the question of Max's[1] fate even after the Liberation, my main goal during those days was to discover what had really happened to him.

Now that the doubt, alas!, has been cleared up, the time has come to reveal to France the first fight of the future head of the Resistance.

When the SS, or some other madmen, drunk on their military success, came to arrest him at the Prefecture of Chartres, on the evening of June 17,

1. *Note by Laure Moulin in the French edition:* The last name used by Jean Moulin in the Resistance.

Jean Moulin was just a Prefect who had remained at his post in the midst of widespread desertion, a civil official carrying out his responsibilities towards and in spite of everything. The miracle which allowed him to survive then could not happen again.

Three years of dangerous life went by, filled with intense work, sleepless nights, much discomfort, constant moving about, physical prowess and sensitive deal-making, as well as sound and intelligent organizing, the founding of the National Council of the Resistance and calling its first meeting in Paris on May 23, 1943. Less than one month later, on June 21, in Lyon, following betrayal by a traitor, he once again fell into the hands of the Nazis. But this time he was no longer an unknown Prefect, he was Max, the most formidable enemy of the Germans, the one who, working for General de Gaulle, had brought together and galvanized all of the surviving forces inside the Nation.

Certainly, in Chartres in 1940, German cruelty was at its height, but torture, as inhuman and as refined as it was to become, was in its infancy and not technically evolved, with hellish torture chambers and carefully measured dosages.

Whatever suffering Max endured, in 1943, in the lair of the Gestapo, we will never know, while carrying within himself every secret of the Resistance, faithful to his friends, fanatically honorable, he withstood in his bleeding body and soul for hours, for days and nights, an eternity of suffering, facing down the enemy to the point of agony, unto death itself!

You who, even while doing all of this, enjoyed youth and life, you who were the youngest Prefect ever in France, you who were your father's pride and the smile on your mother's face, you who combined kindness and strength of character and rose to the challenge to be a born artist and a man of action, to love life passionately and to not fear death, may your sacrifice not have been in vain! May this country of liberty and justice learn how urgent it is that a sense of civic duty takes precedence over partisan politics and that the French people hear the voice of Jean Moulin crying out to them still: "Gentlemen, there is France."

Laure MOULIN

Journal

(CHARTRES, June 14–18, 1940)

Telephone call from Colonel du Tillet,[2] commanding the subdivision, who informs me that the Germans have reached the Blaise and that the greater High Command has decided to call a general retreat to the banks of the Loire. He is surprised to find me still here and that I have not directed what remains of the civil administration to evacuate the city.

I let him know that my intention is to maintain those civil services that are still in place around me for as long as possible.

4:30 a.m.

I called all of the heads of service together in the meeting room of the General Council. While keeping to myself the intentions of the GHQ,[3] I do not hide from them that the situation is deteriorating. I intend to keep them available to me until further instructions whatever the risk that might run. I perceive in their reactions an excellent frame of mind.

5 a.m.

Order from the Government requiring all "specially appointed" individuals[4] to be withdrawn immediately. These are the last instructions that I will receive from the central authority.

This is a serious decision which will deplete the administrative, economic and social services of their strength and vitality. All of the essential positions, or almost, are occupied by men who had to be expressly deferred from the military, such appointments usually involving men who are of age to be drafted but the staffing of whose position is deemed indispensable. My general secretary, my two subprefects and I are all especially appointed.

Furthermore, I know that this order will have the secondary effect of provoking the flight of whatever remains of the civilian population.

2. Du Tillet was the regional commander of the French Army. (See glossary.)

3. General headquarters.

4. Persons who enjoyed a special deferment from military service in order to fulfill important civilian duties.

But the Government certainly has its reasons, and notably the desire to snatch from the enemy's grasp the greatest possible number of men qualified to carry out their duties behind the line of resistance. On the other hand, it was impossible to contact the ministry to discuss the application of this order. I no longer know where it is located and, since nightfall, I have been unable to telephone to anywhere further away than Châteaudun.

Finally, in one of the last broadcasts that we were able to hear before the complete interruption of electricity, the radio announced the news.

I try to soften the rigor of the directive which doesn't allow for any exceptions, by asking those mayors whom I am able to reach to hold together in their service those men whom they deem to be indispensable to the vital services of the community and of the military. Despite these instructions—which strictly speaking ran counter to the decision of the government such as it had been conveyed to me—all or nearly all of them specially appointed apart from those who worked directly for me (employees of the Prefecture, heads of the administrative services, police commissioners) left within a few hours, at dawn on the day of June 14th.

In this way the sense of panic that was already palpable due to the bombing and the flow of hundreds of thousands of refugees through the department[5] was raised to the utmost.

And, starting in the morning, the bombardment of Chartres began again, more intense and more deadly than the day before.

For several days already the network of "links" of aircraft communication had been disrupted due to the retreat of our aircraft, and enemy raids in the department were now only announced by local spotters. Which is to say that usually bombs began to fall before any sirens were heard. But on this day there are no longer any sirens at all, since the military spotters had all departed as soon as they had a chance. The neighborhoods of the airfield, of the Post Office, of the hospital and the train station, and the arteries leading to the south and to the west, and in particular the rue du Grand-Faubourg, were seriously affected. Behind the Post Office, the Hôtel du "Boeuf Couronné" and the entire block of adjacent houses are on fire as a result of incendiary bombing.

We no longer have gas or electricity. Nor telephone, nor radio. I am participating in rescue work. The numbers of members on each team, alas,

5. Chartres is the capital of the French department of Eure-et-Loir.

are going down steadily. But thc brave ones who remain appear to be more devoted and courageous in direct proportion to the decline in their numbers.

Where are the leaders of Civil Defense? The municipal director fled this morning along with several of his colleagues.

Where are the Fire Department and all of their equipment? The Mayor allowed them to depart this morning, with the pumps, led by their captain and the General Secretary from City Hall, riding on the biggest of the pump trucks.

Gone as well was the director of the city's Water Service. In his wild panic, before fleeing, he had dismissed the mechanics from the hydraulic plant after closing all of the valves, so that within a few hours the city will be without water.

I had nonetheless ordered the Mayor myself, during the night, by telephone, to retain all the specially assigned heads in all essential municipal services, and particularly those in Civil Defense and in the Fire Department.

11 a.m.

Along with the young artillery lieutenant who stayed behind to manage the gasoline dump, I take charge of distributing the gas to the refugees, who continue to pour in. I get him to agree that all future gas distribution is to be free and moreover that additional distribution dumps be located on the road from Chartres to Châteaudun, and from Chartres to Nogent-le-Rotrou. We have to keep the roads as open as possible to facilitate whatever the military had to do.

3:30 p.m.

Paris has fallen! The news is brought to us by the refugees. As far as our sector is concerned, I have no update regarding the German advance since the communiqué from the Colonel in command of the subdivision. The telephone connection to Dreux has been cut for several days now and the network of gendarme couriers that I had organized to replace it was interrupted last evening on the orders of the commander because of the intensity of the bombing.

I know, from the messages that were brought to me yesterday, that there are no longer any civilians in Dreux and that the last communities that needed to be were evacuated in plenty of time. For this region of the department, the first affected, I was able to furnish the vehicles and the necessary personnel.

But I am concerned for the mayor and the subprefect who feel it is their duty to remain until the last moment. There are instructions and I would also like to give them moral support. Here people, deprived of news, are giving in to the direst of suppositions. The word is already spreading in town that the Germans have reached Dreux. I need to know, if only to be able to deny it.

I decide to go to Dreux. I have some difficulty finding a gendarme to accompany me, as the commander thinks the mission dangerous and the order having already been given for the entire company to leave in the evening.

I take the steering wheel. We are bombed and strafed the entire way there by successive waves of aircraft coming from the north, flying at between 50 and 200 meters in altitude. On this road where, just yesterday, thousands of refugees jammed the way, no one, except for a few exhausted soldiers who are fleeing without knowing anything. . . .

After several stops under trees along the way, we finally arrive in Dreux. I find the mayor, M. Viollette, and the subprefect, M. Ressier, at the town hall.

They inform me that the depot of the colonial regiment just left the city, but that the Colonel is probably still around. We go to greet him. We find him in the former headquarters making his final preparations before leaving.

I ask him for news. In our region the retreat maneuvers appear to be taking place more or less as planned, and he does not think that the Germans have entered the department as of yet. He tells me that he is sorry that he was not able to obtain orders to defend Dreux. I remain with him until he leaves.

Next, accompanied by the mayor and the subprefect, we take a spin in town. It is entirely deserted, and it would be quiet as well, if it were not for the menacing rumble of German planes that could be heard non-stop.

In the car that carries us sadly on, no one says a word, but we are all thinking the same things. So, it's over. The *Boches* are going to slip into the department without anyone's opposing them except possibly for chance encounters with units that are already falling back.

I look at Viollette seated by my side. It is his town which, tomorrow, or perhaps in only a few hours, is to be handed over to the enemy; it is this city that he led, with a hand that was perhaps a bit coarse at times, for thirty years. There is no quarter, not a single street, not a corner of this ground that does not owe him in some measure.

His adversaries said that he had "construction mania." And it is true. He built, built all the time, hospitals, clinics, schools, sanatoriums, low income housing. . . .

Now as we drive through these streets, cluttered with debris, confronted with this enterprise of systematic destruction, I think how admirable it is to be weighed down with the title of builder.

After assuring myself that all of the measures that I had called for were being carried out, and having given the subprefect, who has a special deferment, the instructions he needed for his departure, I leave Dreux.

One hour later, enemy motorcycles appeared in the town.

The return to Chartres provides us with a gripping sight. A gigantic plume of smoke rises thousands of meters into the sky and seems to weave a shroud of mourning above the cathedral.

It is the air base's fuel dump which exploded and is now burning itself slowly out.

It is around 5 p.m. In the courtyard of the Prefecture I have the unpleasant surprise of finding all of my staff packed into trucks and ready for departure. I had given direct orders that no one was to leave his post.

Furious, I order my people to get out and I instruct each one of them to return to work, until further order.

I can hardly recognize my staff. Some of the women are in a frightening state. Some of the men who only yesterday refused to go down to the basement during an air raid to continue to work by my side are now scared stiff. Idem a veteran of '14, reputed to be very brave, who scarcely hours ago was ready to volunteer for a dangerous mission, has now completely lost control over himself.

The winds of panic which up until now had passed them by now have the better of them. Nerves are frayed. Everybody has just one thought on their mind: to flee.

I exhort them, I implore them. They obey and manage to find a kind of professional automatism, but I immediately sense that for the most part I can no longer count on my chief of staff or my personal secretary.

My waiting rooms are crowded. The heads of services who have not already left on the orders of their departments are hanging around, just ready to leave. The Prefecture appears to be seen as the last safe place.

In the failing light of day amidst the boxes of archives and suitcases I notice the Bishop of Chartres, Msgr. Harscouet, who has come to apologize for not being able to remain—an ordination of priests calls him to the southern part of the department—and the senator-mayor of Chartres, M. Gilbert, who has also come to announce his departure. He appears with his wife and all of their baggage. The tragic events of the past few days, during which time he gave everything of himself, have visibly worn him out. On top of which he lost his sister-in-law and his niece in the bombing. I recognize some of the other usual hangers-on, such as the special commissioner, a bit drunk because he had to empty his cellar. This man, usually very discreet, is talking loudly and handing out English cigarettes. I remind him to show a bit more control.

9 p.m.

It is getting late and I have no further news except a report that a German patrol arrived in Dreux brought in by Viollette and Ressier, who have just returned. Nothing about the big picture either, and as of now we are no longer in communication with the outside world.

I call in Captain Bertrand. He was once the chief of the information service, and I had requested that he be my liaison with the subdivision. He was unable to get any news.

I sense that people around me are losing their nerve and that one thought is on all their minds: the 35 kilometers between Chartres and Dreux.

Up until now I have kept hold of my colleagues, but starting now new decisions are going to come into play as events unfold. I am going to take Bertrand with me when I go interview Commander Bourgeois, who is in command of the —— depot. R.I., who has set up his command post in the chateau of —— in Courville.

I get back into the Citroën.[6] In the dead of night, with the headlights switched off, we head out towards Courville. No more bombs, but trucks and cars full of refugees whose drivers, shaken by the bombings they have survived, whose only concern now is to go west, are constantly about to crash into us.

We find Commander Bourgeois working by candlelight in the main salon of the chateau.

He brings me up to date quickly: "I have received the order," he says, "to take up a position at dawn on the road from Dreux to Chartres via Châteauneuf, in order to delay the German advance. I must try to hook up with what remains of a colonial division that no one has heard anything from. I have about 800 men under me, men from other commands and reservists.

6. Citroën is a French maker of automobiles and trucks.

I only have about twenty machine guns! The situation won't take long to resolve itself, alas! . . . On the other hand, the enemy's scouts arrived this evening to reconnoiter Dreux. Tomorrow morning, at first light, motorized troops will occupy the town and from there continue their advance on Chartres. There will be nothing to stop them except for my weak forces or the possible colonial units. In my estimation the Germans should be in Chartres by early afternoon."

After thanking Commander Bourgeois and wishing him and his troops well, we head back.

Chartres is still in flames. In the rue du Grand-Faubourg the sections of wall that were spared in the bombing have an even more tragic look at night, in the pale light of the burning city.

My chief of staff, Decote, tells me that the gendarmes have just left Chartres. So the last arm of the military is gone. The airbase withdrew three days ago. The garrison left yesterday. The Supply Corps has also gone. Supply is supposed to make sure that the civilian population has food! . . . And we have thousands of refugees to feed! All that remains is the general staff of the subdivision, and its chief, Commander du Tillet, who are leaving early tomorrow.

Considering the very clear assessment of Commander Bourgeois on how events will unfold, I decide to take advantage of nightfall to evacuate everyone from the Prefecture towards the southern part of the department (to Cloyes, 50 kms. from Chartres), under the orders of the general secretary who, depending on how events evolve, will either lead them further on or bring the entire convoy back.

The same decision holds for the chiefs of service who have remained with me. The struggle continues, and they will be more useful on the other side. I thank them for the support they have offered me in these difficult hours.

June 15th, 2 a.m.

I write two letters that I entrust to the general secretary, one for the minister of the Interior, the other for my mother.

The letter to Mandel will not arrive. I was informing the minister that, as I already informed him, I was remaining at my post and that I would not fail to do my duty.

I also brought to his attention the great attitude of some of the people who worked for me, and of some of my colleagues.

5 a.m.

Decote, my chief of staff, and my personal secretary Edouard, both depart, with heavy hearts and on my direct orders.

8 a.m.

This morning I am taking stock of the situation. It is a disaster. There is no longer any economic or administrative organization. An entire social construct to be rebuilt in frightening circumstances, under falling bombs, with an entire quarter of the city in flames, without water, without gas, without electricity, without telephones. . . .

Yet this *must be done*, for the sake of all whose fate is in our hands; it *must be done* in order to present to the Germans, when they arrive, a social and moral framework worthy of our country.

These are feelings that I have no difficulty getting the handful of Chartrains, old people, for the most part, who have offered their services to me, to confirm. (There remain fewer than seven or eight hundred inhabitants out of the twenty-three thousand that once made up the city.)

What a comfort, after the spectacle of failures during recent days, to see these men and women from every political and social quarter, join together in the same conviction, and ready to achieve an undertaking of human solidarity pretty much without precedent.

I divide up the jobs, I dictate instructions; so that someone who, just yesterday, was the editor of a newspaper, is today expected to help me divide up emergency provisions; one of his colleagues, from the competing newspaper, will devote himself to the police and will head the small group of volunteers that we have pulled together. A teacher from a local parochial school has the task of burying the dead, who are, alas! numerous, being piled up in the hospital morgue and at the St. Brice hospice forty-nine were buried straight away in the courtyard of the hospital, thirteen at St. Brice's, and thirty-four in the cemetery; or someone who will direct water duty aimed at assuring from the lower town, the supply of water to welcome centers, public facilities, bakeries; or someone else yet who will organize rounding up abandoned livestock and placing them in enclosures; others, finally, who will be in charge of picking up garbage, of sanitation, of fighting fires, of housing refugees, first aid for the sick and the injured.

In the civilian hospital the mother superior had left, and it is Sr. Henriette who will replace her. She will distinguish herself for her simple devotion and her generosity. She will have by her side the head of the hospital restaurant, M. Fleury, who remained at his post.

I know that I can count on Dr. Foubert, a military dentist, who, although he is a husband, a father, and a head of household, asked to be allowed to remain as a volunteer when the health service people departed. He maintained a calm and courageous attitude in the direst of times.

The military health service left Chartres on the afternoon of the 14th, taking with them thirty trucks filled with the wounded as well as medical and nursing staff. The loading of the trucks took place during an air raid, and the head of the Chartres health service, medical colonel de Fourmestreaux, sustained a minor head wound during the operation.

The convoy, which headed for Vannes, under the command of doctor de Fourmestreaux, included medical commander Baudin, the chief of medicine at the civilian hospital, who had requested, throughout, to be allowed to remain at his post. Doctor de Fourmestreaux preferred to keep doctor Baudin close to him and instead to leave behind military captain Foubert, also a volunteer.

In the end, Chartres has the Sisters of St. Paul, who will rise to the high standard of heroism and of goodness for which they are known. Inspired by the faith of Msgr. Lejards, who is everywhere that danger is to be confronted, everywhere that there is hardship, they will be guardian angels in our darkest hour.

+ + +

But if Chartres is almost emptied of its inhabitants, the monstrous influx from the Parisian region continues to wash over the city unabated.

How many Parisians are there, these suburbanites who have wound up in the Eure-et-Loir? A million? A million and a half?

For sure, they have already felt the overwhelming blow to the morale that war brings. They haven't, for the most part, undergone any physical horrors: dive-bombings, machine-gun fire raking the convoys of refugees. They haven't experienced that, the ones we have seen so far, for weeks, Belgians, people from the Ardennes, the North, Picardy! . . .

Tomorrow they too will have their brush with tragedy. In Chartres itself, some will pay the ultimate price. But, for now, all the Parisians have to complain of is their hunger.

Fortunately, I prepared for this somewhat. In recent days, despite the failure of the Department of Supply which, before it departed, was unable to provide me with food or bread, I requisitioned from the private sector and had stored approximately three tons of canned goods in the three garages belonging to the Prefecture.[7]

I have, on the other hand, received from Blois, thanks to the kind indulgence of my colleague from the Loir-et-Cher, two busses filled with bread. I had asked for eight, which I was planning to send back filled with the wounded and the sick. Only two managed to get through. That represents about 800 kilos of bread. That's very little.

Now we must simply hold out until we can get some bakeries up and running.

At noon, I will have the wonderful surprise to receive the visit of an elderly bakery worker from the rue Muret, the only one to remain behind in Chartres. His employer left, and he has come to place on my desk, carefully folded up in his handkerchief, the recipe for the morning oven-load. He wishes to place himself under my orders, provided that I authorize him to dip into his employer's stock of flour. Not only do I agree, but I round up two volunteers to help him knead, because I need bread, lots of bread. . . .

1:30 p.m.

Into two large trucks which were supposed to go back to the Renault[8] factory in Paris that I stopped as they passed through, I loaded one hundred children from the Aligre Orphanage. They had asked me to try and evacuate them to Limoges. Right after they left the bombing started again, very hard. They just got out in time!

3 p.m.

Toured the city by car just for my own information. I drove down to the lower part of town by the small streets in the neighborhood around the

7. *Note in French edition:* "I should point out in this connection that, before these sad events, the unbounded devotion of one of my collaborators, M. Decote, head of the division which did the work of the chief of staff, had made it possible under the most extreme of circumstances to guarantee the re-supply of the refugees. At the train station alone, M. Decote served more than 172,000 full meals." (*Extract of a report from the Prefect to the Minister of the Interior, July 12, 1940.*)

8. Another major French maker of automobiles and trucks.

cathedral. Doors and shutters all closed. I don't want to say that everything appeared calm, the word appears shocking in this atmosphere of desolation.

Approaching the boulevards life picks up. What passes for life! It is still the same endless parade of refugees rolling out. But the flow is less dense and above all slower. Just two days ago this human mass was still largely motorized. Today it seems to be the large farm wagons that are setting the pace, big wagons that often pull a heavy automobile, now silent, behind them. Bicyclists and pedestrians are in the greater number, all weighed down under heavy loads. Mixed in with them are many soldiers under no military command.

At the place des Epars, the parade continues sadly between two rows of supplicants. Around the statue of Marceau and on all of the sidewalks around the square thousands of people stand extending their arms in desperation towards vehicles full to bursting that will never stop to pick up anyone.

The appearance of a man alone in a car that works sparks their envy. After waving at me from a distance dozens of human beings surge forward and grab onto my Citroën in clusters.

I have a heck of a time getting out of there. Despite all of my attempts to explain my official duties, about my moral duty to remain, they beg me to take them anywhere, towards the south or the west, far from this city of suffering and death, far from the approaching invader. An old lady follows me saying over and over: "I will pay you, sir!" And just so that I don't doubt what she says she desperately pushes a handful of bills at me.

I get free, not without difficulty, and I hurry to put my car back in the garage. I decided not to show it to anyone for now: it's too cruel.

Back at the Prefecture there are a lot of people. They are waiting for me to take delivery of the foodstuffs and bread which are intended for the institutions and rescue centers. After distributing what there was, I returned to the place des Epars to find the unfortunates that I left there.

The two poles of attraction are the two big hotels of Chartres, the Hôtel du Grand Monarque and the Hôtel de France, which face each other across the vast circular square.

The proprietors and the employees have all gone, but the guests have all remained. For the majority of them it was just a run-of-the-mill adventure, only on an endless scale: the car broken down, abandoned somewhere beside the road: the nearest city, reached on foot with whatever could be saved of the baggage: and here, at the hotel, waiting for illusory help. . . .

These initial residents have been joined by others that the road has cast up since.

There are people everywhere, in the rooms, in the lounges, on the steps of every stairway. People are eating on tables that bear still the dishes of prior diners. The silverware is lying about on sideboards. In the corners mattresses where entire families are huddled together, looking harassed. Those who were unable to get inside have settled down outside, on chairs or armchairs from inside, alongside their baggage. All classes, all ages, all sexes are jumbled up together in a tragic promiscuity.

As soon as I arrive, I am surrounded. I try to calm the anxieties of these unfortunate people, while making it quite clear to them that there is no way that they can be helped to get any further along their way. The last train left yesterday, and I do not have any more busses or a single truck. I try to get them to understand that they must accept that they must remain. For sure, there will be problems feeding them, but I will work hard to resolve that. They should not, in any case, set out again on the roads with old folks, children and baggage. We have emergency welcome centers, we will open more of the same, as needed, empty space is not lacking, alas! But the bombings? The Germans? We have excellent air-raid shelters, and the Germans don't generally attack refugees, except from on high with their airplanes, to make them flee. We shouldn't help them accomplish that. Too many refugees have clogged highways, made it difficult for our own soldiers, caused battles to be lost. You should resign yourselves to remaining. I go from group to group repeating my little speech, a speech that I have already repeated so many times. . . . But right away I begin to sense that I'm playing at preaching in the wilderness.

They are still all waving at cars, carts, to any vehicle that passes. Occasionally someone succeeds in getting a driver to have mercy, and finds a place to squeeze in with difficulty next to others; or, having waited for so long, others make the mad decision to start off again on foot. . . .

And new refugees continue to arrive, replacing the ones who leave: it's an unending relay!

I witness some pretty frightful scenes. One woman, on the doorstep of the Grand Monarque, explains her situation to me. She came from Paris on foot with a lady who shared her difficulties, and in whom she had placed her entire trust. But this woman just up and ran off taking 6,000 francs from her, which was everything she had left. I gave her a little something and she asked me for permission to kiss me.

There are a hundred, a thousand, other, more desperate cases. Lost children, wives looking for their missing husbands. A son or a daughter who was supposed to meet their mother, for whom she still waits in vain.

Other dramas are played out scribbled on walls: "We left. Meet us in Orleans," or "We lost Robert. Heading for Poitiers . . . ," and many others.

I make myself useful as best I can trying to alleviate these people's suffering. I am fortunate to find helpers among the refugees, at least among those who have given up the idea of leaving.

The situation at the hotels has to be straightened out immediately. At the Grand Monarque, among the "Guests," there is a former French consul, who accepts, at my request, to take over management of this makeshift relief station. Over the next few days he will prove to be an incalculably valuable collaborator to me.

Aided by his wife, he makes quick work of putting order into this Court of Miracles and arranging for emergency food to be brought over from the Prefecture.

Over at the Hôtel de France, where I thought all of the staff had left—the state of disarray in the establishment moreover supported this conclusion—there was a man acting like he ran the place, and saying that he had been charged as manager by the owner and told to continue running the hotel. The owners, whom I had seen at the time they were leaving, had never mentioned any of this to me, but after all it was possible. The important thing was to see that everybody ate and slept.

(I later learned that this make-believe manager was simply an impostor who liquidated the better part of the owner's cellar and put the proceeds into his pocket. To avoid complicated calculations, and to keep business moving, he charged the same price, 20 francs, for every bottle he sold. The bottles kept sliding across the bar at an unheard-of rate: 20 francs for a Napoleon brandy, 20 francs for whiskey, 20 francs for Clos de Vougeot, 20 francs for Pernod! . . . Having worked for several months for the Germans, which protected him for a while, he was finally turned over to French justice.)

4:30 p.m.

Having no other source of news, I begin to question refugees and soldiers to find out anything I could about the German advance. Contrary to what commander Bourgeois thought, the enemy had turned to force its way west, postponing an advance on places that lay in their direct path to the south.

So the troops that had taken Dreux were ordered to proceed to Verneuil and Laigle, in the direction of Argentan.

It appeared that the attack on Chartres was going to be entrusted to troops from around Paris advancing through Rambouillet and Maintenon, which would give us a little time to breathe.

5 p.m.

I go back home to find that the entrance gate has been pushed in and that my Citroën has disappeared from the courtyard where I left it an hour ago.

Two old-timers from the Hospice who came to the Prefecture looking for bread and food for their institution fill me in on what happened, how they looked on, helpless, as the fence was broken and the car was stolen. "It was some French military people who did it. They got away scarcely fifteen minutes ago."

I don't know what is more disturbing at the time, the shock of learning that I am in a critical situation like this without a car, or my sadness on learning to what a low point some elements of the French army have sunk!

Often I have heard soldiers say that their officers were the first to flee, really, jumping into cars as fast as they could, and I immediately used this to justify these guys who robbed me for doing the same thing.

But what is really incomprehensible, and unacceptable, is that no authority has arrived to replace the gendarmerie which withdrew 24 hours ago under orders from the military command. Everybody around me who lived through the war of '14 remembers how energetic the military police were. Good Lord, how they could make life insufferable for us, behind the front. And now, when we could really use them, there's not a single one in sight! We won't see any, as far as that is concerned, for the three days following the departure of the Chartres troop, leading right up to the arrival of the Germans.

There really are a lot of mysteries about this war!

5:30 p.m.

To make my feelings worse with regard to the constabulary, the few volunteers that I have charged with acting as police have come in to tell me that a number of incidents of looting have occurred.

Our meager police force needs building up. I call in M. Besnard. I direct him to try and round up some new volunteers among the able-bodied Chartrains. But are there any more of those? We doubt it. I will take a walk around the city with a couple of men to see what I find and to try and discourage looters a bit as well.

While on these rounds we notice that a certain number of shops, especially grocery stores, have been broken into and that the doors and the front windows left wide open offer a permanent temptation to passersby. I give orders that these entryways be closed up, with boards and nails if necessary.

Returning to the Prefecture I receive an update from the people whom I charged with looking for two more bakers. Among the Chartrains who have not fled there are none, apart from the old worker from the rue Muret, who is moreover carrying on valiantly in his task. Among the refugees, however, two people have stepped up: a Parisian, who says that he once ran a bakery, and a peasant woman who once upon a time made all of the bread for her farm.

I decide straightaway to open two bakeries: one in the rue du Soleil d'or and another in the rue du Pont-Saint-Hilaire. To give this move an appearance of legality, I go with M. Besnard to break into the two shops. We have the good luck to find a good quantity of flour there, as well as salt. As it happens I have a stock of yeast at the Prefecture, one of the rare things that I was able to get from the Supply Corps! The teams charged with water duty will make sure that there is enough water for the kneading troughs (we found, moreover, a spring in one of the crypts of the cathedral, close at hand) and in the nearby welcome centers, we found several volunteers who will take turns kneading dough by hand. Starting this evening we will get one batch out of each establishment.

The stock of bread at the Prefecture is running out and it is high time we established a regular supply. Finally I am going to have a fully operational bakery!

7 p.m.

I have just learned that a former mayor of Chartres, M. Vidon, has remained in town. I immediately head over to his residence. I know for a fact that he is an energetic man, capable of taking on serious work.

I explain what I need from him, side by side with M. Besnard, for all of the matters that involve running the city, and in particular the public works. We must, first and foremost, get the water back on again, and I know that he is the only one among us, thanks to his experience, to be able to undertake this task.

We have to continue to fight the fire, which is spreading, look out for public safety, and also for the city sanitation. There are some urgent needs in connection with this last. We must clean out the butchers' shops and the *charcuteries* whose proprietors fled leaving their refrigerators full of meat. But the power has been off for a while now, and with the heat, these indoor charnel houses risk becoming focal points of disease all over town. We must also put down and bury the hundreds of dogs and cats that have been abandoned by their masters and are now wandering around the town and becoming a danger as well. . . .

We hardly knew each other at all, Vidon and me; we were at different poles politically. But today we have no difficulty understanding each other. Straightaway and without reservation, he assures me of his complete support.

This will be of a rare quality in the course of the days to come.

8:30 p.m.

Visited the emergency refugee welcome centers. Nearly all of these facilities are now full. But the ones which are proving to be the most successful are the ones that have large cellars or nearby air-raid shelters.

The people have all been fed, for better or for worse. I had some milk distributed, jam, and a little bread. Some women of good will are helping the Sisters of St. Paul, and are shuttling food supplies from the Prefecture to the Sainte-Foy auditorium and the welcome centers. They are also helping out, discreetly and anonymously, with the children and the old people, with the sick and the wounded, whom we can no longer admit to the hospital, because it is full. The abbot Pechetaux, who also stayed behind in Chartres, has been helping out tirelessly as well.

A painful sight was waiting for me back at the cathedral: in the deepest crypt, lit only by a few votive candles, a mass of bruised humanity lay on mattresses and stretchers. On every face, chiseled by candlelight, could be read the signs of lack of sleep, fever, fear. Old people who couldn't keep up, the sick and the injured who found no room at the hospital, all the ones who couldn't get into the air-raid shelters fast enough were brought here, to this place with no air, no light, lacking the most basic facilities. They are safe from the bombing, of course, but you'd be better off dodging bombs than remaining in this stinking place! . . .

Besides, it seems to me that the bombing has grown less frequent and less intense. The Nazi aircraft must be working further away.

It is too late to move these people this evening. But I want them gotten out of here as early as possible tomorrow.

Leaving there, I instinctively look for some more pleasant sight. I head for one of the two bakeries that we opened, where I find my people in the back room waiting for the first load of bread to come out. They open the door of the oven to show me the rows of loaves growing golden brown. Just a moment longer and we will once again taste the piping hot, crusty bread of la Beauce. . . .

I recall, back in my childhood, having heard an old farmer telling how his mother made him kiss every piece of bread that she gave him before he ate it. I never really understood before now. . . . Today I could definitely kiss this white bread which was going to save us.

At the other bakery the load is already out of the oven. I am assured that tomorrow morning there will be another one at each oven.

I leave the place as happy as I could be, just as the bombing begins again, with a tremendous noise. The calm sure didn't last very long!

I decide to appropriate an automobile, because if we were to have injured people, we no longer had any way to transport them.

In the place des Epars, I have the good luck to get my hands on an old Berliet[9] carrying two "special appointment" types who were on the move. I am in a hurry to get to the hospital by car, where I am reassured to learn, thank God, that no new injuries have been reported.

In the meantime, retreating French soldiers have begun to appear in Chartres. Their trucks are parked all along the boulevard, filling the entire roadway. A group of artillerymen have set up their guns under the trees on the square where the Livestock Market is located, in front of the Boeuf Couronné hotel, which continues to burn.

I question some men in an effort to find out where command of the troops that were stationed in Chartres is now. But I only succeed in finding a young second lieutenant who is completely lost in the dark of night and unable to give me any precise information.

I return to the square where my artillerymen have set up tables and benches. I sit down next to these young soldiers and we begin to yak. They are almost hayseeds, guys from the Languedoc and the Southwest. I say how pleased I am that they are going to defend Chartres. They nod their heads

9. A line of trucks manufactured by Citroën.

skeptically. And then all of a sudden they are telling me how surprised they are that the army is pulling back, always pulling back without even waiting to make contact with the enemy. There are things they do not understand.

They seem in good spirits despite that, despite the defeats, despite everything. And I sense that it would take very little to get them to fight with anger in their guts, the way one would have to fight in a struggle where so much was at stake!

Time passes. Now they are talking about where they come from, their families, and what is going to happen afterwards. After what?

3 o'clock in the morning

I am going to bed. The enemy will not show up during the night.

June 16th, 7 a.m.

A severe storm hit the city in the night. The rain, which fell heavily at times, just about put out the fire in the neighborhood of the Post Office. But it also did some damage. Water flooded the interior of the chapel of Sainte-Foy that had become home to many refugees.

I go take a look at the situation. In the nave of the chapel fifty cots are standing in water. A number of old people haven't gotten up yet. The other refugees have moved into the sacristy or the side offices in order to keep dry. I hand out clothing and blankets and arrange for two of the more seriously injured old folks to be admitted to the Saint-Brice hospice.

Together with M. Abdon-Boisson, the ex-consul who took charge over at the Hôtel du Grand Monarque, I take a fresh look at the problem of housing all of the refugees and I make the decision there and then to open up the Guéry institution. It is a vast school complex, located right across the street from the Prefecture, that I have already used as a center for kids from the region of Paris. It has a lot of beds, which I can add to, and kitchens with all of the equipment needed. So we will be able to relocate a lot of refugees together very close to the office, which will make it easier to keep an eye on them and keep them supplied. To begin with, we will relocate the people from the chapel of Sainte-Foy and from the crypt of the cathedral.

I put M. Boisson in charge of getting the Guéry building going, with getting whatever material was needed and finding cooks.

8 a.m.

I have to locate the officer in charge of defending Chartres. After checking out several fruitless leads in town, I am told that there is a commander in Luisant. I go there by bicycle because the truck that we requisitioned yesterday absolutely refuses to start up again.

In Luisant I am told that I have to speak to Commander de Torquat.[10] He has just pulled in and he has set up his headquarters in Chartres, in the boulevard Chasles. I head back to Chartres. Commander de Torquat, of the 7th regiment of mobile Dragoons, is installed, along his officers, in one of the houses attached to the girls' *lycée.*

A friendly welcome, mixed with surprise. I am the first Prefect he has encountered since hostilities began a week ago at the border. We talk about the overall situation. It's tragic. As for his in particular, it can be summed up as follows: his equipment is all worn out, and he really needs to reorganize his unit; but his men are magnificent and will do their duty until the bitter end, no matter what the outcome.

I ask him about the German advance in our sector. He is in fact waiting for a liaison officer to arrive who is supposed to give him an update. Soon the man arrives on a motorcycle. I am present as he is debriefed. The lead motorized German units are on the outskirts of Nogent-le-Roy, 27 kilometers away.

I thank Commander de Torquat and take my leave, after being invited to join him for lunch. I accept with enthusiasm.

9:30 a.m.

Back at the Prefecture, Minet, the journalist that I put in charge of food supplies, informs me that the bakeries are not meeting expectations. There was no second oven load this morning. We concur that our volunteer baker can't be trusted. I instruct him to keep a close eye on the man.

In the meantime I want to get a message to Mécheri, the subprefect of Châteaudun, who might be able to help us.

The other journalist, Rousselot, who still has a working car, volunteers

10. De Torquat was a commander in the retreating French Army.

for this mission. I write out the message for him to deliver. I let Mécheri know about our situation here, and request, urgently, that he send us bread.

With tonight's oven load, we only have 300 kilos left.

Still on my bicycle, I go visit the bakeries, where I try to put a bit of fire under our oven-keepers. I have the growing suspicion that our baker is doing a bad job, and that instead of encouraging the men that I have put at his disposition, he is encouraging them to slack off, giving them drinks, and looking for reasons to delay the work. And a slick talker, to boot. "Boy, they have really filled your heads with a lot of nonsense, my poor lambs. The Boches are just guys like you and me," he says whenever he gets a chance. This individual definitely doesn't please me at all. Only among all of these people he is the only one in this lot who really knows how to make bread!

I admonish him, sharply, reminding him that it is the lives of thousands of women, children and old folks that are now at stake. If his attitude doesn't change quickly, I won't hesitate to come down hard on him as the current situation obliges me.

I don't need to push it. He has understood. Turning back to his assistants he shouts, "Okay, guys, enough joking around, down to business!"

At the other bakery, not a soul! Our farmer's wife has disappeared; the men I assigned to help her have all done likewise. The baker is most definitely not unaware of their departure.

I don't waste any time on useless regrets. We ought to be able to find soldiers to replace them.

I head over to the military command post on the boulevard Chasles to inquire whether there might not be a baker or two in the contingent that they might let me borrow. The captain who is the adjutant to the commander finds me two suitable candidates for today right away, and I put them to work immediately.

In fact, the threat of famine turns out to be difficult to stave off.

11 a.m.

I return to the Prefecture. The food distribution staff are in the public assistance office that we decided to open in order to streamline the distribution of supplies. Starting today it is supposed to provide a meal at noon.

Many people have shown up at the door of the Prefecture seeking rations, condensed milk, and especially bread.

I have been handing out supplies myself. Then, taking advantage of a brief lull, I go and shut myself in my office to do some work.

But very shortly I hear a clamor outside, and I understand enough of what I hear to know that I must go out immediately.

Outside the Prefecture there is a crowd of some two hundred people, led by three or four characters who are talking about "setting fire to the place" and who say they hope to see "the Boches arrive soon to straighten out this rotten mess." My arrival, in uniform, appears to dampen their enthusiasm. But very soon the crowd, encouraged by their leaders, starts to demand bread in the threatening tones of a revolutionary mob.[11]

As soon as I can get a word in, I try to get them to listen to reason: "I am appealing to your patriotism," I say in effect, "I am calling on you to act with dignity and decorum when the enemy arrives. I understand how deeply distressed the situation makes you, but you are wrong to blame the few people who remained behind to help you out."

I sense that my words hit home with many, but I am also dealing with a number of hardened troublemakers who showed up on purpose to stir up a fight. The fifth column is doing its job well.

They don't hesitate for a second and immediately start demanding that we hand out more relief supplies.

I refuse categorically, saying that there will be a distribution at noon at the public assistance office. Old people and children will be given priority, and wise guys who still have the strength to shout will be served last of all.

Now I think I have gotten the best of them. And in fact, after a bit more grumbling the crowd breaks up. But the incident is significant.

Noon.

Here comes Minet to pick up bread and supplies for the noon distribution at the public assistance office. We have to hurry up because a crowd is already beginning to gather.

It's just the two of us to do the job. By borrowing the post office's cart we manage to get it done in only three or four trips. And, because the cart is completely enclosed, we can go straight through the center of town without

11. "*Sur l'air des lampions*": literally, "to the tune of the paper lanterns" that the mobs carried in 1789, singing "*Ah, Ça ira, ça ira, ça ira,*" and so forth.

anybody noticing what a precious cargo we have. We quickly fill our wagon and head over to the office which is scarcely four hundred yards away. In front of the cathedral we encounter a group of people and hear shouting. What is going on?

Some guy has a spot in a ground-floor window of the public school and is haranguing the crowd. He has a wooden leg and is making a lot out of being an injured war veteran. He's calling on people to riot, using language more violent than any I've ever heard, urging them to loot in order to "protest," as he puts it, "against those who have stuffed your heads. It's high time that the Boches get here!" he adds. Again, the big pitch is made. Hitler sent many different advocates, but the message is always the same.

I approach and call out to the "speaker" to try to get him to shut up. Unfortunately my attire—I'm dressed in shirtsleeves—is not about to impress anyone, and I only succeed in drawing a barrage of insults from him and from a number of his supporters. I back off, warning any who would hear me not to follow bad shepherds.

I will be back on the attack.

Meanwhile Minet has arrived at his destination and has distributed the bread and foodstuffs. He has managed to find helpers and he is going back for another load.

The place where the office of public assistance is located is well suited for distributing food, and M. Besnard has organized a security team to get people to keep in line and not to create disturbances.

With the steer that Vidon arranged to be slaughtered, and the loads of vegetables that they rounded up this morning, the Sisters of St. Paul have cooked up a huge stew. I had two thousand tins of *pâté* brought over from the Prefecture, and an equal number of portions of gruyère cream and several cases of condensed milk. The baskets of bread are ready. We can actually begin to serve up food: it is the best answer to the fifth column.

12:45 p.m.

While the food distribution goes ahead without a hitch, I head over to the commander's headquarters. A one-of-a-kind atmosphere where a group of battle-tested junior officers were gathered who refused to let the increasingly bad news get them down.

At this level, in any case, leadership did not collapse.

At the end of the meal, Commander de Torquat says a few words to congratulate me for what he calls, very flatteringly, my "civic courage," and closes by saying that he is proud to name me, in the presence of his officers who he says know the importance he attaches to the distinction, an honorary Dragoon in the 7th R.D.P.[12]

I am quite moved when it is my turn to thank him.

I explain to the commander about my concern regarding the fifth column and my desire to set an example for all to see. "Give me a few men," I said to him, "so that at least we can go arrest the *agent provocateur* over at the school by the cathedral."

Eight men and one hanger-on are now waiting for me outside the command post in order to do just this. It's a lot more than necessary, but at least it will make a real show of force. We head toward the cathedral. We can't hear anything except the roar of airplanes so numerous they are, flying as close as they can to the rooftops, right over our heads. Then about forty or fifty meters away, one after another, they all dive down and unleash their machine guns. In the place des Epars it's like a merry-go-round. The planes come in quick succession at a truly terrifying rhythm. Women and children run screaming every which way. All around the edge of the square, soldiers have taken shelter face down on the pavement just in front of the houses.

We continue on our way, keeping as close to the walls as possible, and pretty soon we're near the school. I go in first and proceed to arrest the man with the wooden leg, despite his protestations and those of a number of the criminal mugs that were hanging around. It turns out he wasn't injured in the war at all, but in a work accident. He is carrying a notebook that is full of suspicious-looking information and addresses that will be very interesting to check out.

While I am handing him over to my men, a woman who has been busily packing up some china starts beseeching me in the name of her five children not to take her husband away from her. When I begin to question her, she admits right away that she has no children and that she is not the wife of our prisoner. She adds that she thinks he was sent here on purpose (by whom? She doesn't know, or pretends not to know) to create trouble, and they decided on arriving to open an aid station the better to get the attention of refugees. I decide to arrest her as well.

12. Regiment of Motorized Dragoons. *Note in French edition:* The exact title, according to Commander de Torquat, was Honorary Brigadier of his battalion.

After having given the commander a written report, I hand the two individuals over to him to be processed by military justice.

I believe that the example had a salutary effect, because the rest of the afternoon and the evening passed without further incident in the town.

The commander and I parted with a firm handshake. We did not see each other again. (Commander de Torquat was killed a few kilometers from Chartres, leading his unit in battle.)[13]

3 p.m.

A group of six or seven employees of the PTT[14] from Paris, led by a manager, show up at the Prefecture. They had to abandon the car they were in, and they are reporting for instructions.

I assure them straight away that there is no hope they can continue in the direction they were going, that they should settle in at the Prefecture. I will find something for them to do.

As soon as they have rested they can start to clean the offices where my employees spent three days and nights, and that they left in a complete mess.

+ + +

I learn that the bakeries have begun to turn out decent oven loads and that they finally have built up a considerable supply. Since the number of refugees appears to be diminishing as well, I now believe that we are saved!

It's just as well, because no help can get in from outside. M. Rousselot, who has come back from Châteaudun, has proudly completed his mission and gives me a complete report:

The bombing was severe. There are both dead and injured. The church of La Madeleine, the Tribunal, the subprefecture are all in flames. The hospital was also hit. The residents who stayed on as well as the refugees are all having great difficulty finding food. There is a shortage of bread, and the subprefect cannot, unfortunately, do anything to help us.

13. *Note in French edition:* Fortunately, this is a mistake based on a false rumor. Commander de Torquat, who later rose to the rank of colonel, commanded the 1st Regiment of Motorized Dragoons in Lunévile until 1946, when it was finally disbanded.

14. The Post Office (Postes, télégraphes et téléphones).

This news is sad, but I am happy to learn that Mécheri, despite the order announced by the government over the radio day before yesterday, including all special appointees, has remained, as I had hoped, at his post, bravely leading relief efforts.

3:30 p.m.

I obtain a bicycle from a soldier from the Second Reserve who is falling back to his depot. (I now have a considerable fleet of bikes at the Prefecture.) He helps me to start one of the many cars stalled in the streets of Chartres. It's a big Renault sedan that could be very useful to me.

4 p.m.

I come back into town. Planes continue to strafe the place des Epars. It's because there is now a column of retreating tanks passing through.

Two young soldiers from the tank corps with a breakdown who are waiting for help come over and talk to me in the center of the square in front of the statue: twenty-one and twenty-three years old. Parisians. Completely gung-ho. It occurs to me that Marceau had this same energy that burns in their eyes. I ask them their impressions. "What do you want?" "They keep telling us to retreat. For fifteen days that's all we've done." "And why?" "Every time we counter-attacked it was hard, but the Boches hightailed it!"

"So?"

"So, once they tell us to make a stand, we'll hold."

"And your equipment?"

"It's true we have very little, but what we have is excellent. What we fear the most are the anti-tank guns that the Germans captured from us."

They leave me to go back and join their buddies. "Don't worry, *Monsieur le Préfect*," they say to me as a farewell. "They haven't licked us yet."

5 p.m.

I return to the Prefecture. One of the employees who is a postal worker has brought a young woman with her who is a nurse. It is a godsend. I am going to take her over to the welcome centers, so that she can put in a day working and then hopefully start to visit them regularly to help the suffering as they arrive.

I take the Renault, which has been fixed. A quick once around. Despite all of their serious problems, the refugees and the Chartrains are for the most part living in satisfactory sanitary conditions. There are exceptions, of course, and these have our full attention. We are told, for example, that a certain number of people, old folks in particular, haven't come out of the cellars since Thursday (June 13).

I gather together some willing souls and we start to visit bomb shelters in the neighborhood of the cathedral, of the covered market, and the flower market. We bring back out a number of families that we try very hard to reassure. I ask the residents of Chartres to remain indoors, and to sleep calmly in their own beds. I arrange for the refugees to be driven to the welcome centers.

At the place du Marché aux Fleurs, in a house that has three levels of cellars, one on top of the other, we bring up, from 15 meters underground an old woman who is virtually paralyzed. She has been down there for five days!

I have her put into my car and send her off to the hospice because her condition is not at all reassuring.

On the boulevard de la Courtille I am broken down in front of a tank unit. A sergeant at arms appears and starts shouting at me: "What are you doing in our way with the German army coming down on us?"

I'm not wearing my hat and my uniform is covered by my raincoat, and though I try to explain that I am the Prefect and that I am trying to get this disabled person to the hospital, he doesn't believe me. "The Prefect? Sometimes, you people! The fifth column, more likely. I'm going to get my commander!"

The commander appears and he asks for my papers. When he sees my card from the Ministry of the Interior he apologizes and introduces himself: "Commander Hugo d'Herleville. It's so unusual," he adds, "to come across representatives of the civil service behind our lines, that we are naturally wary." He calls for a mechanic who fixes my car right away.

Finally I can drop my passenger off at the hospice.

7 p.m.

I go home to sleep for a few hours. My guests decide to spend the night in the cellar. But the nurse agrees to wake me up at 10:30. In fact I promised Commander Torquat's junior officers that I would go to say good night to them at their advance positions at the end of the evening.

11:30 p.m.

I am at the Porte Guillaume, behind the tanks, with a young lieutenant from the 7th Regiment D.P.

The constant sound of artillery that I have had in my ears all day seems finally to have abated. Are the Germans perhaps backing down? We will be receiving a dispatch soon. When it comes it is, alas, an order for the French troops to fall back.

Midnight.

Everyone has gone. I return home, alone.

June 17th, 3 a.m.

The uninterrupted sound of trucks with, from time to time, the characteristic clanking of the treads of assault tanks summons me from my slumber.

The sounds continue so I get up and go down to the garden which overlooks the boulevard Sainte-Foy. In the night, heavy vehicles and tanks are passing by endlessly, coming from the north.

The procession is endless: but are they friend or foe?

I go out and try to catch some word in all of the racket, a command that would help me figure out what was what. Nothing.

So, to put an end to my nagging doubts, I call out to some soldiers whose uncertain silhouette is barely perceptible in the darkness: "French or German?" "French!" come back voices. "What are you doing?" I add. "Everyone has gone. . . ."

I remain in the darkness, until the procession has passed. Next comes the infantry. It is painful to watch, poignant. They advance in groups, in ranks, worn out, without a word.

The groups become further apart. Then, dragging their feet, isolated individuals. Another group comes along and stops right in front of me to catch their breath. They are tired, physically and in spirit. "What do you expect?" asks one of them, who seems to be expressing what they all feel. "They are wearing us out retreating, all the time retreating. We fought, and we were still capable of fighting, us too. But they are wearing us out with these forced marches, without order, and often without commanders. . . ."

"Ah, if we had launched a serious counteroffensive, all of the guys would have done their duty, to the bitter end. . . . But now it's way late and I think everything is fucked. . . . We are worn out! . . ."

I try to encourage them, to tell them that once they get across the Loire they can re-form and that we will hold. . . . "If only you are right," they reply.

These were the last free French soldiers that I was to see for many long months.

6 a.m.

I am awakened by the postal workers who announce that Mgr Lejards and M. Besnard, whom I asked to come, are here. I slip into my uniform quickly and go join them.

The Germans rarely enter cities under cover of darkness, but now they will not delay in coming. Now there is nothing to stop them, except perhaps a handful of Senegalese who, it is said, fought magnificently and made them pay dearly for their advance.

We decide to wait for the Germans in the courtyard of the Prefecture. Mgr Lejards on my right and M. Besnard on my left, we exchange somber comments on the state of affairs. We are facing the flag which still floats over the iron gates of the entranceway. We catch ourselves staring at it, as if we hoped to draw strength from it, to get our fill of it for as long as necessary. . .

Suddenly motors are heard firing. The first motorcyclists pass, not without noticing in surprise the three individuals, immobile under the French colors.

It is 7 a.m.

Next come the self-propelled artillery. They slow down as they pass us, but they do not stop. Soon a big automobile comes and stops right in front of us, and several officers get out straightaway. Military salutes.

The oldest one, who is without a doubt their commander, steps forward and, in French, asks who we are.

I state that I am the Prefect and that I have at my sides the representative of the Bishop and the mayor of Chartres.

I add: "The fortunes of war have led you to enter our city as conquerors. We submit to the laws of war, and I am prepared to assure you that order will prevail if you, for your part, can assure us that your troops will respect the civil population, and especially the women and the children."

To which the officer says to me: "You can be sure that German soldiers will respect the population. I am holding you, *Monsieur le Préfet*, responsible for public order and I invite you to remain in place. Tell all of your staff that the war is over for them."

They left just as quickly as they had appeared. Mgr Lejards and M. Besnard remain by my side while I announce the latest instructions to the general population, as required by my commission.

We can now hear the constant rumble of the enemy armor which must by now be in complete possession of the city and starting to move onward. The Prefecture opens on the rue Colin-d'Herlevile,[15] a small side street, not a major thoroughfare, and all that we will see out front now are occasional cars all alone, and soon a few soldiers on foot.

So it is that we eventually see a German officer and a civilian heading up the street arm in arm, in our direction.

Somehow the civilian looks familiar. I am not mistaken: he's our baker! I was right not to trust him. . . .

Now he taunts us and he introduces his companion: "He's a pal of mine, a great guy. He'd like to visit the cathedral. He is quite knowledgeable about it, you know. . . ."

The officer, wearing a monocle, snickers.

We remain silent. I sense that, unless compelled to do so, none of us will speak to this vile spy.

The German has caught on and, after a moment, he asks Mgr Lejards himself in French for permission to visit the cathedral.

He grants permission and points out, moreover, that the church is always open anyway for worship.

His statement is correct, of course, but I read in the prelate's eyes the combined humiliation of the Christian and the Frenchman.

The morning passes without serious incident. I remain at the Prefecture and see to the removal of my two cars, the old Berliet and the Renault, by the maintenance service, whose first job it is to fix or tow away to the motor pool any and all usable vehicles.

I point out that this is not military materiel and object to this arbitrary sequestration. My remarks go unheeded.

10:30 a.m.

I take the opportunity of relative calm to visit the offices that are now impeccable. I install the postal workers there, and they will also take over the job of reception.

15. *Note in French edition:* This street, the entrance to which has been widened, was renamed the place Jean Moulin on November 11, 1945.

I have asked City Hall to do the same with the volunteer staff that it has pulled together.

Our refugees are now suitably installed, and the locals also seem to be getting on, now that they are assured they will have food. The essential public services can function.

The invader thus has a social organization with which he must reckon. This will have the advantage of sparing us the hundreds of propaganda posters that were inflicted on other cities: "Abandoned residents, trust in the German soldier!"

It would be a few days before a few such posters, aiming to fill in for the government that had abandoned us, would appear on walls of the city.

2:30 p.m.

Once around the city in civilian clothes. Trucks continue to pour in and to park very methodically in every available space. They are on the boulevard Sainte-Foy, boulevard Chasles, boulevard de la Courtille, on the embankments of the Eure, place Drouvaire, on the promenade des Charbonniers. A large group is parked around the center of the place des Epars. Motorcycles and light automobiles constantly come through and go around the heavy convoys.

Teams of signal corps unroll kilometers of telephone wire that they string up on buildings, trees, lamp-posts. . . .

Following the tanks, it is said, a lot of artillery came through. Right now it is foot soldiers parading along, weapons shouldered, bare-headed, their helmets attached to their belts.

Overhead, occasional planes pass on patrol.

Civilians are few and they generally move quickly. Nonetheless I run into a few people who are friends. We exchange what news we have: This morning, when they arrived, the Germans shouted to all the civilians they met: "The war is over for you!" It is the formula. I had already heard it myself.

Now they are spreading the news of the capitulation of the French army and of the flight of Reynaud and Mandel to England. When they can get close to a group of Frenchmen, they turn up the radios in their trucks and simultaneously translate as best they can. Without any local broadcasts, no one can contradict what they say.

But what the Germans don't say is about the atrocities they have already committed in the department.

I learn from a trustworthy man who comes by bicycle from the north of the department, that in Luray a woman of eighty-three years was shot this morning for having protested against the occupation of her home.

I will have the opportunity to officially confirm this misdeed which was moreover worse than I had originally thought. The victim was the widow Mme Bourgeois, née Paucher, who was born in Luray, where she still resided.

At dawn on the 17th of June 1940, Germans broke into her home. Mme Bourgeois appeared and protested against this infraction of her residence. At the order of their commander, the German soldiers seized her and took her into the garden. She was tied to a tree and shot in front of her own daughter, despite the latter's pleading.

But the monstrous carrying on of these new barbarians didn't stop there. Nazis like to raise things to new levels: so they forbid the daughter to take her mother's body down from the tree where she had been so abused for twenty-four hours. And they further required that the daughter dig her mother's grave herself, during the same day, and right in front of her mother's corpse.

So at the very same moment as the German officer was assuring me that the German army would respect the local population, the self-same German army was committing this odious crime against a woman of eighty-three years!

4 p.m.

I go over to City Hall, where I find Besnard and Vidon. The latter has already made contact with the Germans in the interest of getting municipal water flowing again. With Besnard's agreement, I ask Vidon—given the enormous problems that we are going to have to deal with, and to strengthen his position with regard to the occupier—to officially take the title of mayor of Chartres.

4:30 p.m.

I return to the Prefecture via the old town. We were getting used to the quiet of these streets with all of their businesses closed. We thought they were abandoned. So I was surprised, passing in front of the half-open doorway of a bistro, to hear guttural voices, a woman's laugh and the pop of a cork.

(I hasten to note that one should not impute any widespread failing on the part of the general population from a few individual acts of spinelessness. Quite the contrary, and it is my duty here to point out that the population of Chartres and of the Eure-et-Loir, in the great majority, from the very beginning, conducted itself with dignity that in numerous cases showed courage, and occasionally true heroism.)

I realize that looting has risen considerably. It is true that the looters have received reinforcements. On my route I have noticed that several stores that were intact only yesterday have now been stripped bare. In the place du Marche aux Fleurs I see a German soldier coming out of a jewelry store on his hands and knees. Elsewhere it is by the carload, and even the truck load, that I see officers and soldiers taking cloth, preserves, bottles. . . .

At the Prefecture my colleagues tell me that it is the same in other neighborhoods. In many cases, moreover, instead of working on their own, the Germans are using civilians whom they have come upon in the process of looting. Instead of punishing them, they have taken them under their protection and brought them to work in front of stores that interest them and get them to demolish the storefronts. When the way is cleared, they go in right behind the civilians.

This is particularly characteristic of Nazi hypocrisy. How many times did I hear German officers say in days to come regarding these clear cases of theft that I complained about: "German soldiers are not looters; they never commit infractions; but one cannot expect them to not take advantage of property that is left lying around within hand's reach."

6 p.m.

I sit down to share a meal with my postal workers who decided to eat early, because they are eager to get home and shut themselves up tightly for the night.

Scarcely had I begun my soup when the employee who was covering the reception desk hurries in to tell me that two German officers are asking for me on an urgent matter.

"Ask them to wait a moment to give me time to slip into my uniform." In fact, I want to maintain a strict formality in my dealings vis-à-vis the enemy.

I receive them in my office. The one who does the talking, in the purest French that is almost without accent, is a young officer of about thirty years in age. Blond, thin, he is actually quite short, with a disturbing mixture of obsequiousness and disdain about his face. Like his comrade, he is wearing the uniform of the *Wehrmacht.*

(I wondered later whether these men, and in particular the young officer, had the three characteristic letters of the Gestapo on the epaulettes of their uniforms. I can't say now. I was not yet completely familiar with Nazi ranks and army specialties and organization at that time.)

"The General wishes to see you, *Monsieur le Préfet,* for an important communication," he says to me in a deferential tone of voice. "He asked me to come and get you."

"Fine," I replied. "I am ready to follow you."

We got into a car that was parked outside the Prefecture. It pulled away immediately. In the place des Epars they told me to get out and to go and wait in front of the Hôtel de France, which had been occupied since the morning. They say that they are going to announce my arrival to the General. A quarter of an hour passes. Twenty minutes. To pass the time I start to walk around a bit on the sidewalk, when a soldier whom I hadn't seen and who was apparently in charge of watching over me points his rifle at me and orders me not to move. I don't insist.

The young officer happens to return just moments later. He is alone and he asks me to walk with him.

In the middle of the square amidst the noise of motors and the coming and going of soldiers of all ranks, he stops and begins to lecture me about what the General is going to expect of me. With what appeared to be sham indignation, he recounts some supposed atrocities committed by our soldiers while they were falling back. "Women and children, French people," he insists, "were massacred after having been raped. Some of your black troops did this, and France will bear the shame of it forever. Since this explanation of events has been proven beyond a doubt, it is appropriate that a document has been drawn up stating responsibility in the matter. It is in connection with this that the staff of the German army drew up an affidavit that will be signed by our general on behalf of the German army and by you as the Prefect of the department."

I express my complete surprise at this, and object to the charges against the French army, and in particular against the black troops. "Our native infantrymen certainly fight with fierce energy on the battlefield," I add. "But they are incapable of committing any impropriety against the civilian population, much less what you are describing."

I sense right away that we are going to have a serious confrontation over this.

"I regret to say that we are absolutely certain of the facts," he tells me flatly. "In any case, you will follow me to the General's."

I obey.

We arrive at the entrance to the rue du Dr Manoury. I am led into a vast and beautiful house, set back a little from the street. As soon as we cross the threshold two soldiers grab their rifles, fix bayonets, and begin looking me over from head to toe. There can be no doubt that they were expecting me. The officer leaves me with these two men and goes into the first room on the right. He comes back immediately and invites me to go in. I am now in the presence of three officers, of whom two are the original pair that came to fetch me at the Prefecture. The third one is sitting behind a desk that has leather briefcases on it as well as some loose papers.

In a far more abrupt manner now, the man who brought me in here, and who seems to be the one who has been charged with conducting this entire matter, tells me again what is expected of me: "Here is the affidavit you are to sign." And the man who is seated at the table, without getting up, hands me a typewritten sheet of paper.

I answer without even taking the paper: "Do you really think that a Frenchman, and moreover one who is charged with high public office, whose job it is to represent his country in the face of its enemies, could possibly accept to sign such an infamy?"

The reaction is instantaneous. The Nazi master of ceremonies leaps at me, threatening me with his fist: "We will not accept that you mock the army of the Great German Reich! You are going to sign, do you understand? You are going to sign!" He grabbed me by the lapels of my service jacket and shakes me furiously. I do not resist.

"Believe me, it is not by pushing me around that you are going to get me to commit a breach of duty."

So with a remarkable strength for such a small fellow like him he slams me against the table violently. I stagger a bit to keep my balance, which makes all three of the Nazis laugh.

The one who was sitting down now gets up and tries in bad French, but in a calmer tone, to convince me that I absolutely must sign the "affidavit."

The Nazi—We have all the proofs we need that it was your soldiers that committed these atrocities.

Me—I am willing to consider these proofs if you show them to me.

The Nazi, picking up the piece of paper that he offered me a moment ago—As stated in the affidavit, French troops, and in particular black soldiers, in their retreat, took a railway roadbed next to which were found, about twelve kilometers outside of Chartres, the raped and mutilated bodies of a number of women and children.

Me—What proof do you have that the Senegalese infantrymen passed exactly where you found the bodies?

The Nazi—We found equipment that was abandoned by them.

Me—I would like to believe you. But even if I were to believe that they in fact passed that way, how can you prove they actually did it?

The Nazi—There is no doubt about that. The victims were looked at by German specialists. The injuries they suffered show all the characteristics of crimes having been inflicted by negroes.

Despite the seriousness of the circumstances underlying this discussion, I cannot help but crack a smile: "The characteristics of crimes having been inflicted by negroes." This was all they had found in the way of proof! . . .

My smile made them very angry, and my interlocutor curses me furiously in German. Next, the young Nazi says something to the third officer who has remained still and silent. Now this man takes out his revolver, steps over behind me and sticks the barrel of the gun in my back.

Then he pushes me brutally towards the table where a pen with which to sign is thrust at me commandingly.

"Sign," says the blond officer, "or you will soon learn what it costs to taunt German officers."

Since I do not bring myself to bend over and take the pen, I am given a blow between the shoulder blades that makes me stagger. It was the officer behind me who hit me with the barrel of his gun.

I protest this despicable treatment: "I was brought here to see the General. Where is the General? It is with him that I wish to discuss these matters."

My mentioning the General is met by raucous laughter interspersed with joking in German that I cannot understand.

"This is no longer a matter for the General, but we are going to take you to see another officer," the young blond officer says after this, and he calls in one of the men on duty in the hall and gives him an order. The soldier grabs me by the shoulder and pushes me, more than actually directing me, towards another room in the house. As, in his opinion, I do not exit the room as quickly as he would like, he deals me such a blow in the small of my back with the butt of his rifle that this time I actually fall down on the floor.

Before I have time to get up, someone starts kicking me. It's the third officer, the one I had been brought in to see, who is doing this.

I wonder if I will have the strength to get up.

In front of me I now have the blond officer who has followed us, the officer who was kicking me, and the soldier, with a bayonet attached to his rifle.

The little blond officer, whom I will henceforth call my #1 torturer, gives a signal to the soldier, who points his bayonet at my chest and screams in German, "Get up!"

With one painful lurch I straighten up. I am in terrible pain. I feel that my legs can barely support me. Instinctively I move toward a chair to sit down. The soldier removes it brutally and slams the butt of his rifle down on my feet. I cannot help but scream.

Then, when I have settled down a bit: "When is this outrage going to stop?"

"Not until you have signed the affidavit," says my #1 torturer, and he pushes the paper at me again.

Me—I don't understand why you are so obsessed with this, and especially not why you are stooping to such vile methods to get it. I was a soldier myself, in the Great War, and I was taught to respect German soldiers. But what you are up to here is a disgrace to your uniform.

At these words the two officers come at me again, swearing that they will not put up with my insults.

One of them, the one who started kicking me when I was down, a big dark-haired guy with a very athletic build and the face of a brute, grabbed my throat and starts to strangle me. My #1 torturer intercedes and finally gets him to stop.

While I try to catch my breath they continue to hurl coarse insults at me in German and in French.

Now they drag me over to a table where they have placed the copy of their "affidavit."

Me—No, I won't sign it. You know perfectly well that I can't put my signature to a statement that brings dishonor on the French army.

My #1 torturer—But there is no French army anymore. It was defeated, miserably defeated. France has crumbled. Its government has fled. You are no longer anything. It's all over.

Me—That may be, but there is one thing that for the French army will always matter, and that is its honor, and I am not about to contribute to marring that. . . . Moreover, if I no longer have any official function, why does it matter to you so much that I sign your affidavit?

The German—Only because it corresponds to the truth and it serves to establish responsibility.

Me—But if you have proof of what you are claiming, nobody can accuse the German army, and it is not a signature extorted from one of the enemy which is going to make your story hold up.

The German—You are just a smooth-talking Frenchman.

I feel my strength slipping away. Several times I nearly collapsed and each time the soldier hit me in the ankles or smashed the ends of my feet with the butt of his rifle.

Now the other officer starts in on me.

He accuses me of having been a supporter of this unjust war against Germany, of having put up posters inciting the population to resist the Germans.

"I was doing my duty," I say. "You were the enemy."

He also reproaches me for being over-zealous in remaining behind in Chartres in order to provoke the Germans.

"I remained because it was also my duty not to abandon my constituency. In fact, I had been ordered to do so by my boss, the Minister of the Interior."

Then it was my #1 torturer's turn to speak up, in a considerable state of excitement: "Ah! You dare to speak to us about your boss. You dare speak of the Jew Mandel! Of that disgusting Jew who wanted to start a war with Germany! Of that little pig who sold out to the British! Admit it, admit that you were in the pay of that dirty Jew. . . ."

I clarify: "Not in the pay of, under the orders of. . . ."

And he continues, furious now: "You are a country of degenerates, a country of Jews and niggers. . . ."

They took turns like this, in order to wear me down and force a signature out of me.

Once, the big dark-haired officer, my #2 torturer, who has a fox terrier with him, leaps on me in the middle of the discussion, and starts to whip me savagely with the dog's leash. They did not let me sit down for so much as an instant. I am wondering how long I can hold out. . . .

We talk about "proofs" some more. I continue to maintain that their proofs are no more than assertions and that these won't convince me.

My #1 torturer now says: "Ah! You want proofs, do you? Okay, follow me!"

We leave the house. Outside it is still broad daylight. I thought we had been in there forever!

There is a car there, ready and waiting. The two officers get in front with the dog. They make me sit in back next to the soldier. Now we are driving into the countryside. First along the route de Châteaudun, then, after taking a fork to the left, on the route de Saint-Georges-sur-Eure. Not a single civilian in sight. The farms and the fields are all deserted. Where are my torturers taking me, I wonder? What lugubrious move are they scheming on making? I should be very worried, but somehow, after having been pushed so far and having made it through that scene back there, I feel almost happy to breathe the air off the fields, and to sit down at last! The lurching of the car, which is going pretty fast after all, constantly revives my pains. But at least I am sitting down. . . . I would never have thought that just sitting down, when one is utterly exhausted, could make one feel so good.

We pass the village of Saint-Georges on our left and head towards the hamlet of la Taye. Soon I can see the railroad line. It is exactly what I expected. They are taking me to the scene of the crime. Less than fifty meters from the level crossing the car turns right as if to go to the little station of la Taye, and stops in front of a large building, part farmhouse and part café; it is the only building still standing in the vicinity of the station.

We get out. The terrier goes and smells the body of a dog that is lying next to the wall, with a bullet-hole in its head.

My #1 torturer goes straight to a door and, taking a key out of his pocket, he opens it for us. We enter a common farm courtyard, filled with farm machinery and household objects.

The officer approaches a hangar, on the right-hand side at the back of the courtyard, and opens both doors wide. He turns to me: "Here are your proofs."

And with a sweep of his arm he shows me, lined up side by side, nine poor corpses, bruised, disfigured, shapeless, their clothing so torn and stained as to make it hard to tell the men from the women. There are several bodies of children. Two or three of the victims' limbs appear twisted or convulsed, suggesting a painful agony.

Surrounded by the silence of death, this is truly a sad sight. But, alas, I have seen so many such sights in the past month. . . . Peasants dead next to their horses, refugees burned to a crisp in their cars, women massacred with their children in their arms. . . . I have seen so many that it has become easy to control my emotions.

The Nazi—There is what your good niggers have done. And he takes care to point out to me that some of the victims are women and children.

Me—I am not denying this last point.

The Nazi—In that case I hope that you will have no further objection to signing the affidavit.

Me—There are two possibilities here but the result is the same. Either your trust is being abused by someone, or you yourselves have concocted a horrible deception. You don't have to be a great specialist to see that these unfortunate people, whose bodies have been torn apart by explosions, are simply the victims of the bombing.

Alas, I have said too much, I have seen right through their macabre charade. So, their faces twisted by all that a human being can conjure up in the way of hatred, they throw themselves upon me and begin to beat my head, my shoulders and my chest repeatedly with their fists.

The soldier, who had been standing to one side, comes running over with the butt of his gun at the ready to help in the beating, but he is stopped by a gesture from one of the officers. It is clearly important not to mess me up too much right away. With one knee and one arm on the ground I try to muster what little strength I have left. I finally get up and I sit down on a crate nearby. They let me. I must look pretty bad already.

But soon they come over and tell me to follow them to a small outbuilding and they throw its door open wide.

"You see, this here is the body of a woman whose arms and legs were cut off by your black men," says my #1 torturer.

Indeed I see, inside the shed, stretched out on a makeshift table that takes up nearly all of the space inside, something that must have been the torso of a woman, a horrible sight, half naked, with a shirt on which blood had plastered to her skin in places, her legs cut off right across her upper thighs. No arms either. In their place, two bloody stumps. The head was just a bloody sphere, with hair sticking to it everywhere, hanging limply to one side.

"Was it the bombing, then, that cut off her limbs this cleanly?" And, grabbing me by the shoulders, he throws me forcefully on top of the mutilated body. The door to the shed slams shut behind me.

I had been thrown onto these human remains, and its cold and sticky touch chilled me to the very bone.

In the darkness inside the shed, with the dull stench of the corpse filling my nostrils, I feel a cold sweat like the start of a fever come over me. And I felt for the first time that I would not be able to hold out any longer.

I try to open the door. Nothing doing! How long did I remain like that, broken, waiting for them to come and get me out of there? Ten minutes, a half an hour? I don't know. But when they finally come to get me, night was beginning to fall.

They only let me out in order to offer me the paper to sign again, that wretched paper. I still have enough strength left to refuse.

While this is going on, in the middle of the farmyard, the big Nazi raises his fist to hit me again. . . . To avoid being hit, I duck to one side and run towards the open door. Three shots ring out, one after the other, loud in my ears. I am not hit, but I collapse, unable to take another step. I have only run a few meters. I am exhausted. The two officers put away their pistols. The big guy takes his dog's leash and, helped by the soldier, he ties my hands behind my back.

They drag me to the car and throw me on the backseat. The soldier gets in next to me. We head back to Chartres. Along the way the soldier grabs the leash that is serving as handcuffs for me and gives it a fierce twist every time a bump in the road forces a whimper from me.

Now we are back in the place des Epars. Night fell. The car stops in front of the Hôtel de France. One of the officers goes inside, and then comes right back outside again. In the light of the doorway of the hotel, about three meters away I see a civilian whom I recognize. It's Vidon. I call out to him and say that I am under arrest.

I am immediately punched squarely in the jaw, followed by several blows in the shins with the rifle butt. The officers swear at me.

The car goes around the square once before stopping in front of the house where I first met my two torturers.

The officers both go inside, leaving me in the car guarded by the soldier.

A quarter of an hour later, someone comes and gets me, and I am led back into the room on the right. In this room, now lit by candlelight, I find an officer who is not the one we were with a while back. He is older and no doubt of a higher rank. Despite the state I am in, I try to lodge a protest with this officer regarding the way I have been treated. I point out the state of my uniform, my swollen lip, my bloody left hand.

He doesn't want to hear any of it, and in broken French he limits himself to repeating "You must sign."

I don't answer. The officer goes out with my #2 torturer, leaving me with his buddy and the soldier. At a sign from his superior, the soldier comes over and unties the leash that binds my hands.

My #1 torturer takes the affidavit out of his briefcase one more time, spreads it out on the table and says to me: "Why this pointless resistance?

We know very well that we are going to get you to sign it. . . . I'm going to let you think about it."

I say nothing. What good would it do? He goes out.

The soldier who remained with me immediately makes it clear to me that I am not allowed to sit down or to walk away from the table. He hits the floor regularly with the stock of his rifle to remind me that he will be delighted to smash my feet if I disobey in any way.

Neither of us says anything now. From time to time, when our eyes meet, he points with a commanding finger at the odious affidavit.

Time passes slowly. I am in terrible pain, and I wonder how I am still managing to hold on.

Finally my torturers both return, they take a look at the paper, and then indicate to the soldier that he should bring me outside.

The car is still there, its lights off. We get in. Where are they going to take me now? The car goes four or five hundred meters in the darkness, enters a gateway, and stops among some trees.

They get me out of the automobile and lead me several steps until we enter a freestanding building. A sergeant greets us, a lantern in his hand. Inside is a large room that has been turned into a guardroom. German soldiers, some of them with bayonets fixed on their weapons. In a corner a negro, who must be a captured Senegalese infantryman. Bare feet, in shirtsleeves, he is eating a piece of black bread.

I am still standing, I have been for hours, with unbearable pain everywhere, but especially in my back. And my feet, my poor feet, can no longer carry me.

I feel that if they don't let me sit down, or lie down, soon, I am simply going to collapse in a heap.

The junior officer who appears to be the commandant of the post comes over to me upon a sign from his superiors and searches me from top to toes. I have nothing in my pockets. In fact I had changed clothes very quickly and left everything in my civilian clothes.

This being done, my #1 torturer stands in front of me and states, pounding out each of his words: "Listen to me carefully. I am giving you one last chance: *Tomorrow we will make you sign.* Only, by signing this evening you will save yourself a number of additional complications that will cause you to regret having waited so long."

He holds the affidavit in his hand. I look at it but say nothing. There must be sufficient contempt in my face for him not to insist. He turns quickly to the sergeant and issues a brief order. The sergeant signals to two soldiers, takes a ring of keys and heads for a narrow corridor, lighting his way with a flashlight. The two soldiers push me along after him, taking advantage of the darkness to hit me savagely with their rifles. At the end of the corridor, the sergeant opens a door, on the left, and shines the beam of his flashlight into a small square room. It is a plainly furnished dining room. The drawers of the buffet are open and have clearly been searched. The table and the chairs have been pushed into one corner to make room for a small mattress. The Senegalese who was in the guardroom earlier is already lying on it.

My two torturers, whom I can hear behind the soldiers, have followed in order to enjoy the spectacle. With a snicker, my #1 torturer shouts at me: "Since we know how much you love niggers, we thought we'd do you a favor and let you sleep with one of them tonight." And the soldiers, on orders from their superiors who continue to laugh loudly, grab me by the arms and throw me on top of the unfortunate infantryman who draws back in fright. My head smashes into the wall. The door slams shut.

Despite the blow that I received, I did not pass out, and I can still hear, outside the door, the voice of the head Nazi giving strict instructions to the guards, telling them to watch over us closely. Several times he repeats, and pardon me if I quote him: ". . . *sehr interessanten Leute, sehr interessanten Leute . . .*" [very interesting people].

In the darkness, the good Senegalese gave up his place on the only mattress to me, and went to sleep a little way off. I pass him the blankets, because the floor is covered with shards of glass from the windows that were broken in the bombing.

But I cannot get any sleep. A short while ago the alarm clock on the sergeant's desk said it was 1 a.m.[16] I had been physically and psychologically tortured for seven hours.

I realize that during the course of this day I had reached the limit of my endurance. I also know that if this goes on again tomorrow I will end up by signing.

The choice is becoming clear: sign or disappear. . . .

Flee? That is impossible. I hear the regular footsteps of the guards, not only in the hallway but right under our only window.

Yet I cannot sign. I cannot be an accomplice to this monstrous machi-

16. This is in the early morning of June 18, 1940.

nation that could only have been thought up by sadists running amok. I will not sanction this insult to the French army and bring dishonor on myself.

Anything other than that. Anything, even death.

Death? From the outbreak of war, like thousands of Frenchmen, I have accepted this. Since then I have seen it again close up many times. . . . It does not frighten me.

If it had gotten me a few days ago, it would have created a void here, right now, on the side of the resistance.

Now, I have accomplished my mission, or rather, I will have fulfilled it completely, when I have prevented our enemies from dishonoring us.

My duty is clearly spelled out. The Boches will learn that a Frenchman is capable of falling on his sword. . . .

I know that the only human being who could still demand that I account for myself, my mother, who gave me life, will forgive me when she learns that I did it so that French soldiers cannot be treated like criminals and so that she does not have cause to be ashamed of her son.

I have already figured out what I can do with the shards of glass that are scattered everywhere on the floor. I figure that they can slit a throat just as well as the knife that I don't have.

Once I have decided this, it is simple to go through the physical movements that are necessary in order to carry out what one believes is one's duty.

+ + +

The Senegalese is sleeping deeply, not suspecting in the least the drama that is playing itself out less than one meter from him, and in some small part for him.

+ + +

Five o'clock rings somewhere outside. I have lost a lot of blood. It ran, warm and slow, down my chest, to collect in big clots on the mattress. . . . But life has not left me. . . . As long as it is over when they come in and find in my place a still lump, that cannot sign anything!

But soon the locks squeak, steps approach. So soon! Since that is how it's going to be, I will face them standing up!

The door opens. It's two soldiers, with fixed bayonets, here to tell us that we can come and perform our morning needs. They have noticed nothing yet. Then, all of a sudden, I see them begin to perk up as they register the vision that is in front of them, a man dressed in glittering braid, staring at them, standing up, covered with blood, a gaping hole in his neck. . . .

The post commander must not be around because he would have run in right away in response to the soldiers' shouts.

They make me come out and sit down. I realize that we are in the courtyard of the civilian hospital, and that the little house we were in is the concierge's loge.

A German officer, who must be a medic, hurries over with a male nurse. First aid. A dressing is applied.

Once I feel that I can speak, I exonerate the Senegalese infantryman whom they had begun to suspect.

The medic, helped by the guards, gets me across the pathways leading to the hospital, and places me in the care of Dr. Foubert, who is quite surprised to find me in this state. Once the Germans have left, I hasten to explain to Dr. Foubert, to the best of my ability, everything that had happened to me since the prior evening. Soon, Sr. Henriette shows up. The doctor brings her up to speed. I believe, rightly or not, that since luck has had it that my torturers did not appear before I was brought in here, my only chance of getting out of this now might be that the matter blow up into a scandal so that they can't hush it up much as they might like to.

+ + +

I am now in a sunlit room, surrounded by white wimples. Is all of this in fact a bad dream?

Alas, the sad reality is not far off!

I have been in bed scarcely ten minutes when a nun comes to tell me that the Germans are asking for me urgently and that Sr. Henriette is downstairs bargaining with an officer as we speak.

Soon the door bangs open and it is my #1 torturer who enters to deliver the order to get up and follow him.

I am gotten out of bed, dressed, and several minutes later, helped by Dr. Foubert and the sisters, I am outdoors, facing the officer.

In the presence of Dr. Foubert, and with the most blatant hypocrisy, he asks me why I tried to take my own life: "You know perfectly well that after the treatment I was subjected to by you it was the only way for me to not sign your affidavit." And turning to the doctor: "The affidavit in which I am to certify that French soldiers raped and massacred women and children. . . ."

I stop at that, exhausted.

The Nazi now states for the doctor's benefit that he is of the utmost integrity and that I must have misunderstood, and that this "misunderstanding" should be forgotten immediately.

And heads in the direction of the front gate where he hails the car that is supposed to drive us away.

During this time the doctor told me about the outrageous things the officer said about me to Sr. Henriette: "You didn't know, did you, Sister, that your local prefect had some strange ways of carrying on. He wanted to spend the night with a negro and this is what happened to him. . . ."

They load me into the car that had now pulled up, and I am driven to the place des Epars, to the Hôtel de France, which appears to have become the headquarters of the Kommandantur. I am told to sit down in the reception area, while the officer is led into one of the living rooms.

Soon I hear raised voices that make me think that a stormy argument is going on about me.

After twenty minutes my torturer comes out accompanied by another officer who after many greetings and much clicking of heels says that they are going to take me back to my residence and that German doctors are at my disposition.

It is my torturer who is responsible for accompanying me back to the Prefecture.

Once there, I immediately run into the postal workers who, seeing me in such a wretched state, decide to flee at once.

3 p.m.

In the absence of the mayor of Saint-Georges-sur-Eure, the Chartres City Hall will be required to bury the bodies of *nine victims of the bombing* at la Taye.

It is M. Rousselot who will be charged with this task. The tenth body, that of the horribly mutilated woman, has disappeared. There is no longer any mention of atrocities.

June 22

My fever has broken at last. I take up my administrative responsibilities again, with a new Kommandantur.

November 14, 1940[17]

Months have gone by without a single German officer ever mentioning my little misadventure.

Today I am invited to the office of the Feldkommandantur, in the big French Workers' building.

At the entrance, guards snap to attention, the officers salute me in regulation style.

A speech by the Feldkommandant, a Major Ebmeier, translation provided by lieutenant Zeitler, that closes with these words: "I congratulate you for the zeal with which you were able to look out for the interests of the civilians under your administration and for the honor of your country."

17. Three days following the arrival of a letter from the Ministry of the Interior in Vichy, suspending Moulin of his functions as prefect of the Eure-et-Loir.

Appendix

[These notes were appended to the original French edition.]

BEFORE THE INCIDENT

Prefect of the French department of the Eure-et-Loir.

January 21, 1939. Jean Moulin is appointed Prefect of the Eure-et-Loir. His active duty begins one month later, on February 21, 1939.

The patriotism and republican[18] ardor of Jean Moulin were already made known in Chartres during the year 1939, in particular at the Marceau Banquet,[19] in the *conseil général* of the Eure-et-Loir, and on the very eve of war, during the preparations for the celebration of the 150th anniversary of the French Revolution.

EXCERPTS FROM THE SPEECH DELIVERED BY JEAN MOULIN IN CHARTRES AT THE MARCEAU BANQUET

(March 5, 1939)

> "I am among those who believe that the Republic should not deny its origins and that it should, on the contrary, remember accurately, and with respect, the great events that marked its birth. And that is why it is with infinite pleasure that I learned that, in this department, men gather together each year, united in the same fervor, to honor the memory of one of the people who did the most to promote our ideal of government.
>
> Gentlemen, in a time when, throughout the world, spiritual values, the principles of liberalism, even human dignity itself, are constantly under

18. In French political culture, *républicain* refers to belief in liberal democratic values of government, separation of church and state, and an embrace of the ideals expressed in the Declaration of the Rights of Man, a document that emerged from the French Revolution of 1789.

19. The Marceau Banquet is an annual regional celebration of the Radical Party, often convened in Chartres, named after François-Séverin Marceau. Marceau was born in Eure-et-Loir on March 1, 1769, and died in battle on September 21, 1796. He became a soldier at age sixteen and participated in the storming of the Bastille. He was made a captain in the Army of the Revolution in 1789 and rose to the rank of general through his own strength in battle and by the wise management of conquered lands. Lord Byron addresses lines to his memory in *Childe Harold's Pilgrimage*, canto 3, stanza LVI: "Honor to Marceau! o'er whose early tomb / Tears, big tears, gushed from the rough soldier's lid, / Lamenting and yet envying such a doom, / Falling for France, whose rights he battled to resume."

attack in the name of some political reality or another, I can hardly tell which anymore, it is not without emotion that we evoke the image of this adolescent who appeared out of the blue, without ulterior motives, from the bourgeoisie to the people, to work with the people to set it free, with all of the courage in his heart and with the strength of his patriotism.

I understand, gentlemen, your being proud of Marceau, he is one of the most attractive and endearing figures to come to us from the French Revolution!

As for myself, great-grandson of a soldier of the Revolution, grandson of a man who knew the inside of a prison under the Empire for having dared to proclaim his attachment to the Republic, it is not simply lip-service that I am paying to your great Marceau. And if you will permit me to slip a fervent wish into this tribute, as threatening clouds continue to gather over our borders, I wish that the memory, the example of a man like Marceau can incite us to forge in France again the strength and generosity of soul that was his back when those admirable volunteers from Eure-et-Loir hastened to the border to fight and die for Liberty. . . ."

EXCERPTS FROM THE SPEECH DELIVERED TO THE OPENING SESSION OF THE CONSEIL GENERAL OF EURE-ET-LOIR (May 8, 1939)

"There are times when serving one's country, in whatever capacity it might be, is such a compelling obligation that it is only natural and even with enthusiasm that men of good find the strength they need to lift their assigned load. . . .

Mr. President, I thank you for having underscored my very keen sense of the need for impartiality; I have never hidden my political beliefs. Yet, as I wish to serve an ideal that I hold infinitely dear without the slightest compromise, I can assure you that my administration will try, in every circumstance, to remain impartial and free of partisanship. If one day it decides to act a little less rigorously, I would like that only to be in favor of those who are struggling in life or of those who suffer.

Gentlemen, while the people of France are presenting such a fine example of national effort and dignity, at a time when with such calm and resolute men have left their homes to serve their country, I believe that these sentiments should be reaffirmed with even greater resolve. That is why, in closing, I would like to follow your example, Mr. President, and call upon all of you to unite in order to give those people who bear the heavy weight of the nation's destiny the strength and the faith they need to tend firmly to the preservation, not only of the integrity of our territory, but also of our patrimony of honor and liberty."

A PREFECT WHO WANTS TO FIGHT

Jean Moulin wrote to the Minister of the Interior on many occasions to express his wish, in the event of a general troop mobilization, to be drafted along with the rest of his age group.

Here is one such letter, dated March 30, 1939:

Mr. President:

In response to your dispatch of March 28th, regarding my military status, I have the honor to inform you that, as I have previously stated, in the event of a general troop mobilization I continue to wish to be treated as any one of my peers.

I will permit myself to point out to you the very real need to begin dealing now with the replacement of Prefects who are to be mobilized and to make it clear to potential replacements that they must make themselves available, on a regular schedule, to be brought up to date on the state of affairs, and in particular on plans to mobilize the departments that they will have to administer. This is an important practice that has been adopted in numerous agencies that, in my opinion, can be expected to produce the best results.

Jean MOULIN

His request was not met.

On September 24, 1939, he wrote a letter to the Air Ministry, to request admission as a trainee machine-gunner in one of the schools that were being organized, with a view to being assigned to a unit on the front lines, even though he was eighteen years over the age limit for admission.

Despite this, Mr. Sarraut[20] *kept the Prefect in his post for two more months.*

On November 15, 1939, he wrote again to the Minister of the Interior:

Mr. President:

I am taking the liberty to renew the requests I have made to you on September 14, 1938, on December 1, 1938, and on March 30, 1939, regarding my being permitted to be called up for service with the rest of my age group.

A bachelor, belonging to the youngest group of the second reserves, I continue to believe that my place is not behind the lines, at the head of an essentially rural department where mobilization has made deep gaps and where the Prefect is at all times required to call on the patriotism and spirit of sacrifice of those left behind.

20. Albert-Pierre Sarraut, minister of the interior, 1938–40.

This is why I continue to respectfully request that I be permitted to join my unit this upcoming December 12, and as a consequence of which that all necessary steps be taken to designate, as of right now, my eventual interim replacement.

I believe I should remind you in this connection that M. Caillet, a war veteran and a former Prefect without a current assignment, could very well be named to the post in Chartres, which he already filled, to widespread satisfaction, for four years.

In the unwavering hope that you will not be unmoved by my request, I beg you, Mr. President, to have complete confidence in my respectful devotion.

Jean MOULIN

Such was his insistence that his name be put down for a place as a trainee machine-gunner. On December 12 Jean Moulin rejoins his unit and so notifies M. Sarraut.

The Minister of the Interior retaliates and gets his colleague in the Air Ministry to reclassify Reserve Sgt. Jean Moulin, Air Battalion 117, as specially deferred for an undetermined period of time in light of his service as Prefect of the Eure-et-Loir.

The decision is dated December 21.

On December 24, Jean Moulin lodges a protest with the Minister of the Interior. Here are his notes regarding the interview:

M. Sarraut receives me in a friendly manner, says that he understands my motives for requesting to be allowed to fulfill my military duty and promises to consider my wish with good will.

On December 26th, I go see M. Berthoin, Secretary General of the Minister, and the head of Human Resources, to learn the final decision of the Minister.

It hasn't changed. I must demobilize immediately and go back to my post in Chartres without delay.

Forced to remain at the Prefecture, Jean Moulin praises the patriotism of the citizens of Chartres and looks out for their safety. He has a brochure printed up entitled "What to Do in Case of an Air Raid." In it, the necessary instructions are given in clear and straightforward language.

On June 11, six days before the Germans arrive in the department, he has the following notice posted:

RESIDENTS OF EURE-ET-LOIR

Your sons are resisting the German onslaught victoriously. Be worthy of them by remaining calm. No order to evacuate the department has been given, because none is called for.

Do not listen to people who encourage you to panic, who will, moreover, be reprimanded. Sanctions have already been adopted. Others will follow.

Everyone should remain in place. Economic activity must continue.

Elected officials and civil servants must serve as an example to others. No excuse for failure will be tolerated.

I have confidence in the capacity for wisdom and patriotism of the residents of this department.

I am confident. We will prevail.

The Prefect of Eure-et-Loir

Jean MOULIN

LETTER FROM JEAN MOULIN TO HIS MOTHER AND HIS SISTER

June 15, 1940

My dear mother,

My dear Laure,

I have written to you very little in recent days. The fault is in the tragic events I have been living through. I have witnessed a great deal of human suffering. My comfort has been in observing simple acts of kindness, acts that no one will ever know about, apart from a few eyewitnesses.

My poor department lies wounded, bleeding from everywhere. The civilian population has been spared nothing.

By the time you receive this letter, I will no doubt have fulfilled my final duty. By order of the government I will have received the Germans in Chartres and I will be a prisoner.

I am certain that our imminent victory—thanks to an outpouring of indignation on the part of the rest of the world, as well as the heroism of our own soldiers (who often are worth much more than popular opinion would have it)—will come to rescue me.

I didn't know it was so simple to do one's duty when one is in danger.

I am in good health despite the exhaustion of these past days.

I am thinking of you with all my heart.

Jean

P.S. If the Germans—they are capable of anything—made me say things inimical to honor, you know already *that they are not true.*

AFTER THE DRAMA

RESISTANCE TO THE GERMANS

Jean Moulin assiduously defended the local population against abuses, thefts, and violence perpetrated by the army of occupation, filing a protest in each and every incidence with the Kommandantur.

Chartres, July 14, 1940

I have the honor to file an urgent complaint against the methods adopted by certain German authorities against the first magistrate of the department, that which I am.

Without consulting me, the Kommandantur of L'Aigle, charged with taking care of the French prisoners of war, has decided to draft and to append to it the signature: "The Prefect" on a poster whose use of certain terms I cannot accept.

This poster says, among other things, that in the case of any infraction on the part of the prisoners, their families would be held responsible.

This clause is absolutely contrary to all of the rules of war and the basic rights of all human beings.

But what is even more inadmissible is to attribute this decree to the representative of the French government, when this latter was never asked to give his opinion and that he only learned of the text of the poster when it was already printed and distributed by the German authorities.

The Prefect

This protest was followed by a response. The Feldkommandant replies to him: "You are absolutely right to complain about this incident, it is regrettable to the nth degree," and he includes a disavowal to the Feldkommandantur in L'Aigle.

As the thefts and the abuses continue, the Prefect files yet another complaint with the Feldkommandant on July 27th:

I have the great regret to have to come to you again about a series of complaints and demands for compensation in connection with the confiscation of crops, of farm animals, of vehicles, etc., by the German army, which are not covered by any payment or by regular requisition.

As you will be able to determine by reading some of these letters, in no case were the officers willing to give either their name or the number of their regiment.

These facts are unfortunately not of the kind that might reassure the peasant population on the eve of the work of the harvest that they must bring in.

On August 10, 1940, there is a new complaint:

The Prefect of Eure-et-Loir
to the Colonel in command
of the 751st Feldkommandantur in Chartres

I have the honor of transmitting to you along with this communication a letter from the mayor of the city of Dreux that I absolutely must bring to your attention.

The situation that it makes reference to, the seriousness of which I needn't point out, is not unique to Dreux. For over a week now all of the mayors of the larger townships are being asked to deliver supplies that clearly exceed their share of "occupation reparations."

Thus a number of radios, refrigerators, armoires, mirrors, flower vases up to and including frames for photographs, and rugs valued at several thousands of francs are being requested daily under threat of the severest sanctions, notably in Bouglainval, in Maintenon, Luisant, Châteaudun, Nogent-le-Roi, and Dreux. In Dreux, it was even officers stationed *in another department* who are requiring the delivery of household furnishings of very high value.

There is no way that I cannot bring these facts to your attention, and I urge you to please have a care to put an end to this abuse.

The Prefect

In response to a particularly despicable expulsion, the Prefect spoke up with his usual courage. (September 17, 1940.)

The Prefect of Eure-et-Loir
To the Chief of the
751st Feldkommandantur in Chartres

I have already had, on a number of occasions, the need to bring to your attention inhuman methods used by some occupation forces with respect to residents who have simply been expelled from their homes without consideration either for their age or for their sex.

I have just been informed that again at Meslay-le-Vidame, on September 1, a noncommissioned officer appeared at the home of a widow aged 72 years, who lost two sons in the 1914–1918 War, and ordered her out of her home in *one-quarter of an hour.*

The circumstances of this order, of which there have been many in the past three weeks have stirred up a lot of hard feelings in the population of the department.

The Prefect

The same day, another complaint regarding forced loans:

The Prefect of Eure-et-Loir
To the Chief of the
751st Feldkommandantur in Chartres

The right of requisition having been suspended, in principle, for transient troops, as you have so kindly informed me in recent days, these latter have in the last month taken to using a different procedure: *that of the loan.*

They have notified the population via the mayors that residents must loan a certain number of household furnishings for the duration of the troops' stay in the town.

The population has generally responded to these orders with diligence, convinced, as in fact they had been assured, that these objects would be given back as soon as the troops departed.

But, frequently, when the military units temporarily stationed in the department move on they take with them the items that were "loaned."

In Voves, for instance, the unit designated by the number 15836E departed on September 7th, taking with them eight radios that had been loaned to them.

I would be particularly beholden to you if these incidents ceased immediately and if all necessary steps could be taken to reimburse the owners.

The Prefect

TESTIMONIALS

TESTIMONIAL OF THE SQUADRON LEADER DE TORQUAT, COMMANDER OF THE FIRST BATTALION OF THE 7TH DRAGOONS (4TH ARMORED DIVISION), REGARDING THE PREFECT OF CHARTRES: JEAN MOULIN

During the night of June 12–13, 1940, the 4th D.C.R. [Armored Division] covering the left flank of the Army of Paris, which under threat of encirclement, gave up its defense of the capital, fell back towards the south.

The 1st Battalion of the 7th Regiment of Motorized Dragoons, that I have the honor to command, after having passed several hours at Gambais in stationary alert, received the order to move to Chartres and to take up positions on the left bank of the Eure in order to defend the bridges leading to the roads coming in from the west.

We took up these positions during the afternoon of the 13th of June, while the local airfield was being bombed by enemy aircraft. My command post was at Nogent-le-Phaye.

On June 15th, at 3 o'clock, I received an order to change the direction of the defense of Chartres and to bring my units around to the west of the city to cover the Northwest, North and West.

Starting at sunup, I established my command post in Chartres itself, in a huge mansion that was open on all sides, situated on the exterior ring boulevard on the south side of the city.

The city had been completely abandoned by the local government: there was no municipality, no city officials, no firemen. . . . On the street there was an abandoned Paris city police truck that contained hundreds of rifles. There are many refugees wandering the streets, looting food stores for anything to eat, or simply filing down the avenues, on foot, in cars or in automobiles. Many ask me for help, as if I were responsible for directing the evacuation of the country! . . . I have my team of repairmen fix a number of cars. . . .

In the course of the afternoon, we are bombed by enemy aircraft. There are a number of civilian casualties that our battalion's medic (Dr. Erbéia) attends to immediately.

I am informed that enemy armored vehicles have entered Ablis.

On the 16th of June, the flow of refugees through the city continues. I try to put some order into this disorderly mass of people, and to help those in greatest need. I have to stop people a number of times, in particular to order farmers to take exhausted pedestrians into their cars.

In the morning the Prefect of Eure-et-Loir, M. Jean Moulin, comes to see me. He is in uniform, and he is using a bicycle to get around, which is a somewhat striking sight. I express my surprise to him about finding the city deserted by those who were responsible for protecting it.

"*Monsieur le Préfet,*" I say, "you are the only public official of the city that I have seen!"

"Indeed, all of the civil servants have gone; even my staff has deserted me. Better than that, someone stole my private car right out of my garage! So, you see, I am reduced to getting around by bicycle."

Jean Moulin then told me what he did to help feed the roughly five to six thousand people (residents and refugees combined) who are in town now and hungry. He found flour and started bakeries up again with the help of some bakery workers.

He asks me to find him some qualified helpers, and I assign to his service a couple of my tank drivers who are bakers by trade.

I am immediately sympathetic to this young, brave and energetic official, who knows how to face up to his responsibilities.

"And you yourself, *Monsieur le Préfet,* how do you manage for your own meals?"

"Oh, I manage. . . . But I will admit to you that I haven't eaten anything that was hot in the past 48 hours, and that I really miss it. . . ."

I inform my cook right away and he brings a nice hot cup of coffee. But I immediately insist on inviting Jean Moulin to join our mess, for as long as we are in the area.

He accepts enthusiastically, and the next we see of him he comes into our mess at 12:30, apologizing for being late.[21]

A very cordial lunch. I do not fail to warmly congratulate the young prefect in the presence of my officers for his courageous manner, which is so different from that of so many other officials. Over dessert, I name him an honorary Brigadier of our battalion.

"And I," he says to me, "I name you an honorary citizen of Chartres."

At 1300 hours, officers and men from the 4th Zouaves, who were withdrawing, told us that the enemy, having reached the Oisème–Nogent-le-Phaye line, was in fact at the outskirts of the city. I doubled the alert, and forbade civilians from leaving the city.

Around 1500 hours, Jean Moulin comes back to see me. He has switched out of his uniform this time, and instead is dressed in "civilian defense" garb: a blue raincoat and a helmet of the same color.

When I express surprise at this disguise:

"Don't talk to me about it!" he says, laughing. "Just imagine that I was almost torn apart by all my starving constituents who are holding me responsible for the lack of food! So I swapped my uniform for this one that lets me move about without being noticed. . . ."

In the evening, we learn that enemy columns have for the most part swept past Chartres and are threatening Orléans. At 1830 hours, I receive an order from General de la Font, who took over command of the Division on the 7th of June when General de Gaulle left, to prepare to withdraw.

We sit down to table to eat a quick dinner eaten with our fingers, our supply vehicle having already fallen back toward the rear, the danger of being surrounded growing greater at every moment.

Jean Moulin was with us at this last meal.

"And you, what are you going to do?" I ask him when I have told him that the Battalion is pulling back.

"I will wait for the Germans to arrive in Chartres, as is my duty."

"I congratulate you, *Monsieur le Préfet.*"

"Goodbye, Commander, and thank you for everything you have done to help me. I will not forget it."

21. *Note in French edition:* I learned the following day why he had been late: one of my men had spotted the Prefect personally accompanying a blind man who had asked that someone conduct him to the road out of town.

We leave Chartres a little before midnight, without the enemy's ever having attacked our roadblocks, leaving our positions occupied until 200 hours by the motorcycle squadron which takes up the defense of our rear and which only gets away itself at the agreed-upon hour under a hail of artillery and mortar fire.

I never saw Jean Moulin again.

After the Armistice, I made a point of reporting officially via Regiment channels on the particularly distinguished conduct of this prefect.

Later, when I went to draft an account of the history of the 7th Dragoons,[22] I made a point of inserting the following sentence (page 40, June 15th):

"Only civil servant remaining in the city, M. Jean Moulin, Prefect of Eure-et-Loir, has just been in touch with the squadron leader commanding the 1st Battalion and, in agreement with him, he is organizing food supplies for the inhabitants—some tank drivers who are bakers in civilian life have been put under his orders for the time being—and he has also generally tried to put order into the place, showing great courage and an exemplary sense of duty."

TORQUAT

RESISTANCE TO THE GERMANS

DEFENDING THE POPULATION

[by Laure Moulin]

Here are two examples, among others, which I have from my brother's lips:

(1) *Aided by employees of the SNCF,*[23] *the Prefect was able to wrest from the rapacious Germans entire trainloads of foodstuffs from trains that were stalled on sidings: sugar, cocoa, flour, etc. . . . , which were then distributed to hospitals and school cafeterias;*

(2) *The question of fuel for heating provides an example of how the Germans worked and of how the Prefect looked out for his people. The Germans overlooked entirely how the population of Eure-et-Loir was supplied with charcoal. Noticing this, the Prefect took the necessary steps, in consultation with the farmers whose land the wood was on and the merchants who sold it, to guarantee the supply to hospitals and schools as well as to the general population. Cutting was undertaken, but as soon as the wood was stacked by the sides of roads ready for pickup, the enemy's motorcycle patrols noticed it, and military vehicles appeared im-*

22. *Note in French edition:* Published in 1942 by Charles Lavauzelle.

23. The French National Railways (Société nationale des chemins de fer).

mediately to pick it up. Mayors complained to the occupier about the scarcity of firewood; the Germans responded by accusing the French authority of carelessness and the Prefect of neglect. In order to set matters to right, Jean Moulin called together the mayors of the region of Chartres in the presence of the Feldkommandant and forced him to admit in front of them that the German army had been systematically stealing it.

The arrival of the soldiers of the occupation was always accompanied by confiscations, requisitions without vouchers, evictions, the theft of livestock, automobiles, radios, refrigerators, etc. . . . , as well as by looting and at times by ill treatment, rape and murder, just like that which was described in the Journal, above.

As soon as he was informed of these abuses of power or of such atrocities, the Prefect lodged vehement protests, in writing, with the Feldkommandant. Here is one of the more serious incidents. I quote verbatim from the complaint filed with the Prefect, changing it only to drop the names of the people and places involved:

July 6, 1940

Monsieur ——, living in ——, town of ——, declares the following facts:

On the night of July 5 to 6 at 12:30 a.m. (German time), there was a loud knocking on his door followed by two German soldiers shouting: "Patrol, patrol!" Monsieur —— opened his door. Then the two soldiers entered his house and went into the bedroom where his two daughters, aged sixteen and a half and fourteen and a half, were sleeping. They stripped them both bare and took them by force. The two children screamed and their father and mother heard it, but they were unable to help, because they were being threatened by two revolvers that the soldiers were carrying. The soldiers left the room at 3:15 a.m. this morning.

Signed ——

From the inquiry conducted by the mayor of ——, it emerges the allegations related above are exact and, moreover, that probably the same individuals perpetrated the same acts at the home of Madame —— and that they attempted to do the same kind of thing at the home of Madame ——, farmer at ——.

The Mayor of ——
(Signature of the Mayor)

And finally, here is a letter from Pierre Lefebvre, Mayor of Boissy-lès-Perche, member of the conseil général, *to the prefect, following an intervention in his favor. It reveals the Germans' bad faith:*

November 13, 1940

Monsieur le Préfet,

It seems to me that it would be useful, if only to document the case, to let you know what follow-up there was to the complaint that I sent you on October 18, along with the expressed wish that you bring it to the attention of the Feldkommandantur regarding regrettable incidents which can be laid at the feet of German soldiers in my own house.

In the same good faith as I, you expressed the belief that these were serious incidents, and that it would suffice to inform the German high command about them honestly and without getting carried away, in order to receive an assurance that they would not happen again.

Let me take this opportunity to thank you for having acted as you did at that time.

The officer commanding the unit that was stationed in my house at the time, when he came back from leave, also expressed his regrets, without any prompting, adding these words: "When the cat is away, the mice will play!"

But, last Tuesday, November 5th, a German policeman from the Feldgendarmerie in Dreux appeared at my residence.

After a quick questioning of the several low-ranking military personnel present, and without ever contacting their officer, he proceeds to interrogate each member of my staff and my children, including my daughter, aged six. He then called me in and began to read to me in German the text of the letter that I sent you—a far too literal translation in which all of the nuances of the French had disappeared—and, sentence by sentence, he attempted to convince me that my exposé was crawling with errors: there are no officers in the Pferdelarzarei,[24] only veterinarians; the words "Army of Occupation" have a pejorative tone; the French should not know only German soldiers; to speak with a few buddies in a room is enough for there to be noise, and there needn't be any reason to complain about that; the Germans—who do not resemble the French—do not drink; the man who was wearing heavy hobnailed boots who fell in the stairway can be forgiven for having slipped on the steps; how could anyone be surprised that this woke up some children;

24. Literally "Horse-doctory," the Veterinary Corps.

finally a junior officer was billeted to my house today, he didn't know the upstairs at all; he had a lot of trouble finding his room, which explains why he tried to open a lot of doors, even the cupboard in one of the toilets!

He concluded by saying that my statements were inaccurate, that I had lacked respect for the German army; that moreover I had no right to inform you of what was going on regarding such matters—only the Kriegskommandantur was supposed to know about such things—nor even, as Mayor, to request sanctions against German soldiers.

He did nonetheless conclude in what seemed to me a conciliatory manner, saying: "Let's let it go for now, after all peace is only a few days away."

How unsurprised I was, on Saturday night, when I returned from a thirty-six-hour absence in Paris, to learn that this very same policeman had returned to my house during the morning, quite annoyed to find that I wasn't there, and declaring that I had been condemned to twenty days in jail, which I could defer on payment of a 5,000 franc fine, to be paid by me in person to the Feldgendarmerie, the following morning by 11 a.m. in Dreux, failing which they would send someone here by noon to bring me in for imprisonment.

The reason for being condemned: he addressed a report that was *contrary to the truth* that bore prejudice on the dignity of the German army.

The means by which the judgment had been delivered was not specified; there was no document delineating the judgment included; no impartial inquiry cited, no means of redress specified.

I bitterly handed over the 5,000 francs, Sunday morning, believing that I was henceforward personally on their blacklist, and that I would probably run into further difficulties because of it.

Our poor country is not out of the woods yet. All of which, this time, is for your eyes only.

Please accept, Monsieur le Préfet, etc. . . .

Signed: Pierre LEFEBVRE

A handwritten note from Jean Moulin, at the bottom of this letter:

M. Lefebvre had complained to me about the attitude of the Germans that were occupying his chateau: depredations, noise, drunkenness, attempted theft from his chambermaid, etc. . . .

M. Lefebvre, a devout Catholic, father of ten, found himself forbidden to enter his own chapel (where he went frequently to pray). The Germans closed the chapel, and kept the key.

It was following my complaints that the Germans brought the charges against him that are detailed in this letter.

Prior to this, a number of depositions on the part of the Prefect had already borne fruit. The initial Feldkommandant, baron Friedrich von Gültlingen, an old squire of the Prussian persuasion, a veteran of World War I and an admirer of William II, who sometimes appeared to be beyond the reach of reason, who had suddenly been sent into retirement, doubtless for having been too tepid on the subject of Nazism, was replaced at the end of September with a more orthodox officer, Major Ebmeier, with whom relations would prove to be more tense. It is at any rate without any doubt that it is because of him that Jean Moulin was relieved of his duties as Prefect in November of 1940.

THE DISGRACE

On November 11, 1940, a letter from the Ministry of the Interior arrives in Chartres instructing the Prefect to step down from his functions. Here it is in its entirety:

Paris, November 8th, 1940

General Delegation of the French government in the Occupied Territories.
The delegated Prefect of the Ministry of the Interior

Monsieur le Préfet:

I have the honor to inform you that, by decree of M. le Ministre, secretary of State for the Interior, that as of November 2, 1940, as noted in the *Journal Officiel* of November 3, 1940, you are placed in the position described in Article 1 of the law passed on July 17, 1940.

Please accept, M. le Préfet, this assurance of my high regard.

The Prefect
By appointment of the Ministry of the Interior
Signed: [Illegible]

As soon as the news that this position was open got around, which is to say a few days before the official notification (Jean Moulin himself learned it from the Germans), an outpouring of letters and visits to the Prefect expressed the indignation of the city of Chartres and of the entire department and the virtually unanimous regret that his departure caused.

The local press expressed the sentiments of everyone by bravely going on record in his praise.

An article that appeared in the Dépêche d'Eure-et-Loir, *Thursday, November 7, 1940:*

A PREFECTORAL SHAKE-UP

M. JEAN MOULIN

The Prefectoral shake-up that was recently announced concerns the Eure-et-Loir. M. Jean Moulin, Prefect of our department since February 1939 (and prior to that of the Aveyron), found himself the target of the law of July 17, 1940.

M. Jean Moulin, who has now got twenty-three years of service in the prefectoral corps to his credit, was the youngest subprefect and the youngest prefect in France.

During his tenure in Eure-et-Loir he demonstrated, in every circumstance, a broad and quick intelligence, an absolute commitment to egalitarian principle, and an unflagging wish to serve the local population.

He had the difficult task of serving during the war. Remaining at his post—he did not leave it for an instant—during the evacuation, which he tried to slow, he demonstrated a devotion to duty that everyone is pleased to acknowledge, to protect the interests of the inhabitants and to ensure the supply of food to those who stayed behind.

Included in this were: his success in getting 800 kilos of bread delivered to Chartres and Châteaudun from Blois that permitted him to feed the population during the first days, when all of the bakers disappeared; creating a stock of foodstuffs at the Prefecture which were distributed through the Office of Public Service which he himself helped staff, in person, sharing in the work of people who were charged with transporting and distributing bread.

It is appropriate to remember this exemplary behavior as M. Jean Moulin prepares to leave office.

We wish to send him, along with our best wishes, our feelings of respectful sympathy.

Article that appeared in La Vérité d'Eure-et-Loir *(the newspaper of the Archbishopric) November 9, 1940:*

TO THE PREFECTURAL TERM OF M. JEAN MOULIN

M. Jean Moulin, Prefect of Eure-et-Loir, will be leaving us, in accordance with the administration instituted by the law of July 17, 1940.

M. Jean Moulin will leave behind in Eure-et-Loir keen regrets, the memory of an understanding and energetic administration, righteous and obliging, and also courageous. He demonstrated that courage during the tragic days of June.

La Vérité d'Eure-et-Loir respectfully invites M. Jean Moulin to kindly accept this expression of our deep and very sincere sympathies.

Excerpts from an article that appeared in Le Patriote de Châteaudun *(early November, 1940):*

THE PREFECTORAL SHAKE-UP, M. JEAN MOULIN

"Surprise and emotion"—such is the mildest reaction of the residents of Eure-et-Loir on hearing of the measures that have just been leveled at M. Jean Moulin, Prefect of the Eure-et-Loir since October, 1939. . . .

Enjoying a wide circle of acquaintances and possessed of an alert intelligence, he may be counted among the high-level administrators who, through their uprightness, their courage and their clear-sighted patriotism, have faithfully "served" France and who, throughout the cruel trial that she has been put through, was able to preserve her dignity.

All of these qualities conspired to make him loved by the population of the Beauce and Percheron provinces to which he showed an unfailing devotion, and a kindly, as well as a friendly, understanding.

His attitude at the time of the evacuation *en masse* of the civilian population—which he attempted to slow down—and during the dark days that followed, earned him the gratitude and the admiration of the entire population of the Eure-et-Loir.

At the moment when M. Jean Moulin must leave the Prefecture, it was imperative, trust us, to mention his admirable attitude, recalling which only makes one regret even more a decision that fairness and simple good sense refuse to accept.

It is a truly great administrator who is leaving, to the unanimous regret of everyone, even—we are certain of it—of the occupying forces, who were able to see in him a citizen who loves his country and an excellent organizer.

HOMAGE OF THE CONSEIL GENERAL

A farewell luncheon is organized in Châteauneuf, November 15, 1940. M. Billault, President of the Departmental Commission, made the following speech:

Monsieur le Préfet,

At our meeting of the Departmental Commission, last Saturday, I allowed myself to speak on behalf of my colleagues to tell you how much we all regret your departure.

Today, when the members of the General Council are meeting "probably for the last time," on the occasion of this lunch, you will allow me to express again our very keen and very sincere regrets on seeing you leave our department.

Since February 21, 1939, the date when you took up your mandate in the Eure-et-Loir, you were able to make everyone appreciate your qualities and your worth, you knew how to make the working people of this department appreciate you, and you know that they will only bestow their confidence and their sympathies on someone who truly deserves them.

Allow me to tell you that these people think that you are an exceptional civil servant, welcoming and cordial, with wide-ranging knowledge and a lively intellect, fair and impeccably loyal, and motivated by clear-sighted patriotism.

We are all aware of the courage and the dignity that you showed in the dark, sad days of June, during the mass evacuation, as well as the energetic stance you have always taken in the face of the occupying authorities, and this always in defense of the interests of the department.

This, my dear Prefect, we shall never forget!

Believe me that the sanction that has been brought to bear on you does not leave us indifferent—it is with sadness that we have learned of it—but we have the abiding hope that . . . the day will come when we will have the joy and the pleasure to see you take up your noble duty again, in a position similar to the one you are leaving today.

It is our dearest wish, and you may be assured, M. le Préfet, that in the difficult hours that we must now pass through, we will be inspired by your example, holding close to us a warm and friendly memory of you all the while.

During this ceremony the members of the General Council presented Jean Moulin with a handsome copy of Jean-Christophe, *by R. Rolland.*

On the flyleaf they inscribed these lines, followed by their signatures:

"In recognition of services rendered and in homage to his proud attitude in the face of the enemy, the General Council of the Eure-et-Loir presents this to Jean Moulin, their great Prefect, their friend."

November 15, 1940

HOMAGE FROM THE EMPLOYEES OF THE PREFECTURE AND FROM THE SUBPREFECTURES

It is through the voice of M. Decote, the faithful chief of staff of the prefect, that the employees express their gratitude and their regrets to their former boss:

Monsieur le Préfet,

On June the 15th, heavy of heart, I left you, alone, in the courtyard of the Prefecture. The city was deserted, its buildings still burning.

For several days and as many nights you fed the Chartrains and the many transients by distributing food that you had gathered at the Prefecture for the unfortunate refugees who didn't stop pouring into Chartres ever since the 10th of May. In your shirt-sleeves you transported these supplies to the Office of Public Assistance where they were distributed.

On the morning of June 17th, when you received the German authorities, your very first words were to enjoin them to respect the seniors, the women and the children.

The next day, having refused to be a party to dishonor, you endured, in a neighboring locality, the most severe abuse[25] You were brought back to Chartres where you were imprisoned, abused, and you only owe your survival to the swift departure of these initial occupation troops.

You bore these humiliations, without shirking, with sublime courage, you stood up to it all, and your French heart did not fail you.

You returned to your Prefecture without talking about these painful events, and it is only because you were physically scarred by them that certain of your closest colleagues finally came to know of the actual suffering that you endured.

+ + +

The people you have served, like your colleagues themselves, learned of your imminent departure with regret; they are dismayed to see you leaving this department that you have so honored; you were their defender; you were their respected and beloved guide; they are proud of their great Prefect.

Henceforth your name belongs to History; it will be a symbol and synonym to all for goodness, energy, courage, loyalty, honor and patriotism.

POSTHUMOUS HOMAGES EXCERPTED FROM SPEECHES DELIVERED IN CHARTRES

Speech by M. André Mars, Commissioner of the Republic, August 18, 1945 (the anniversary of the liberation of Chartres):

25. *Note in French edition:* It was actually the same day. See the *Journal.*

How, on this beautiful day, could I fail to evoke, in the front row of our glory, of our joy of today, our ever-abiding anguish, the name of Jean Moulin?

This war has chosen, among the heroes the country will always remember, the one who, above and beyond all virtues, of all acts of courage, of all acts of self-denial, will forever embody the living, vibrating image of our national honor?

Jean Moulin is worthy of being that one. . . .

Speech of M. Chadel, Prefect of Eure-et-Loir, November 11, 1945, at the dedication of the place Jean Moulin:

. . . The name of Jean Moulin, which was at first that of an obscure Prefect of the Republic, became that of one of the most prestigious in the history of our times. . . .

Jean Moulin? I invoke it, this name, as an exorcism of cowardice, of despair, of pettiness, of neglect. At this time when what we all need the most is civic strength, we would be wasting our time to look any further for a greater example than this little forty-year-old Prefect who devoted his life and his death to an ideal made up of two inseparable ideas: France and the Republic. . . .

It was thus that he was among the first to follow General de Gaulle, that he was among the first to take up the struggle, the struggle of the knife and clandestinity. It was in this way that he founded the CNR [Conseil national de la Résistance], organized the French resistance, that he galvanized faltering courage. . . .

Yes, Jean Moulin. . . . It is of you that we thought, on August 16th, 1944, when we broke our chains, while the German beasts ran rampant in the courtyard of this Prefecture, harassed, beaten, consumed with anger in their hearts and with fear in their bellies. How could I not believe that I saw your very shadow pass among us, a frail and beaten silhouette, wearing a white bandage around your neck, as you are forever engraved in our memory? You who stayed to see the enemy arrive in his brutal arrogance, and who foresaw immediately, in the mist of what was to come, the day of anger, the day of vengeance. This heated mob of fighters who, on the other side of these very same iron bars, where forging a new epic, possessed of a soul, it was you!

Speech of M. Maurice Viollette, at the Marceau banquet in March 1946:

How can I not think about this pure hero, who was one of us and who, in the department of Eure-et-Loir, began this heroic enterprise that was to end in I don't know what prison, where torture broke him forever? Who can say or measure what France might have become if Moulin had been able to remain as the wise counselor to I don't know which leader, loyal, smart, and enthusiastic as he was, and who can say what Republican France lost when he was so horribly pitched into the void? We who knew him, we who loved him, we know, and that is why we have absolutely no difficulty in comparing him to Marceau, whose memory we celebrate today. . . .

Commemorative plaque in the meeting room of the conseil général, *dedicated May 8, 1946:*

"To the memory of Jean Moulin, Prefect of Eure-et-Loir.

Who refused, even under torture, to sign his name to defame the French army, as the German General demanded, at the time of the occupation of Chartres.

Recalled by Vichy in November 1940.

As a hero, organized the French Resistance and became one of its greatest leaders.

Arrested in Lyon in 1943, he died the victim of new and terrible tortures.

He never spoke, never betrayed anyone, neither the Republic, nor France."

FIRST RESISTANCE IN THE OCCUPIED ZONE

Editor's Introduction

On Sunday, October 31, 1943, a group of prisoners arrived at the Frauen Konzentrationslager[1] in Ravensbrück, a locality in the Brandenburg district of Germany, about sixty miles north of Berlin. They were forty-three French women who had been deported from Paris in smaller batches, in passenger-train cars, held for shipment in Aachen, and from there sent to Fürstenberg, less than two kilometers from the camp itself. One of these women was Germaine Tillion. She had been arrested on August 13, 1942, for acts of resistance against the Reich. This earned her the status of *N/N—Nacht und Nebel* (Night and Fog)—in the hierarchy of the German penitentiary system. This meant that she would be housed in a special block and that she would never be allowed to associate with the common prisoners in the camp. Despite these restrictions, and the special prejudice that was directed at such detainees, Tillion survived Ravensbrück's Block No. 32. She tells her own story and many more in *Ravensbrück*, an astonishingly clear and compendious archive of the camp and of the entire concentrational system of the Third Reich. It is a unique account by a survivor who was a trained anthropologist and ethnographer. Tillion rewrote it twice for publication in French, substantially updating it each time. *Ravensbrück* was translated into English in 1975 and is a must-read book for anyone who wishes to study this grim subject.

The document presented here is Tillion's brief account of the activity that landed her in the hands of the German security police. It describes how resistance groups of the first hour formed, what motivated the people involved, and what they actually did. Tillion was one of the earliest members of the now-celebrated Groupe du musée de l'Homme resistance network and one of the last five members of the group to be rounded up. This network—which called itself the Comité national de salut public (National Committee for Public Well-being)—is now diversely called the Groupe de Boris Vildé, the Groupe de Vildé et Lewitsky, and the Groupe Vildé-Hauët, after its principal early leaders, as well as the Groupe du musée de l'Homme, after the ethnographic Museum of Man in Paris's Sixteenth District, where many of its members worked. This is how we will refer to it henceforth, as well as simply "the group."

1. "Concentration Camp for Women."

Tillion had been out of the country during much of the run-up to the war. A graduate of the École pratique de hautes études, where she had studied under Marcel Mauss,[2] she was doing fieldwork on Berber tribes of the Aurès Mountains in Algeria in the 1930s. She returned to France in May 1940, arriving in Paris five days before the German army. As unprepared as anyone in France for what then transpired, perhaps more justifiably so, she was shocked at France's quick capitulation and deeply disgusted by Philippe Pétain's June 17 speech seeking an armistice. Tillion is one of a number of French men and women who reported having literally been moved to vomit upon hearing the famous speech.[3] She vowed never again to be so out of touch with her country's affairs as to feel such surprise and disappointment. Within a few days, long before becoming involved in the group that would form around Boris Vildé, Germaine made contact with a former colonial army officer turned businessman, Col. Paul Hauët, and began to work for him.[4] Together with his friend and colleague Charles de la Rochère, also a colonel in the *coloniale* (the French colonial army), Hauët had begun organizing a string of contacts with the aim of smuggling men on the run, soldiers mainly, out of the country. At this time he called his group the Union nationale des combattants coloniaux (UNCC). It is also around this time that Germaine and her mother, Emilie, decided to give their identification papers to a family of Jewish refugees to help them escape from what was now Occupied France. It is noteworthy that these two men, Hauët and de la Rochère, who certainly came from the traditional right in France, were immediately actively opposed to the French government that was forming in Vichy, and its self-proclaimed Révolution nationale. Whether their initiative took strength from a belief still held by some in France that the country might continue in the war from the vantage point of its colonies is never made explicit, but all of this was happening before Charles de Gaulle became recognized, as he would be in months to come, as the beacon of hope for a Free France.

In the summer of 1940, France was divided into a northern zone, occupied by the German Army, and a south-central and western part of the country,

2. Marcel Mauss, 1872–1950, is often familiarly referred to as the father of French anthropology.

3. Recorded interview, France Culture, 1987.

4. In an on-camera interview in the 2000 documentary film *Sisters in Resistance*, by Maia Wechsler, Tillion tells the story of how she met Hauët at the suggestion of a worker at the French Red Cross office in Paris.

which called itself the French State, to distinguish itself from the former French Republic. This zone was, and still is, sometimes misleadingly called the "Free Zone." It could also be more accurately called "Vichy France" after the spa town near the border between the two sectors, where the newly formed collaborationist regime headed by Philippe Pétain settled itself in the summer of 1940. We will simply call it the "southern zone." The business of smuggling people out of France at this time usually involved first getting them from the northern into the southern zone, and from there over the Pyrenees Mountains into Spain and on to Portugal, where there were still boat and air connections with both England and America. There were also many refugees crowded into the port city of Marseilles, hoping to find passage to anywhere from North Africa to Madagascar or New York.

By summer's end, Tillion was back in Paris, where her scholarly work naturally led her to the Musée de l'Homme. Her mission to Algeria had been sponsored by the museum's director, Paul Rivet, and her appearance there at this time brought her into contact with Boris Vildé, in her own words "a brilliant ethnographer" of Polar peoples, as well as others working at the museum, notably Anatole Lewitsky, also an ethnographer, and Yvonne Oddon, the librarian. Germaine could not have known in advance that the three had begun to organize "to do something" about the situation in France, but it clearly did not take long before she joined their number. By October 1940 she had brought Hauët and de la Rochère into the group. At this time, in addition to the Comité national pour le salut public, a part of the group also began to operate under the cover of being a writer's fan club, the Société des amis d'Alain-Fournier.[5]

Organizing escape routes to exfiltrate soldiers and downed airmen continued to take precedence over other activities, out of urgent necessity. The group began to exploit new escape routes via the Pas-de-Calais and Brittany. By wintertime their underground publishing activity had begun, starting with translations of speeches by Franklin Roosevelt and Cordell Hull, then the creation of a newsletter. This latter project took a while to get off the ground. Editorial work was led by Lewitsky, with assignments being farmed out to some major literary figures who had returned to the capital, writing under pseudonyms, of course: Claude Aveline, Jean Cassou, and Jean Paulhan

5. Alain-Fournier is the pen name of a French author who died tragically young in the opening year of World War I, leaving a single albeit a great debut novel to his name: *Le Grand Meaulnes.*

all took part in writing the newsletter. The first four-page-sheet *Résistance* appeared in December 1940.

By this time the group was also engaged in gathering intelligence, even before they had made contact with anyone to transmit it to. One of their escape-route contacts in Brittany, a boat captain, had provided them with an opportunity to gather information about the growing German submarine base in St. Nazaire. It would take some time before they made contact with an agent of Britain's Secret Intelligence Service (commonly abbreviated as the IS) and succeeded in passing this information along.

The history of the Groupe du musée de l'Homme is now as well known as that of any of the secret organizations that began at this time. Henri Frenay[6] had written his call to action, *La Libération Nationale,* by November 1940, the same month that the France Liberté group started meeting in Lyon. By December 1940, Libération-Nord (led by Christian Pineau) was also in the early stages of formation. These groups apparently all became immediately involved in a similar agenda: organizing escape routes and publishing news and calls to action, followed by gathering military intelligence—as well as recruiting. This last activity is really the focus of Tillion's article.

Early in 1941, due to several simultaneous mistakes, the group was betrayed. In January a member of the group, the lawyer Léon Nordmann, was caught distributing *Résistance* newsletter number two (published December 30, 1940). Nordmann was the first to be arrested. The indiscretions of a very young courier, René Sénéchal, and the jealousy of a disgruntled subaltern at the museum may also have played parts, at almost exactly the same time, in the group's being penetrated. In February, Yvonne Oddon, who had helped choose the newsletter's title, and Anatole Lewitsky, who had somewhat reluctantly approved it, were the next to be arrested. The German secret police had by this time also placed a mole in the group in the person of Albert Gaveau, a Frenchman with German roots who was working for an officer in the Sicherheitsdienst,[7] a Captain During. Gaveau gained Vildé's confidence and subsequently personally betrayed several members of the group, including Vildé, who was arrested in late March. Soon after that (April 1941), Agnès Humbert,

6. Henri Frenay, 1905–1988, a French Army officer who became an important Resistance leader. (See his *National Liberation,* in this collection.)

7. The German state security service, of which the Gestapo was also a part.

who worked at the Musée d'art et de traditions populaires across the hall at the Palais de Chaillot, who had typed the newsletters, was arrested. The men around Vildé were tried and executed near Paris in February 1942. The two women who were arrested in this first wave were sent to Germany, where they served as slave laborers until the end of the war.

Emilie Tillion, Germaine's mother and herself a writer, and Germaine both escaped arrest at this time, as did Hauët and de la Rochère. The two former army colonels took over leadership of the group when the people around Vildé were arrested, and work continued, with a focus on the ever-pressing need to smuggle refugees and downed airmen out of France and on to England. Under the cover of his earlier group identity, the UNCC, Hauët not only continued his escape-network activities but also stepped up the gathering of military intelligence. By now he had reliable connections with the British Intelligence Service for getting information—largely communiqués on German troop dispositions—out of the country. But again it was through the work of a traitor, this time a Catholic priest named Robert Alesch who was working for the Gestapo for bounty money, that the story of this group of early resisters was brought to a close. De la Rochère and Hauët were arrested within a few days of each other in early July 1942. De la Rochère's testimony exculpated Hauët entirely—he took all of the blame onto himself—and he was soon deported to Germany, where he died in the camp at Sonnenberg. Hauët was released. However, he was arrested again on new charges in July 1944 and deported to Germany, where he died in the Neuengamme camp. Germaine and her mother remained free until August when they, too, were betrayed by Alesch. Germaine tells the story of her arrest for Maia Wechsler's camera in *Sisters in Resistance,* a 2000 documentary film.

Emilie Tillion was murdered at age sixty-nine on March 2, 1945, in Ravensbrück. Her daughter was still in the same camp at the time, albeit in the infirmary, one of the most dangerous places in the camp under any circumstances. Scarcely one month later, Germaine managed to escape from Ravensbrück aboard a Swedish Red Cross White Bus, an escape organized by a Swedish count, Folke Bernadotte. Until her death in 2008, aged one hundred, the younger Tillion was one of the most highly revered doyennes of the French Resistance, recipient of the Grande Croix de la Légion d'honneur and the Grande Croix de l'Ordre national du Mérite, among many other distinctions. Her long career as an anthropologist and a historian was as distinguished as her five-year stint as a resister, and the list of her published writings runs to over a dozen major works, several of which have been translated into English.

The article presented here for the first time in English translation was initially published as "Première Résistance en zone occupée" in the review *Histoire de la Deuxième Guerre mondiale* in April 1958. The Comité d'histoire de la Deuxième Guerre mondiale was formed in 1951 out of an already existing Commission for the Liberation of France and a committee for the history of the war that had been formed in 1944–45.[8] The review was the committee's forum for advanced scholarly discussion. Of course her motivation is, as Tillion says, at least in part to honor the memory of people both living and dead who were part of that struggle. It is a brief and candid history of the earliest hours of the French Resistance, though we must also recognize the imprint of some subsequent twentieth-century French history in her text as well.

Written thirteen years after the end of the war, and eighteen years after the events it describes, it is in any case an eyewitness account of the formation of what is arguably the first resistance group in wartime France. That distinction is of little matter. Again, Henri Frenay was making the first contacts that would lead to the creation of the Mouvement de libération nationale at precisely the same time, and so was Emmanuel d'Astier de la Vigerie with respect to the movement that would call itself simply Libération-Sud. And they were all doing these things independently of each other, and of London. The first newsletters from these groups appeared at about the same time, which is to say in December 1940. What makes Tillion's testimony so remarkable is the independence of her point of view, and the objectivity that she brings to her discussion of these matters. Tillion was not from a military background, and the fact that she met and started to work with two colonels from the coloniale owes more to chance than to any preexisting social and political connections. This in itself is revealing of the utter chaos into which the country was plunged. Their meeting took place during the summer following the Collapse of France, the so-called *Débâcle*. In the interview for the Wechsler film, Tillion describes having been directed to Hauët and de la Rochère quite by chance, by a worker at the French Red Cross, in July 1940. She then took these men and the network they began to create in August into the fledgling network at the Museum of Man when she and the rest of Paris observed the seasonal return to the city known as *la rentrée*, which must have been anything but usual in the autumn of 1940.

8. This is the same group that commissioned the 1955 Alain Resnais documentary *Night and Fog*.

The strength of Tillion's article lies in her discussion of membership and recruitment. She recounts the winter of 1940–41, during which a number of independent groups began to come together out of the shared revulsion of otherwise fairly diverse individuals, and their simultaneous desire "to do something."[9] Faith in existing political parties was at a low point due to what the country had just gone through, the gridlock engendered by intense left/right confrontation throughout the 1930s that had led to the Débâcle itself, so it is perhaps not surprising that personal acquaintance and word of mouth would count for more in these times than prior political affiliations. Tillion describes a world in which the networking of individuals and extremely small groups had replaced recruitment at rallies and mass meetings. The need to operate without attracting attention was also clearly apparent, and intense discretion obliged activists to find new methods for making new contacts. The way in which the group came together has a lot in common with the way in which the Mouvement de libération nationale and other non–party-based groups at the time were born. Use of the term *mouvement* for this kind of group was frequent, but Tillion appears to prefer less politically charged terms such as "nucleus" and "network." She likewise avoids calling groups "cells." She points out that groups emerging from Communist organizations were different both in not being as spontaneous and in having a predetermined ideology or political agenda.[10]

Tillion's account tries hard to avoid political ideology, but it is by no means unsophisticated. She is aware that the mixture of backgrounds in her group is unusually broad, with social scientists, art historians, and retired colonial army officers working together and recruiting each among their own. One occasionally wishes that she was more interested in telling stories of direct action, but in fact this is not what is on her agenda. She does refer to meetings, but these were usually between two people, and are presented without drama, as indeed they probably were. Her goal in telling these stories appears to be to show how decision making went, along with the personal nature of everyday

9. A 2013 documentary film by V. Goubet that includes interviews with many of the last survivors of this period uses this iconic phrase as its title. The phrase resonates in several of the pieces in this collection.

10. The story of how the Communist groups formed in the Resistance is inevitably influenced by the events of August and September 1939: the Molotov–von Ribbentrop Pact and the subsequent banishment of the Communists from French politics following the declaration of war.

contacts within her group. Even when she is critical of someone, it is not her aim to draw political caricatures of the individuals she names. She makes it quite clear that they did come from very diverse backgrounds—the traditional far right and intellectuals rather to the left, including, she says, only a few Communists. This is not surprising in the political climate of France following August–September 1939, when the French Communist Party saw its press banned (August 26) and the party itself dissolved (September 26) after the signing of the Molotov–von Ribbentrop Pact and France's declaration of war on Germany. Communists in France, until then a large and well-represented party, remained in political limbo until Germany turned on the USSR in June 1941.

Tillion occasionally remarked that she thought indignation to be the most powerful of all human emotions. Here she describes how these early groups came together, primarily as individuals who knew each other already and who shared a similar indignation and, because of it, a shared willingness to face the risks involved in taking action. They began to discuss among themselves what shape this action might take. Then these largely spontaneous, tiny clusters of individuals that she calls "nucleuses" joined with others to form larger "networks." And she notes again that this coalescing of energies happened across class and existing party affiliations, and that they definitely took place before any top-down guidance started coming from London.

Not that London, home of de Gaulle's Free French organization, ever claimed to have invented the Resistance. On the contrary, it appears that de Gaulle scarcely had sufficient belief in "the resistance" (always lowercase) to embrace it, let alone to really shape it. What the Free French did for these groups they did from afar, and they did not have high hopes for their success.[11] De Gaulle's open contempt for the rank-and-file resistance fighters (not just Communists, either) who paraded in front of him immediately after the war, sometimes wearing *espadrilles* instead of boots, and the disdain with which he dispatched them back to their prewar jobs, were already legendary in 1958. Tillion wrote this article immediately prior to the long de Gaulle presidency (1958–68) that began the Fifth Republic, during which time this picture

11. In the days of the Liberation of Paris, de Gaulle would, however, occasionally say things that would later appear to be exaggerated praise, even to many in the Resistance, and certainly to many outside it: "Paris libéré, libéré par lui-même" (speech at Hôtel de Ville de Paris, August 25, 1944). And when de Gaulle returned to public life in the late 1950s and 1960s, he famously entertained a myth that the Resistance was far more significant than collaboration.

changed somewhat. Tillion goes out of her way to say that the Groupe du musée de l'Homme was on its own in 1940, and not getting directions from London, and this is clearly intended to mean from de Gaulle as well as the IS and Churchill's Special Operations Executive (SOE). On the one hand she wants to record what happened, and on the other she wants to pay tribute to the individuals who took this dangerous initiative. But the reason she does this so explicitly is probably further connected with the time and collateral circumstances at the time she wrote the article. This was in 1958. The need she felt to write the history of this group appears to have still been quite real and present. We ought to ask ourselves: why?

Tillion says at the outset that she had hoped someone else would record this history, and in fact she and a number of her colleagues in the Comité d'histoire de la Deuxième Guerre mondiale had been hard at work for years doing similar work, but none had focused on the creation of this group as she does. Henri Michel's groundbreaking *Histoire de la Résistance* was published in the same year. And the official work of the French government to authenticate claims of resister activity, validating pensions to affected families and retired participants, had largely taken place by this time and had involved serious historical research. Anyone who wishes to pursue this should trace the status of persons carrying a *carte de combattant volontaire de la Résistance*, issued under law no. 49.418 of March 25, 1949, as amended. Somewhere around 250,000 official cards have been issued to such persons, some as recently as 1996, and Tillion does not appear to be making a claim for anyone hitherto unknown. As this status had been established for almost ten years by 1958, and was under no threat in the last days of the Fourth Republic, it seems unlikely that anything connected with this effort was what motivated Tillion to write the article.

It seems possible that Tillion was moved by a desire to put forward the roles of her earliest colleagues, colonels Hauët and de la Rochère, lest their roles in the Groupe du musée de l'Homme, or the Groupe de Vildé-Lewitsky as it was primarily being called, might have been somewhat eclipsed in the ten years just past. This would be gracious and quite typical of her. If she did want to remind the public of their critical contributions, she may have succeeded. If she wanted to add their names to the popularly used title of the group, alas, she did not. The role of the ethnography museum and its fearless scholars appears to have a firm hold on the public imagination. In truth, the group might just as well be named after Tillion and her mother. Although Hauët and de la Rochère clearly emerge as the first resisters that she met, and appear to have been the last members of the group to be arrested, the museum group remains the Groupe du musée de l'Homme, and its principal leader is considered to have been Boris Vildé.

In April 1958, France was becoming deeply mired in the next great crisis of the national conscience following that of World War II, the loss of Algeria. To link Tillion's writing with the events of that cataclysmic upheaval in French society should provide today's readers a glimpse into how the *memory* of the Resistance, and the adherence to its ethos, played out in the first decades—if not in the entire seventy years—since World War II. The defeat of the French Army at Dien Bien Phu and the loss of Vietnam as a colony in May 1954 had been deeply felt. In some ways, it increased anxiety and hardened reluctance to suffer a similar setback as calls for Algerian independence sharpened following the Toussaint Rouge of November 1, 1954.[12] To evoke the memory of the Resistance, and particularly the Resistance pre-1942—when the story becomes infinitely complicated by the struggles around the mission(s) of Jean Moulin and the reentry of the Communists into the fray—invites readers to feel a pride in their past that might provide a healthy tonic in newly troubled times.

It would be easy to trivialize the anguish of the French at the time of the Algerian crisis and characterize it simply as the inevitable End of Empire blues, but Algeria was more than just another colony. It was considered an administrative department of the French state, and as such comparable to what Alaska is to the United States today. The Algerian separation had begun in an ominous preview of things to come on Victory in Europe (V-E) Day, May 8, 1945, when the French Army fired on crowds of civilian demonstrators in two Algerian cities, Setif and Constantine. The struggle did not really explode until the mid-1950s. By 1958 Tillion had become very much involved in helping the Algerian people to assert their independence. She had just met (in July 1957) with one of the principal leaders of the Algerian Front de libération nationale when this article appeared, and she had begun actively protesting, among other things, the French use of torture in the ongoing Battle of Algiers. In early 1958—when her article was in preparation—the besieged French military authority in Algiers had publicly begun to seek the intervention of General de Gaulle, then in retirement, to intervene personally in Paris to lead

12. Toussaint Rouge (or Toussaint Sanglant), "Red All Saints' Day," is the name given to November 1, 1954, when the Algerian War nominally began. Dozens of bombings and acts of sabotage occurred across Algeria. The Algerian people's struggle for independence lasted until 1962.

the nation through the crisis. De Gaulle agreed to do just that in the weeks immediately following the publication of Tillion's article (May 1958).

Leaving aside for a moment other questions about the Algerian situation, it is safe to say that, in April 1958, Tillion was thinking about Charles de Gaulle in more than just his role as the man in London who in 1940 was struggling to become the leader of a Free France, or, in his own words, Eternal France. Neither she nor any one of her readers could help but think of him as the man now called upon to save the country once again. Graciously, and wisely for the quality of her discussion, she does not say what she thinks about him in this new context. She does mention torture, however, although only once, and while she does not explicitly connect her reference to Nazi torture of resisters post-1941 with events in 1950s Algeria, what she says about it in the earlier context is expressed in terms that easily allow its transposition to other struggles. What clearer message could she send to her countrymen about torture than to point out that, through its use, "immeasurably greater became the cohesion and the capacity to attack of the oppressed people"? That is to say, independently of any discussion of its immorality or of any putative human rights, the use of torture would inevitably help any oppressed people to resist. But by choosing to describe the resisters as "oppressed people" Tillion is calling to mind her solidarity with the Algerians, and inviting her co-resisters and their admirers in 1958 to identify with them as well, in effect equating the Algerians' struggle with that of wartime French patriots like the members of the Groupe du musée de l'Homme.

Although she never wanders from the history of a specific group of French resisters that survived for scarcely more than one year, Germaine Tillion has in fact given us a document that also shows the nature of organized resistance to oppression anywhere. She explicitly calls on us to think about the struggle and the experience of the French in World War II as a typical example of resistance to tyranny. Her account of this brief history will naturally be of interest to students of the broader history of the French Resistance in the war. It certainly bears critiquing in the light of Daniel Cordier's argument about the relative value of document versus memoir in studying the Resistance. But, as a historical document of mid-twentieth-century French history, it reveals other complexities. The final page, entitled "The Lacunae in Our Historical Documentation," would bear analysis simply as an example of writing on the anthropology of politics. And as a description of the day-to-day evolution of a politically engaged activist movement, from the initial experience of individual outrage to the formation of a nationwide complex of groups and political movements, it is unparalleled for its explicitness and its concision. For these reasons, I offer this translation into English not only for students of Occupation France, but certainly for others whose interest goes to the tumultuous fifteen years that followed, and quite possibly for people who are studying activism and political struggle on other fronts.

First Resistance in the Occupied Zone

GERMAINE TILLION

For thirteen years I have been hoping that someone would write the history of our resistance organization, so as not to have to do it myself. But the years are going by, and it is unfair to withhold from the public, and in particular from that part of the public made up of the survivors of our groups, an account of what remains following the inevitable loss of people and of memory regarding a past that we deeply care about.

Despite the number of years that have gone by, we are still just learning the facts: the links between countless events, sometimes set apart from each other by gaps and areas of darkness. These can seem insignificant to people who didn't take part in them, while for others who did they may have taken on quasi-religious importance. But they are not only either fascinating or entirely lacking in interest; for the principal witnesses, they trail in their wake memories that are quite literally unbearable to this very day.

An unbelievable combination of circumstances was necessary for anyone who chose to actively fight in the Resistance beginning in 1940, first of all to avoid death, and then to overcome physical and mental cruelty the duration and intensity of which are scarcely imaginable. Following which, among the survivors, a latent exasperation developed, which took many forms: an obsession with memory, frightened refusal of memory, sometimes both at the same time. None of which reactions facilitates the job of the chronicler, especially not when she shares them.

Translation of Germaine Tillion, "Première Résistance en zone occupée," *Histoire de la Deuxième Guerre mondiale* (Paris: University Press of France), no. 30 (April 1958).

1. Political Opinion and Parties in the Resistance of 1940

What were the people who fought in the Resistance thinking? What did they hope for following victory? How did they imagine France's future would look? Why had they sought to join a group? I hardly talked about these matters with anyone at the time. I did know, however, and very precisely so, by whom and at what date they were put in touch with us, as well as exactly what they were capable of doing, what they actually did, and through what sequence of events their involvement in our movement was broken off.

In the groups of 1940 whose beginnings I was able to determine, the start of recruitment was often the meeting up of old friends who decided to start getting together regularly "to do something." Sometimes, too, people who barely knew each other were drawn together because they realized that they felt the same way, and some of them also began to distance themselves from other people that they knew well because they suddenly found themselves put off by their attitude. The Armistice caused an almost immediate split across all of French society, and this split could be perceived in every milieu.

Very soon this core group began to expand and began to include ever more heterogeneous individuals who began to coalesce into a *movement* or a *network,* in which the principal concern was effectiveness.

Within the groups that were created by Colonel de la Rochère, from the very first day, the homogeneous milieu from which he came (religious, anti-revolutionary, even monarchist) was outnumbered by people who, apart from an unwavering sense of patriotism, had no particularly well-defined opinion, and who came from every class of French society: for example, administrative personnel from the prefecture of the Seine, monks, firemen, a neighborhood bookseller (who, starting in 1940, began printing Churchill's speeches), the corner shoe repairman, rural small-business owners.

Colonel Hauët was not religious; he had left the army a long time before and was running a factory which took up fairly little of his time: he recruited former soldiers (commissioned and noncommissioned officers), engineers, railroad workers, factory owners, doctors.

Boris Vildé, an extremely brilliant ethnographer, knew university professors, lawyers, people in the sciences, but in order to create an effective group, he soon began recruiting people from outside Paris where, through networking, he came into contact with like-minded individuals who to all appearances had very different occupations and preoccupations from his own.

Any and all recruitment that I did myself occurred among my friends, an extremely varied lot from the outset.

All political parties were represented in our group—from extreme left Socialists to monarchists—with the exception of the Communist Party. Why this exception? Because our recruitment took place almost entirely before Hitler attacked Russia, consequently at a time when the Communist Party was in a compromised position vis-à-vis the Resistance. When the Communists were being persecuted, I helped some escape whenever I could, but neither Vildé nor Hauët, nor La Rochère, nor I ever inducted any into our groups, and as best as I can recall we never talked with each other about this because the question never came up. I suppose that the Communist Party, which had its own structures, took care to see that its members never went astray in areas that were outside of its control.

The active Resistance, in its earliest beginning, consisted of a very small number of people; as the repression gradually built, the Resistance grew, without ever becoming very large.[1]

We were only a handful in 1940, but were we already representative of a considerable segment of French opinion? As far as I was concerned, I believed so from the very first day and it seems to me that none of my comrades ever raised any doubts about the matter in front of me. But if this had not been the case, what would we have done about it? The same as we did do, I think, always hoping that our compatriots would end up by following our example.

I believe to this day, however, that we did reap the benefits of fairly widespread passive sympathy from the very start. Thanks to German repression (which began to play an active part in *recruiting for the resistance* during the second half of 1941), this latent sympathy became more and more active as the years went by.

Our people coming from widely varied, even contradictory, backgrounds and opinions for the most part put on an optimistic outward appearance that I shared in completely, which seems excessive in retrospect (even though circumstances ultimately justified it).

In 1940 there was a fundamental belief that it was not only inevitable that

1. *Note in French edition:* Even among the people who were deported, by definition a select group, all of my inquiries revealed a minority from the Resistance: one-third "resisters," one-third common criminals, and one-third made up of hostages and innocent bystanders—not including the unfortunate Jews who, in principle, were not in the same prisons as we.

Germany would be defeated, but that it would happen soon; beneath this confidence that was proclaimed loud and clear there could nonetheless be found lurking unspoken thoughts that conformed better with the outward reality of the situation. *Liberation was inevitable and there could be no doubt about its being possible*—only when would it happen? And would we still be around to witness it? Looking ahead from the point of view of 1940, the institutions of France seemed intangible, and vanished in the background of our true preoccupations. At the end of 1942, and the beginning of 1943, people interested in the "political" began to think and put some ideas forward. By this time, the people who had been active in 1940 were largely in prison or dead. Among the few virtues that it is possible to claim for this first wave of resisters, the first is certainly that they did not act out of self-interest. . . .

What political doctrine did we see as belonging to the future? I do not remember ever trying to find out my comrades' ideas about this for myself. Like myself, they had all lived through the shock of the collapse of France, and they were all sufficiently shaken up by it at least momentarily to have thrown off the baggage of their prior beliefs (that they, moreover, nearly always picked right back up again if they had the good fortune to survive). The thought did dawn on some of them that eventually it would be necessary to find some healthier and more effective political ideas than the ones that had led us to this disaster. When the time came to vote on a new constitution—an expiatory ceremony corresponding to the rite of casting off of sins in less complex societies than our own—the results immediately punctured this lofty hope, allowing it to slowly collapse.

When I try to reconstruct my opinions at that time, I remember first of all Pétain's speech about seeking an armistice.[2]

I had not foreseen the collapse of France. I had scarcely even felt it coming, and it hurt, it was unbearably painful when it happened and was made worse by my reproaching myself for my prior neglect, since the dignity and the independence of my country were so fundamental to me, I had no excuse for

2. *Note in French edition:* I was not well-informed about our public affairs, since I had come back only two weeks before from the mountains in the south of Algeria, where I had been on an ethnographic mission since 1934. There were still no roads up there, no mail and no radio (this has changed since), and there was nothing there to distract me from the subtle polemics of my interlocutors: Chaouia peasants, crafty, loquacious, and litigious. At that time their natural eloquence exercised itself on politics a bit more archaic than those of Vercingetorix. (This, too, has changed.)

having entrusted them to the care of persons unknown. During those awful days in June 1940, I decided from then on to try and pay more attention to our public affairs. Without particularly admiring the men who—for better or for worse—had represented us, I always felt that I supported their decisions, and that I consequently had a duty to keep the commitments that they made. As an example, in 1940, France having undertaken to wage a war side by side with England, I felt that I was personally obliged to consider the English as allies and to act accordingly, which did not prevent me from feeling a certain repugnance at the perspective of seeing our resistance effort coordinated from London by employees of the Intelligence Service.[3]

Col. Hauët, moved by loyalty to the army and to French traditions, after the meeting in Montoire,[4] following a number of pro-German speeches, after the return of Laval, chewed on his big white moustaches and remained somber and silent for days on end, while he received with eager joy the news about Laval being put out of the government, the arrest of traitors in the Free Zone and in North Africa, Pétain's receiving people from the Resistance, as well as some orders given to civil servants (in particular regarding Alsatians during the first period, or to the struggle against the S.T.O. in the next).[5]

I did not have the occasion to discuss these matters with Col. de la Rochère, whom I only met once, but how he felt about them was known to me through his family and Col. Hauët. Before the Armistice, and therefore on a purely military basis and independently of having to choose, Col. de la Rochère did not have a high regard for Marshal Pétain, but in contrast he very much admired Colonel de Gaulle, whose works he had read and whom it appeared he had met. The Call of the 18th of June excited him very much.

Vildé, who escaped on July 5th, and Lewitsky, who was freed in August,[6] had found Yvette Oddon at the musée de l'Homme. All three of them found National Socialism revolting, and it was this revulsion that was their principal spur to their subsequent deeds.

Whenever one studies a period in history that is decidedly closed, and

3. The British Intelligence Service.

4. In Montoire-sur-le-Loir, on October 24, 1940, four months after the French surrender, Marshal Pétain met and formally shook hands with Adolf Hitler.

5. The STO (Service du travail obligatoire) was an obligatory work service instituted by Vichy in February 1943 that aimed to send young Frenchmen to work in Germany. (See glossary.)

6. These are presumably the dates when Vildé and Lewitsky escaped being POWs.

about which there are few dated documents, there is a great danger that memories will shift: it is easy to believe in good faith that what one believed in 1942 was the same as what he believed in 1941. But I can put an exact date on my last conversation with Lewitsky, and it was almost entirely about Pétain; it took place at the musée de l'Homme, at lunchtime, in February 1941. We spoke without constraint, in good spirits and mutual understanding, and we enjoyed being able to understand each other without having to spell things out, all the more because we were so tired of the daily dose of defeatist humiliation and whining heard on Radio-Vichy. Vildé and Lewitsky were excited about the prospect of reprinting Poincaré's *Memoirs*, including his sharp criticism of the victor of Verdun. They especially wanted to stress the serious matter of the call for an armistice, which Pétain supported in 1917. As I left, Lewitsky ended our conversation saying: "In short, the Old Man was prone to betting on Black. This time Black came up a winner: he won." Lewitsky laughed, then we shook hands, and I never saw him again.

I can also put a precise date on a conversation with the mother of a particularly shameless "collaborator," the minister Abel Bonnard, because it occurred exactly three weeks before the execution of my comrades (so it was in January of 1942). The old woman talked a lot about her maid and her nurse, and repeated what they said about the German repression. She herself was completely spineless, which prevented me from being able to determine whether she considered them to be less reliable reports or if she believed them; doubtless she was unable to decide. But I felt at the time that the mere fact that our antennae extended right into the kitchens, the back rooms and even the families of our adversaries, was a victory, and in fact it was.

During a conversation (no less easy to date, since it took place two days before my own arrest, therefore at the beginning of August 1942), Jacques Legrand, the head of an Intelligence Service network, and I were discussing the French radio broadcasts from London—"our radio"—that we all listened to religiously. Legrand was criticizing the harshness of his own attacks on the government in Vichy, which he felt inadvertently hurt many French people, and he compared it with how Swiss radio managed to make no concessions to the enemy while at the same time acknowledging a broad range of sympathies inside the country. —It was a beautiful summer afternoon, the window was open onto a garden full of flowers and we were six people: two days later five of us were arrested and deported—of whom I alone survived. The sixth was the traitor who turned us in—he was shot following the Liberation.

Other conversations come to mind, which are harder to connect as exactly with an event that sticks in my memory: for example accounts of people who, in 1941, after a trip to the Free Zone, told us (in shock, indignation or plain jest) the inanities of the cult of Pétain. But those people were not involved in the Resistance.

It would be foolish to conclude from these few memories that, in our groups, we excused the politics of Vichy and that quite often collaborators with the enemy frequently turned into admirers of General de Gaulle, but it does seem to me that differences of opinion were not as great as people have made out, between people who belonged to the Resistance and the ones who did not. The differences among us were primarily ones of degree: reaction to the behavior of people working for Vichy was more often defiant, in 1941, than among people who belonged to the passive population—but it was also present among them. Conversely, these groups were not at all immune to the reverence that enshrouded the old Marshal at this time. Public opinion is a fluid against which no impermeable barrier is known: there is no one worker opinion, for example, nor one women's opinion; there are opinions which are widespread among workers, there are women's reactions.

Moreover, beliefs are not the only thing that leads to action: all French people were hurt by the defeat in 1940, many felt shame in abandoning their allies in the heat of battle, or viewed the new world that was being built before their eyes with revulsion—but pain, and shame, and revulsion were only intolerable for some people, and they were not necessarily the ones who were best equipped from a dialectical point of view.

I do not recall at what time they began to call us Gaullists. Not right away, in any case. Nonetheless, Gaullists we were, in the sense that from the 18th of June, 1940, on, we considered General de Gaulle as "the man who was right," or rather as "the man who was of the same opinion as we"—but we knew next to nothing about him, apart from the position that he had taken, about his brief tenure at the Ministry of Defense and the titles of some of his books (that few among us had read and that we could not obtain). Among the "resisters" of 1940, I know some who did not become "Gaullists" until 1942, and others who never did: they couldn't tolerate the presence of Germans in France and needed no other motivation to act. As for myself, it was only during captivity—in short out of action and even outside of life itself—that I learned real-life facts about him: I learned them with infinite gratitude. *We had been right,* and about that, I believe, none of us ever doubted—but what an enormous relief it was to learn that all of the hardship was not in vain, that it was directed and taken full advantage of somewhere, with a reasonable end in view, by a clear-thinking, right-minded and unflinching man, in a way that matched the enormous sacrifice that our support entailed.

2. "Nucleuses" of Resistance

The ideal network arises from a decision taken, in London or in Algiers, by a high command. Next, volunteers offer their services for work that can be expected of them; then, one fine night, they all set out with a certain number of addresses on slips of paper or in their heads. And, depending on the usual turns of fortune, either they are destroyed by the enemy, or they make it to the glory days of Liberation. From the first day to the last, the life of this ideal network is framed by a specific chronology: it started on such-and-such a date, and it ended on another.

Even for a network that fits this model exactly, this is only an administrative ideal: the historical reality is far more complex. The "Network of 1943," like our own, had to recruit members in order to accomplish its mission. It had to recruit among sympathetic milieus, of course, and these might already have been semi-organized and semi-clandestine; it did not always recruit isolated individuals, but sometimes entire groups—whose subversive activity predated their official co-option into a recognized organization.

Such groups constitute the smallest units of the Resistance that is in the process of taking form; as such, they can be considered to be "cells" in the larger body to which they belong. By designating them in this way, however, we risk confusing them with a political construct whose formation is not the same; for this reason, without abandoning biological terminology, I propose to call them "nucleuses." And it is also true that—like in biology—these "nucleuses" of resistance were more unsophisticated than the classic revolutionary "cell."[7] They were more spontaneous, but less complete and evolved.

In order for a party to exist there must be semi-public recruitment around a program; a central body must record the membership and assess the capability of individual adherents with an eye to designating who among them will take charge of this or that geographical area. Nothing of this sort happened with the Resistance, which did not have the luxury of a period in which to

7. *Note in French edition:* The "cell"—a designation popularized by the Communist Party—is, in reality, under different names, the basic unit of all clandestine parties. But it presupposes the existence of a party—and therefore also of a doctrine. The Resistance was not a party and had no doctrine. This became very clear at the Liberation.

prepare: France was occupied without having put anything like this into place, and no such leadership had been designated before the widespread collapse. All prior social structures (political parties, religious groups) appeared to be unsuitable in entirely new circumstances, and, from one day to the next, all experienced an internal split that, from that moment on, cut across the entire population.[8]

Regarding these "nucleuses" of resistance, we see three different ways they come into existence:

In the first case, a nucleus forms when a group of individuals sets its sights on getting some predetermined strategic information or on pulling off a specific action. The network makes contacts and has to place trust in them. This kind of group is fundamentally different from the "cell" in that it is not directed towards propaganda, but it is like one in the way it is organized. In 1940 and 1941 it was by far the least frequent kind.

In the second type, creation is spontaneous. People linked by friendship first of all happened to share the strong feelings that the new situation provoked in them; they decided to get together to talk more freely and to try to decide how to behave; then they sought to decide "what to do." . . . They almost always found it, as far as I can tell, and without too much difficulty.

That is because, at this time, "what to do" began to take on a life of its own and to impose itself more and more clearly just about everywhere. Soldiers who had deserted, and who needed to be provided with false papers and civilian clothing, British soldiers who needed to be gotten to the Unoccupied Zone, Jews to hide, and then (later on) men dodging service in the STO that needed to be gotten over to the *maquis*—all of these were obviously needed, in addition to the more considered options that people came up with.[9] "What to do" would underlie the third type of recruitment—if in fact it is different from the first kind, because who can say what is predetermined without one's first having asked himself what is to be done?

In 1940, the prisoners of war had not yet been shipped off to Germany, but the gigantic net was already closing around them. The job of rescuing them was at first fairly simple: an ordinary suit of civilian clothing, a few addresses, was all that was needed to rescue a man. Only a short while later, one needed

8. *Note in French edition:* The responsibility for this secession falls upon Marshal Pétain, for, without him, "collaboration" would have found itself in a morally indefensible position.

9. The *maquis* were young men who dodged participation in the STO by escaping to the countryside. The word is often used by extension for the Resistance as a whole. (See glossary.)

to get false demobilization papers, to find passers, transportation, a series of contacts. But circumstances forced people to learn how to do all of this.

It was the rare group that was so childish as to ascribe to itself an exclusive title in 1940 or 1941. The names, the labels, were created in the second phase of the Resistance—following November of 1942.

By definition almost, each "nucleus" included one or two leaders, but they were not necessarily officially recognized—a spontaneous hierarchy that generally did not give rise to inner conflicts, unlike the formal hierarchies that followed.

No specialization either: each team took on many jobs and organized escapes, printed and distributed tracts, gathered intelligence, gathered and hid weapons, all at the same time.

All of this required secrecy, a spontaneous organization in which the members saw each other, spoke to each other and exchanged information frequently. As the group grew in size, bit by bit, the amount of information increased. How to handle this? The ones that handled it the best found ways to pass information along and became the first networks.

Once such a pipeline was established, the group that controlled it would start to gather around itself as many as possible of these little autonomous nucleuses whose development we have been talking about. In so doing we enter a new phase—perhaps the most dangerous one—the first resistance.[10]

3. Networking

In order for these connections of group to group, and from these to a larger network, to be possible, a large number of personal contacts was needed linking the people specifically charged with outreach within our resistance nucleuses. These contacts wove a vast spider's web that covered all of France, and this is one of the most characteristic and important phenomena of a period of insurrection. Except when they were needed to create the link between a group and a network, in all likelihood they would remain hidden forever. Without these contacts, however, there would not have been any Resistance, nor any groups or networks. . . .

10. *Note in French edition:* It was these spontaneous nucleuses that made up the membership of our network, and during numerous inquiries about the Resistance and deportation, every time I explored the origins of an organization, I discovered the remains of these nucleuses more or less intact within the membership of the subsequent group.

These relationships between agents of different networks were dangerous, and should have been forbidden, at least according to the "Handbook of the Perfect Clandestine Agent." In actual practice I don't know of any team that could have functioned without this happening, and I scarcely know any that failed because of it. Indeed I could cite a considerable number of rescues that were necessitated because of personal relationships that existed—outside of the work of their groups—among resisters of the 1st hour. When the enemy's use of torture became an everyday reality, the dangers caused by these relationships became immeasurably greater, but so, too, did the cohesion and the capacity to attack of the oppressed people become immeasurably greater. And it is always the enemy that loses the most.

Following this, these interconnections, instead of taking place through personal connections, began to be run via London, and managed by specialists. This development was necessary and one could even say inevitable. It sometimes caused damages to escalate, because of the increased difficulty of protecting groups against betrayal while dealing entirely with strangers.

Through loyalty to friends whose lives one was personally familiar with, one had to keep their secrets even from companions in resistance, unless it was agreed on in advance that these latter could in fact be informed. This is why everyone only knew his own network of relations. This is why it is impossible to assess the extent of this gray area in our colleagues' activity except when they lived to tell us about it.

What were Boris Vildé's contacts outside of the network? I don't know. What were those of Colonel de la Rochère? Likewise, I have no idea. As for those of Colonel Hauët, at least I can say that I positively do know, from countless allusions made to them, that they were numerous, but I don't know the details. As far as my own are concerned, I didn't talk to anyone about them, and even Col. Hauët (whom I met every day until his first arrest, July 5, 1941) didn't know about them—thanks to which he was not arrested again until June of 1944, two years after my own arrest, which was in August of 1942.[11]

In 1945, I found a note written in cipher that I had drawn up shortly before my own arrest (the Gestapo never found it and, in any case, it couldn't have compromised anyone but me). In it I classified a number of groups of resisters,

11. *Note in French edition:* I naturally didn't write anything down, and it is entirely from memory that I note:

In December of 1940, I was supposed to meet an officer named Jean-Pierre who was coming in from London. He was supposed to stay with the wife of a friend, the painter L. A meeting

the causes of whose arrest were known to me, by how they had been arrested, in order to examine how we could reduce the losses that we were suffering. Very small was the number of arrests due to carelessness, stupid mistakes and idle chatter (we note with both surprise and satisfaction); twice as costly, according to my reckoning, were arrests due to motorized triangulation units; as for the evildoings of double-agents, they make up more than two-thirds of the total number. (I was myself, a few days later, given up by a double-agent.)

---

was set up at which Jean-Pierre failed to show up and I subsequently learned that he had been arrested under circumstances that were impossible for us to clarify at the time. Six months later, when my friends from the musée de l'Homme wound up in the prison of Cherche-Midi, I learned through a clandestine correspondent referred to me by them that Jean-Pierre had been Estienne d'Orves's commanding officer. [Estienne D'Orves was a naval officer, and widely revered as the first martyr of the Resistance.—Ed.]

When one of my old friends, Jacques Lecompte-Boinet, joined a group that at the time was run by Elisabeth Dussauze, he told me about it at once, and subsequently kept me informed about his activity almost daily, through accounts that were incredibly alive and picturesque. In case of disaster in any of my own networks, it might be an asset to be in possession of this information to repurpose any of our people by hooking them up with another group. As it happened she went down first, and I was able to help Jacques Lecompte-Boinet to take over the group at that time.

Following the execution of my comrades from the musée de l'Homme, I don't remember how but I came in touch with a teacher from the Lycée Buffon who belonged to a "nucleus" whose name I did not know (Valmy) until after the Liberation. A posthumous name, no doubt. As far as I could judge at the time, in February 1942, this group was more interested in propaganda than in action or intelligence, despite which this teacher was subsequently arrested and beheaded. He had put me in touch with one of his friends who belonged to the IS.

The head of this network of the IS wanted to organize an escape from Fresnes: I was arrested with him at this time. I was informed by him of the procedure for contacting a group in Lyon that was led by M. de Vomécourt, and I was able to get in touch with Jacques Lecompte-Boinet.

During the course of 1941, the painter A. got in touch with a police commissioner who had been dismissed by Vichy. This man was devoting all of his time to resistance activities, and I knew the organization to which he belonged that went by the name of "Belgian Volunteers." I entrusted to this commissioner a portable printing kit that belonged to me in order for him to start a small clandestine periodical. He had the people in place to undertake the physical work of doing this, and I could take on the job of providing copy. The periodical never appeared because the commissioner was arrested along with his group; he died in deportation. Upon my return from captivity, I tried to get in touch with the "Belgian Volunteers" among the known networks of the Free French Forces and I found no trace of them. Perhaps their existence is recorded in Belgium.

In 1942 I put up a Belgian man who belonged to an entirely different group from the preceding one for several weeks at my own home. His name was Debisy and he was with the IS and

But I did not keep records on most of the groups whose development and end I did research on back then, and they do not figure in the listing given in note 1 on the previous page. Nonetheless, I knew them well enough to be able to say what happened to them, which was in principle a secret.[12]

One can conceive of the Resistance of 1940 and 1941 as a crystallization; each crystal was connected to an infinite number of analogous groups along its many facets, and gradually as they entered into contact with the inert and still

---

was being sought by the Gestapo (I found in my mail in July of 1945 a card mailed from London in which he sent news of himself).

I knew Col. Hauët's contacts with the network set up in Vichy by some former officers of the 5ème bureau and on one occasion I even met with a man from this group. [The Cinquième Bureau was a special counter-espionage unit of the regular French Army headed by Col. Louis Rivet.—Ed.] As far as my participation went, this meeting was set up by Col. Hauët, but I later learned that this man didn't know the colonel, and he had been sent to meet me by Captain d'Austrevaux. Because I met him again later on, this event has stuck in my memory.

I recall, for the same reason, my meetings with two members of the Johny network that I had been sent to warn about certain dangers to which they were exposed.

(The contacts which I have listed here all took place outside of my own resistance network.)

12. *Note in French edition:* On the other hand, I remember having exchanged information with Mr. Jamati, an employee of the Center for Scientific Research. His group, organized under the name Maintenir, was led by Claude Bellanger. I did not conduct a systematic survey of relations between Maintenir and our group, and I offer the following as raw information:

Apart from contacts between Mr. Jamati and me, Maintenir was also in contact with Léo Leymarie, who was one of the principal information agents (in the sector in which I was engaged with Col. Hauët), as well as with Théophile Perrier, his sister, and Mme Fort, who were active in the same sector. In the sector of Vildé, Claude Bellanger also knew Yvonne Oddon, Agnès Humbert, and Professor Fawtier.

Let me state in passing that if Yvonne Oddon belonged to the nucleus created by Vildé, from the very first hour, Professor Fawtier was himself at the center of another nucleus which continued its activity after the destruction of the team of Vildé and Agnès Humbert, with, in particular, Marcel Abraham, Claude Aveline, and Jean Cassou, and belonged to another group of ten people from the very start which in principle was to remain entirely separate.

In this same sector, the lawyer Jubineau had formed another group in August of 1940: he was put in touch with Henri de Lipkowski (who died in deportation), who was theoretically to be responsible for his communications, and later with Lewitski [*sic*] and Vildé and, from this period onward, became a part of the latter's organization. It was as a member of this group that he frequently met up with the small group that was directed by his colleague Séjourneau and, at the same time, at the request of Vildé (who wanted to connect up all of the Resistance groups in the North) and, under his direction, Jubineau entered into contact with the Transler group, the Gauthier group, and with a group led by a pilot who had a route to Spain, and who was shot within a few days of Vildé's execution.

liquid mass of French society—but saturated with salts—this mass became crystallized in its turn.

In the process of hooking up with one another, these teams increased their share of danger. We were aware of this, but we could not avoid taking this risk if we also wanted to increase our effectiveness. Because in order to be effective the group had to constantly recruit and increase the number of its informers, of its passers, of its safe houses, and the places it worked from, and even, possibly, in order to find or to reconnect with a "network," which is to say a means of transmitting whatever information it had obtained.

This lack of separation constituted a great weakness: we recruited excessively in order to ensure our survival. Whenever a traitor, like a toxin, managed to infiltrate a part of the organism, its one ambition was to move through the arteries towards the heart: this was only too easy, and when it succeeded there was one less network and a few more people dead. The surviving groups, who sometimes were not aware of each other's existence, were thrilled to learn of the existence of another network—they almost always found it without any difficulty. And so on until, from one incarnation to another, they disappeared in turn. This crisscrossing can be compared to a card game in which each card would represent one of these nucleuses that I have just described, and in which each player would then act as a network. The cards would circulate from hand to hand; sometimes a player would be eliminated and another would take his place; finally, if the game went on too long, the trump cards turned up in front of the banker—the enemy—but then new cards are dealt to other players.

It's easy to see how little chance we had to avoid arrest; but it is also too simple to accuse the people of this first resistance of being careless or unaware of the dangers involved: we had no choice, and it was necessary either to abstain from any activity at all or to submit to the rigors of clandestine action, in the context in which we encountered it. What is more, we had no experience of this kind of struggle—students, workers, businessmen, people trained in law, medicine, architecture, or in scientific research, were completely unfa-

---

For his part, Col. Hauët spoke to me about his contacts with Gauthier and with the pilot who was making flights to Spain, but was it Hauët who introduced them to Vildé? Or was it Jubineau who informed Vildé, and through him Hauët? Or was it a third group altogether (for example what remained of the Deuxème or the Cinquième Bureau) that informed one or the other of our sectors? Jubineau was also in contact with Pierre Mars (died in deportation).

Transler's group, Gauthier's and the pilot's, like that of Séjourneau, *were not administratively part of our network,* even though Jubineau was one of the leaders of Vildé's sector.

miliar with it. The former officers in military intelligence who popped up in some of our groups were not, I recall thinking, any better prepared than the others for the kind of battle that we had become engaged in: their choice of what information was significant was better informed, but when it came to getting caught, we were all pretty much equals, for it's one thing to be the hunter and quite another to be the hunted. Nonetheless, if the damage caused by enemy agents—despite its seriousness—never resulted in the loss of all of our people at any one time, we owe it to the very high moral quality of this first phalange, that made it possible for the majority of our people to hold up under interrogation, and to the reliance on personal contacts, generally of long standing, at the start of our recruiting, for protecting some of our sectors. In fact the enormous losses that we suffered were no greater than those within organizations set up by trained specialists.

I had the opportunity to talk at length to my comrades who lived through the intense and technical resistance of 1943 and 1944 about what I recall, and they told me about the networks that were created by the IS or by men of the BCRA.[13] In contrast with us, they were handicapped by their lesser knowledge of the milieu in which they were operating and of the people whom they had to employ; this explains some of the errors that they committed.

To understand their other errors, one must assess the difference in recruitment: in 1940, just as in 1944, there was an impressive percentage of well-rounded people, insightful, courageous, an absence of self-interest, even abnegation; naturally, on the mediocre fringe that every human group drags along with it, there was also a reasonable proportion of clumsy, loose-tongued, eccentric, weak and vain people—but it seems to me that the fringe in question became a little thicker in 1944. That is moreover quite logical.

4. Federation and Organization of the Resistance

The majority of these little autonomous groups that we have been calling "nucleuses" multiplied like protozoa in tropical water, and they all communicated pretty much with all of the others, through one or the other of their constituent elements. The milieu was ripe for fermentation, and essentially favorable to "structuration," and this happened under two different influences:

The first is the impulse to organize in its purest state: people organize

13. The Bureau central de renseignements et d'action (BCRA) was an office in de Gaulle's Free French organization situated in London.

themselves in order to be organized. This gave rise to what were often called *movements.*

The second had to do with the need to be in touch with London, for any team that had adopted the gathering of intelligence as part of its activities: once a nucleus had established "contact," it became an organizational center for all of the groups with which it was in touch. Today we call this kind of organization a "network."

In 1940 and 1941, in the northern zone, I don't think there were any *movements* that were not organized as "networks"—they were all at least partly doing intelligence work; but these networks, as much from the point of view of their goals as of their structures, resembled the *movements* enough that one could easily confuse the two.

In a recent book on the history of Combat[14] we read about a few dozen members recruited in Marseilles by Henri Frenay in December of 1940; at this time this *nucleus* called itself the Movement for National Liberation.

Two months later, Capt. Guédon leaves to go up north. Before leaving he happened by pure chance to run into Capt. Frenay, but he is also charged with a mission by Col. Baril, of the Deuxième Bureau, located in Châteauroux.[15] For the former he starts to organize a kind of secret army in the northern zone, an offshoot of the Movement for National Liberation; for the latter he starts to recruit members for an intelligence-gathering network.

Once in Paris, he pays a visit on the directress of the School of Supervisors,[16] whose address was given to him by Frenay who held it in turn from Bertie Albrecht. The School of Supervisors was becoming the center of a nucleus that, in June of 1941, would merge with another which met at the Union of Metallurgical and Mining Industries, but it was already older than the one into which it merged. . . .

In February of 1941 Capt. Guédon met Lt. Pierre de Froment—who at this time had just formed an important network, in the Loire-Inférieure, in the Somme, in the Nord, in the Pas-de-Calais. . . .

In the Nord, in the Pas-de-Calais, the elements that Pierre de Froment

14. *Note in French edition:* Marie Granet and Henri Michel, *Combat* (Paris: Presses Universitaires de France, 195), 33–34.

15. The Deuxième Bureau is the external military intelligence agency of the regular French Army.

16. The Ècole des surintendantes was founded in 1918 to train women to do social work in France's factories. It became a hotbed of Resistance activity.

recruited were already organized when he came into contact with them, and they were publishing a newspaper (whose first number came out in December 1940): *Les Petites Ailes du Nord et du Pas-de-Calais*. This paper, co-opted by the Movement for National Liberation, will for a time lend its name to the entire organization.

This is merely one example, chosen at random. The Arabs of the Middle East often call a man by the name of his father, "the son of Louis," but even more readily by the name of his son, "The father of Little John." After 1945, when the networks were being dismantled (and often, too, their founding myths), it was sometimes the same.

The network of the musée de l'Homme Hauët-Vildé stands apart from this custom of naming the father after the son: our organization was entirely in place starting in October 1940. Its current name was chosen in five minutes, by me, one day in 1946, for the purposes of closing the book on it.

5. The "Affairs"

In this tangled but far from impenetrable underbrush, betrayal will soon forge alleyways both straight and wide.

In 1941 and 1942, after each arrest, we never spoke of this network or of that movement, but of such-and-such an "affair," and each one of them had contours that were as distinct as those of the movement or the network were not. Each one had a name.[17]

Starting in February of 1941, there was first the affair of the musée de l'Homme, followed soon after by the affair of d'Estienne d'Orves.

Colonels de la Rochère and Hauët (July 1941) were arrested together, but Col. de la Rochère, who was implicated in both affairs, managed to clear his friend Hauët, who was released prior to the trial. When Col. Hauët and I spoke about this trial we never called it anything other than "l'Affaire des Pompiers . . ." [the Firemen's Affair].

The very same day that Elizabeth Dussauze, her brother, Jeanne Sivadon and her entire team were arrested, Jacques Lecompte-Boinet warned me. Following that, we had to work together quite often. As far as I can recall we always said at the time: "l'Affaire des Surintendantes" [the Supervisors' Affair].

17. The contours were distinct, but not the name that was empirically used; this was often as much of an approximation as, say, the title of one of Proust's books: *Swann's Way*.

We would have been more accurate historically if we had named them in the manner of Proust: *du côté des Surintendantes,* or *du côté du musée de l'Homme,* but if we had known everything then that we know now, we could have given to each of these dramas its true generic title: Affaire Devillers, Affaire Albert Gaveau—after the two enemy agents who sent our comrades to their death.

Every day during the trial of the musée de l'Homme network I met with the lawyer of one of the accused men, Maître Wilhelm, and one evening he told me about a conversation he had had that afternoon with the president of the German military tribunal: Roskoten.

Allow us to recall that this trial took place a year after the arrests, during which time the Gestapo had shown an extraordinary zeal—doubtless in order to prove that their presence, disproportionally larger than any real threat to German security, was actually justified in "gay Paris." Voluminous files had been filled and, for some key indicted figures, the police had drawn up time lines in which all of their movements were chronologically laid out.

Roskoten (a professional jurist who appears to have had respect and even possibly some sympathy for the people whom he condemned to death), leaving the courtroom in the rue Boissy-d'Anglas where the case was being heard, exchanged a few words with the lawyer about the charges that hung over each of the accused. He concluded by remarking, "We know everything that Gaveau knew and nothing more than what Gaveau knew. This case ought to be called the Affaire Gaveau." And in fact all of the accused about whom Gaveau knew nothing more than their names escaped with their life. Our comrades knew how to remain silent. (It is true that the use of torture was not widespread at this time.)

The screenplay for each of these affairs was the work of the traitor. As it happened, in this case the latter used partial information to cause a series of arrests that only cut off a portion of a nucleus. Even though the traitor had successfully penetrated the network, while the resulting affair appeared to reflect the group's true contours, it never really gave an accurate projection of them.

The affair, nonetheless, has an undeniable historical quality to it: this group was arrested on such-and-such a day, was judged on another such, was executed on another—those are facts that can no longer be contested by anyone. All of the people arrested (who in many cases never knew each other prior to this) will straightaway be linked in unbreakable solidarity: first they will try to communicate with each other just as insistently as they will be forbidden to do so, to coordinate their stories under interrogation, thanks to which, the day when they wind up in the same cells they will already be friends. Their families, during this time, are already meeting up outside the gate of the prison, exchanging news; following which they continue to keep in touch. Following this, it is deportation or death, a great shadow that falls over the future, and sometimes over the past as well.

6. Administrative Liquidation of Resistance Organizations

Following the Liberation, the need arose to bring order into the chaos that existed among what remained of our organizations. A difficult task, because of the disappearance of the principal witnesses; but an absolutely necessary thing to do because of the need to provide sustenance to the families of victims and get rid of profiteers. After many years of effort, these goals have been achieved, and the number of inequities today is quite small.

For the majority of networks, however, going on the record has not always corresponded exactly with the actual history of the organization.[18] One has to recognize that this latter has not been easy to trace. Except for a very few monolithic organizations that had been created and run from day one until the end of the war by a single leader who survived, we were faced with organisms whose component parts could accurately claim several different successive incarnations, or even sometimes simultaneous ones, of which the principal leaders were dead.

Administrative deactivation had to simplify, to attribute a "nucleus" to such and such organization, to designate an official start date when this relationship began (and in doing so to not recognize prior activity): it also strengthened those relationships that it authenticated; and it necessarily weakened those that it did not officially recognize.

Did the affair that we mentioned earlier (the Overseers' Affair) arise out

18. *Note in French edition:* As far as the network whose liquidation I personally administered is concerned, I strove relentlessly to follow the historical contours of the organization as it was in 1940. I didn't always succeed. Consequently, at the specific request of the leaders of France combattante, I paid particular attention to the files of the group Adam. The men of this group were only linked to elements of Vildé's group in having also been sold out by Gaveau and in having planned to escape to England on the same boat: the tuna boat *La Monique*. On the other hand, there were quite a few groups that were actually federated with our group that I reconnected with, in 1945, upon my return from captivity, and found that they had hooked up administratively with other networks. I tried to straighten this out, but I ran up against insurmountable material obstacles.

of the Combat organization? Doubtless so, but only in part. After the disaster caused by Devilliers, the strands reformed, under the command of Jacques Lecompte-Boinet, into a single network, Manipule, and in a movement, the CDLR.[19] Who is going to take charge of liquidating the groups that were betrayed by Devilliers? Neither Manipule, nor Combat, nor again the CDLR, but a network known as Hector, which was, I believe, in contact with the team in the Pas-de-Calais who printed the first issues of *Petites Ailes*: the uncle of the brother-in-law of my nephew is also related to me. . . .

That is not surprising for very long. If one looks carefully at the realities of the period, one immediately notices:

1. Clandestine periodicals. They are written, printed and distributed. People who undertook the first two activities can lay unimpeachable claim to the label of choice as their title in the newspaper (*Résistance*, *Les Petites Ailes*), but the people in the team of distributors are included as well—and indeed they were often arrested and shot along with the rest. The distributors often had a principal activity in some other aspect of resistance work.

2. Networks dedicated to gathering intelligence. They collect information, and they transmit it. Two separate activities, the first of which reaches far outside the *network* itself.

3. Organizations in which weapons are gathered and military preparations are undertaken. Drawn into contact with a newspaper or a network, these groups will become a part of it, or will take it over entirely.

4. Escape-route networks that should have been autonomous (but all the other organizations also had people who needed to be smuggled out).

In 1940 and 1941 many nascent groups whose organizers were extremely active undertook all of these activities. This was the case with ours. But we do find groups that, for example, gathered intelligence for one network and

19. Manipule (named for a unit in a Roman legion) was a network of the Free French in London, also known as the direct action section of Ceux de la Résistance (CDLR). CDLR was one of the eight major groups that sat on the Conseil national de la Résistance.

distributed newsletters for another. A fusion of the two elements might have occurred, but in fact it did not. This was all evolving very quickly: sometimes a contact made between the leaders of two different nucleuses led to the formation of a solidly constructed network, and sometimes it merely happened and left no trace.

The Lacunae in Our Historical Documentation

Today the history of this period can only be roughly sketched; it will take a lot of time to do it right, and someday it must be undertaken.

Documents exist, but dry and formal documentation only amounts to an archive, not to a history. Moreover, these archives are not even complete, because, for example, I was not able to trace the origins of some groups that had become absorbed into another network once I had succeeded in obtaining the recognition of our own. I know, however, that they belonged, historically, to our organization, but I already had my hands full with the groups that I was charged with describing.

Another lacuna: the questions that interest the historian, and that interest me today, are rarely the ones that I asked back then, so many others were there whose very urgency made it necessary that we not put them off. The very same urgency when, between 1945 and 1954, I attended to what we called the "disbanding of the network": at that time I was called upon to furnish a crushing load of affidavits and official texts (of which I did keep duplicate copies) that contain a massive amount of exact and precise facts—yet lack human detail.[20]

During this second phase, however, each time that the opportunity arose, I carried out a broader inquiry than what was strictly required, sometimes out of historical curiosity, but more often because of the deep sympathy that linked me to my companions in those events and in that struggle, a sympathy that endowed all of the details of their lives with interest—all of which is now only preserved in my memory.

In addition to which, I was constantly supported by materials with which

20. *Note in French edition:* In October 1940, the size and complexity of my sector appeared to me to require a general description that I of course destroyed after taking the necessary precautions. It is not this type of document that I am thinking of, but rather of the ones that I drew up, following an inquiry, between 1945 and 1954, for the disbanding of the network. Their volume is so great that I could not keep them at home, and I was only able to keep the most important ones: these alone fill a large closet.

I could make fruitful comparison, because, during three years of captivity, I never ceased informing myself about the origins and the avatars of the resistance organizations that came up in conversations, and I recorded a great number of characteristic anecdotes. During this phase of activity I sought to compare, to categorize and to understand the facts about detention, and to this extent I was conducting a structured inquiry. The rest—the Resistance—my comrades and I spoke of this too, afterwards, for distraction: countless little stories, some bad, some good, heroic or grotesque that, "in addition to everything else," I recorded as time went by.

Before setting out to *tell* the events of this period, I wanted to conduct this summary and very compressed analysis of what is on offer, because it permits us to take stock of the resources and the pitfalls that the historian will encounter; if the resources are occasionally revealed to be insufficient, the pitfalls, at any rate, will never be found lacking.

NATIONAL LIBERATION

Editor's Introduction

Henri Frenay was probably the single most important leader of the French Resistance next to Jean Moulin. Frenay led a group called Combat that had begun in the heart of Vichy itself, among officers of the French Army and their close sympathizers. Mostly very traditional French, they became part of the right wing of the French Resistance. Frenay was not, however, the second man of the Resistance to enter the Panthéon. That honor went to Pierre Brossolette, less well known now, much less powerful at the time.[1] Why? The answer to that question lies at least in part in the document presented here. *Libération nationale* is a tract, certainly not a handbill. It is a ten-page spirit-applicator-printed document that the mayor of Saint-Raphaël found, barely one year into the Vichy era, and thought worth bringing to the attention of the prefect of the Var department. It contains Frenay's statement of his intention to resist. It contains what his detractors today see as one major problem: his support for Philippe Pétain. But his relative unpopularity in the public mind today probably derives more from something else. As with Moulin's *Premier Combat,* few Frenchmen today have actually read this text, and it would appear that much of what they know about this man derives from an enduring public image as a rather cold military guy, whose rivalry with Moulin did him, and the Resistance, no service—either during the war years or in the forty years he lived afterwards. He was, despite this unpleasantness, an important figure in our story, and the recruitment tract presented here is a unique document of the struggle that deserves to be made available in English to students of the Resistance.

Frenay was a captain in the French Army at the time the Germans invaded the country. His unit was surrounded on a mountaintop in Alsace. Together they heard Marshal Pétain's speech in June 1940, calling for an armistice,

1. Pierre Brossolette (1903–1944), a Socialist, escaped the cracking of the Groupe du musée de l'Homme, and was a founder of Libération-Nord. He killed himself by jumping out of a window while imprisoned and under torture at Gestapo headquarters on the avenue Foch in Paris. His ashes were transferred to the Panthéon on February 21, 2014.

and they wept. The Germans who received their surrender were cordial, but Frenay did not believe their reassurances, and he and another member of his unit, only one, a man he did not know prior to that time and never met again afterwards, decided to flee in the night. Consequently the two of them were spared being among the 1.8 million French soldiers imprisoned in Germany for the rest of the war. With only a Michelin map and the clothes on their backs, the two men walked most of the way south to the Jura Mountains, where a sympathetic civilian agreed to drive them in his truck across the border between the occupied North and what was fast becoming Vichy France, toward Lyon. Frenay tells the story in his memoir *La Nuit finira*, a dense tome that is essential reading for anyone interested in the French Resistance.

He had grown up in a military family in the traditional capital of the Gauls, Lyon, which was to become the capital of the Resistance. His father was career military, an officer but not a high-ranking one, who died in the Great War. His mother raised the family on a widow's pension, and Frenay recalls growing up in a rather Spartan but happy household in a France that, though it perceived itself as having won the previous war, was by no means at peace with itself. The family was nonpolitical, very traditional French Catholic, but not by any stretch of the imagination of the upper class associated with the senior officers of the day. He went to the military academy of Saint-Cyr, then served under the flag for nine years before entering the École supérieure de guerre in Paris. He was in service in the south of France in 1934 near Sainte-Maxime, where his mother had moved, when he met an older woman, Berty Albrecht, who would be enormously important in his further intellectual development, and his partner in the French Resistance.

Albrecht was married and a mother of two, but by the early 1930s she had separated from her Dutch husband and was living in Sainte-Maxime. She had trained as a nurse, was politically of the left, and still extremely active in human-rights circles in Paris, having founded a feminist journal, *Le Problème sexuel*, in 1933. Berthe Pauline Mariette Albrecht, née Wild, born into a Protestant family of Swiss origin, was also highly sensitive to German culture and had begun to receive refugees from the collapsing Weimar Republic at this time as well. Albrecht was a supporter of the Popular Front in 1936, which Frenay certainly was not, but their friendship did not suffer for that. She was doubtless responsible for making Frenay aware of the danger of Nazism, and for encouraging him to pursue studies at the Centre d'études germaniques in Strasbourg in 1937, where he apparently learned German and read Hitler's *Mein Kampf*. In that same year Albrecht enrolled for training as a social worker at the École des surintendantes d'usine,[2] where she made a number of important personal connections that she would put to good use during the Resistance.

When Frenay reached Lyon in mid-July 1940, he immediately took a train to Marseilles and continued straight on to Sainte-Maxime, where he was warmly received by his brother and their mother. He began at once to get in touch with the French Army, now the army of Vichy, and offered his services. One night not long after his return home, he sat up in his room and wrote the first draft of the document presented here. There is an account of him writing it in the memoir, where he incidentally says that he no longer was in possession of a copy of it himself, and wishes he did. In the chapter that immediately follows this account, Frenay tells how he and Berty Albrecht proceeded to recruit and to train the Mouvement de libération nationale (MLN), which would soon become the resistance group known as Combat. Together they created a great deal of the tradecraft that would become common throughout the Resistance, the formation of cells known as *sixaines*, the use of liaison agents and drop boxes for communication, and the division into propaganda and information services, and action units known as *groupes de choc*.

National Liberation was Frenay's first statement of purpose and a recruitment document. It may have arisen out of a need to formulate what he was thinking, for himself, in a time of enormous turmoil. He soon showed it to Berty, and with some revision over time, the two of them used it to reach out to others until at least the middle of 1941, when the movement was renamed Combat. He called the document *La Libération nationale*, in the version we have used, found in the archives of the department of the Var. It can also be found in a slightly different form, perhaps an earlier draft, which Daniel Cordier found in the archives of the BCRA in Paris.[3] In *La Nuit finira*, published in 1973, Henri Frenay called it *le Manifeste*, or *Manifesto*, and this curious name has stuck. It would be easy to go through it and single out the characteristics that have raised eyebrows, the evident Pétainophilia, first and foremost, followed by the rejection of foreigners, specifically the Jews, and the stated aim of making Communists the next target after getting rid of the Nazis. These

2. L'École des surintendantes d'usine, a school for social workers in Paris. (See glossary.)

3. Daniel Cordier was Jean Moulin's secretary from 1942 to 1943. He has since dedicated himself to documenting the institutions and events of the Resistance (see bibliography). The Bureau central de renseignements et d'action was the intelligence unit of de Gaulle's Free French office in London during the war. (See glossary.)

aspects cannot escape the reader's attention, but it might be fairer, and more useful, to try looking at it afresh.

The document falls roughly into three parts: in a carefully worded introduction of less than two pages, Frenay positions himself squarely behind the National Revolution, the program for changing the system of republican government that Vichy began promoting immediately behind its standard-bearer, Marshal Philippe Pétain. In summer 1940, this revolution could only be concretely seen as including the dissolution of Parliament and the settling of all legislative powers on an unelected government that itself did not vote on anything. This, according to Frenay, could be counted on to improve the French economy and restore public virtue ("prosperity" and "moral values"). Frenay's argument is that, if France had undertaken this revolution of its own accord, in peacetime, with its borders intact, the revolution might in fact have succeeded. But, given the current reality, that the most vital two-thirds of the country are occupied by an invader, he thinks that it cannot possibly work, that it would not be in the interest of the invader for it to succeed being the first, and really the only, reason that he offers for this impossibility. But, this being the case, the only way for the National Revolution to succeed is to give the Germans the boot, and then follow the marshal on to victory.

This may all be quite true in practical terms. But it certainly does not constitute either a clear expression of what the National Revolution entailed, nor does it provide any justification for abandoning democratic principles in order to achieve it. There is at least one good reason for this lack of substance: there never was a clear statement from Vichy as to what the National Revolution was. It can, in fact, only be defined in retrospect, by looking at what the regime did, over four years. We could enumerate the policies that best define the Révolution nationale now, but we cannot imagine that Frenay knew what they were to be in mid-1940, nor if he really would have endorsed them if he did. At the end of the war, during the trials of the Épuration,[4] a number of Vichy officials, Pétain included, admitted that they never really knew in any detail what the revolution was to involve. Calling their agenda thus appears to have been a way for Vichy to foster a notion of change that was at once broad and yet profound, without at the same time being particularly meaningful. The choice of this name appears to be an attempt to co-opt the vigor, though obviously not the program, of the much detested (and feared) Communist

4. *Épuration* means "purification," and it specifically refers to the period immediately after the war when the French punished collaborators. (See glossary.)

movement. The French Communist Party (Parti communiste français, or PCF) had been banned from politics in the wake of the Molotov–von Ribbentrop pact, so this rightist National Revolution could have been the only show in town. Ironically, however, the German victory had immediately called into question the exclusion of the Communists, who were naturally quick to ask the occupier for a redress of their status.

Frenay clearly hated both National Socialism and Communism. He states his utter revulsion to Nazism immediately in part two of the document here, and then he undertakes a description of his own movement, which he does with relative clarity. In a postscript he states emphatically that, once the Germans are kicked out, his movement's next job will be to get rid of the Communists once and for all. The Mouvement de libération nationale relates to resistance as a state of mind and of engagement with the enemy. Frenay reaffirms his support for Pétain, who according to Frenay cannot help but bend to the will of the occupier. This section, as in the version found by Cordier, begins with a reference to Montoire, the town where Pétain infamously shook hands with the Führer on October 24, so we can be certain that neither is the original draft of the text that Frenay wrote in the summer of 1940. Frenay does not reproach the marshal for his actions, as he recognizes that it is Pétain's job to guide France through these dark times, and any hint of the government's wanting to do otherwise would necessarily result in serious consequences for the country. Indeed, Frenay sees Pétain's acquiescence as filled with dignity. But, says he, the French people never promised any such posture, and they need not remain silent. They want to *shout* their objection, and clearly the MLN will help them do just that. He immediately goes on to condemn Nazi Germany; the Nazis are seen as practitioners of a "cult of strength and blood," and Germany is the country "from which free speech has been banished forever." He clearly knows what he is talking about, and this in itself is remarkable. Although he never cites *Mein Kampf* here, he does mention Rosenberg and Dietrich, and he is not taken in by Vichy's call for collaboration with Hitler. He is the "lord and master" who has "broken his word at every turn." There can be no trusting him, and the people (presumably in Vichy) who are trying to persuade the French people to do otherwise are wrong to hope otherwise. That is as hard as he will be on Vichy.

Next, still in this second section of his statement, Frenay turns to close argument. Victory has not changed Germany—far from it—and the war rages on. If the French do not want to throw in their lot with the Germans, they have no other choice than to side with the British. It is not out of love for the

English, or their culture, that France must do this. It is the lesser of two evils. In this discussion he does appear to have at least momentarily abandoned the principle of free speech in favor of opportunism. Perhaps he can be excused for this: at least he makes it quite clear what he means. It is France's defeat that has forced them into this position. But support Britain they must. In autumn 1940, it must have taken Frenay a great deal of honesty, and even courage, to come to this conclusion. For one thing, there is a long-standing idea in France that England is France's "hereditary enemy." This attitude goes back many years, and Vichy exploited this ancient sentiment to try to align the country behind Germany's ongoing war effort, and they had recent events on their side as well. Mers-el-Kébir, which Frenay cites as an unforgettable treachery on Albion's part, was fresh in their minds.[5] If it was not, Vichy propaganda and the daily papers would be sure to remind them.

In the Army of Vichy, a force of over 100,000 in metropolitan France that Frenay had initially joined, the dominant culture was Anglophobic, and the fact that England was where the rogue general Charles de Gaulle had fled in hopes of rallying a Free French force certainly did not help Britain's stock in military circles. Frenay argues to convince himself as much as the men he will soon seek to recruit: "We will never act as the mercenaries of England. We will accept neither orders from her, nor subsidies." But supporting Britain is the issue he realizes will be the key, or the stumbling block, to his future co-conspirators' allegiance. In part three, where he gives specific instructions as to how to recruit members and what the first order of business should be after that, he is quite specific: "In no case should one try to convince someone who is not already of our opinion." Sound people out in steps, and don't tell them where the conversation is heading until you are absolutely certain that they have already come to these same convictions on their own.

The National Liberation Movement that he envisages will be an entirely French organization. This is where Frenay turns to the question of the Jews, where some critics feel that he condemns himself as squarely as he does with his Pétainophilia: "Jews will not have the honor of joining us unless they already fought for us in one of the two last wars." In part three, Frenay also enjoins his followers to recruit from among their close friends and colleagues whenever possible, since their attitudes and reliability would already be

5. Mers-el-Kébir is a port on the North African coast where Britain attacked and sank a large contingent of the French Navy, in July 1940, to keep it from falling into Axis hands. The attack killed 1,300 French sailors.

known, and in practice the MLN's membership did continue to come predominantly from military circles. That there were French Jews who were in the military there is no doubt, and it is certain as well that a number of Jews became members of Combat. Ultimately there would be both former military as well as nonmilitary Jews who distinguished themselves within Combat, so this injunction has to be understood as it was meant to be: it is a directive rather than a proscriptive. He will not reject those Jews who had fought in two wars, as others in Vichy certainly did, but he certainly does not take any pains to assert the rights of Jews whose families had been in France for centuries, whether or not they had served in the army. He never mentions the Jewish exclusion laws that Vichy used to throw Jews out of public-sector jobs, teaching, medicine, and law, whether they had been French since before the French Revolution or not. The first round of those statutes had been promulgated in early October 1940. What is without a doubt is that Frenay's group, and perhaps the Resistance in general, did not make the plight of the Jews in France one of its priorities, if they gave it any consideration at all. The fact that Frenay mentions excluding Jews from the MLN can certainly lead us to conclude that he was aware of their being likely postulants. And more than this is at best unclear.

How this directive is connected to the following two sentences in this same paragraph of part two is also unclear: "The money that will be needed for our activity will be French money. We will not ask for a shilling from Great Britain." The logical thread may lie in a perception (and not just Frenay's) that many of the Jews in France in 1940, like shillings, were foreign. He might think that this refusal of foreign funding is simply another nationalist ideal. But it might also be read in the context of propaganda at the time that widely blamed the war on bankers in London in particular, often characterized as being Jewish. In any case, we think it fair to surmise that the author is at least pandering to popular xenophobic stereotypes, if indeed he was not a xenophobe of some stripe himself. Frenay's stated intention not to accept any foreign money for his movement was probably sincere, whether its motivation was based on xenophobia or simply idealism, but it was certainly unrealistic. In 1942, the arrival of money from London became a key to the survival of all of these groups. The basis of its distribution would also become a source of contention between them, but about that this document tells us little. Necessity, one can certainly say, required that they accept such support. But here we are interested in what the man thought, what spirit motivated his urge to resist, and how he saw that as taking place. Our assumption is that he felt he had to say some of these things in order to convince others to throw in their lot with Britain. (In the following year, Frenay may well have convinced himself that the money Jean Moulin was bringing back from London was only French money, but his subsequent efforts to secure independent funding from American sources in Switzerland in 1943 certainly show that this ideal, at least, was short-lived.)[6]

In part three of this statement, Frenay turns to a very interesting discussion of whom and how to recruit, and for what jobs first, and so forth. But he also reminds his readers immediately that, among the preferred qualities and antipathies the candidates should share, they should be "deeply French." He repeats and refines his exclusion of Jews who had not *really* fought under the French flag in either of the two world wars. And at the same time he adds that recruiters must exclude any Frenchmen, true or otherwise, who had been swayed by Jacques Doriot's French Popular Party (Parti populaire français, or PPF). Few people would fault him for that today. And it is worth noting that Frenay was not taken in by just any form of right-wing nationalism. Still a Communist during the events of February 1934, Doriot had left the PCF by end of that year, and in 1936 he founded what was to become for a while France's largest fascist party, with a membership in large part made up of former Communists and Socialists. In 1940 it was for a while illegal in the southern zone, however, but Doriot managed to bring it back in 1941, and along with its rival, the National People's Rally (Rassemblement national populaire, or RNP), it would remain one of the two leading parties of collaboration in all of France until the end of the war.

While it may well be Doriot's political past that made Frenay suspicious of the man and to single his party out for exclusion, this is not what he says. Frenay rejects the PPF for embracing collaboration "as a path to the future," not just as a "necessary evil," which he has already said is how the marshal must view the situation. This leap of understanding is fundamental to Frenay's mindset. He does not say what he thinks about the National Revolution, but he does go on to specify that candidates should be committed enemies of "communism, Freemasons and international finance." This is more recycled Vichy propaganda at best. Freemasonry is a secular philosophical movement advocating free-thinking that has deep roots in republican France which, given his previously stated regard for free speech, one wonders if Frenay really

6. The story of *l'Affaire suisse*, as this murky bit of intrigue has become known, is best described in Robert Belot and Gilbert Karpman's 2009 book of that title. (See bibliography.)

understood. But lumping communism and international finance together in this list of the greatest moral enemies of the era is reminiscent of some of the worst fascist oratory on record.

The bulk of part three is concerned with a discussion of whom to recruit for the MLN and what tasks to staff for in the immediate future, and some of it is extremely clear and vivid: "we must try to recruit people from all walks of life: Bourgeoisie, army, civil service, farming, factory workers, etc. . . . A traveling salesman who makes a regular route must let the person who recruited him know about it. The same goes for businessmen who have many branch offices, postal workers who are assigned to mail trains, airplane pilots, etc." But how Frenay can imagine he is going to recruit among some of these categories without embracing people sympathetic to international finance remains a mystery, and one would certainly have to doubt the possibility of recruiting postal or railway workers in 1941 without entertaining some Communists. The modern reader (with hindsight) must also be indulgent when confronted with statements like "The movement must remain a secret movement for the time being, because if the German police found out its existence, it would require us to disband." Less than a year later, following the treachery of the double-agent Henri Devillers, Frenay himself surely would have winced at the utter foolishness of such a statement.[7] Order them to disband? How about execute them? Yet this was a man who knew more about the German and Nazi culture than most French men and women of his day. But there can be no doubt that Frenay was a true patriot, whatever his political orientation, and a man who was ready to break the mold, to think for others and himself, and to take significant risk for the country he loved.

Whatever shortcomings of its author this tract reveals, and whatever it cannot tell us about later events—Frenay's conflict with Jean Moulin, for example, or his 1942 trip to London when he finally met and embraced de Gaulle—we must not lose sight of what it does contribute to our emerging picture of the French Resistance in the early months of what was to be a four-year struggle. First of all, it confirms that resistance began almost immediately. We believe that Frenay began drafting what became this very text in August 1940. (We cannot say for certain how much of it was there in the initial draft, of course.) Second, and this is quite remarkable, it shows that some resistance also began inside Vichy, in otherwise loyal Pétainist circles. It demonstrates that there was a right wing of the Resistance. Although it cannot show us just how

7. Henri Devillers was a traitor who infiltrated Frenay's group in 1941. (See glossary.)

strong Combat would become, it does give us an idea of how early resisters set to work.[8] And third, it confirms an emerging model that resistance began as a patriotic impulse informed by a sense of duty to others, and not out of self-interest, even if in this case the "others" in question were all to be "deeply French."

This is in every regard an unusual Resistance document, whatever title Frenay, or we, might give it. That Henri Frenay did not have a copy of it when he was writing his memoir is a shame, as he himself said, because he might very well have had the honesty to explain some of its inherent contradictions. As it was, lost in time, he called it a *Manifeste,* which it never was. "Manifest" means "clear, and easy to understand," before the derivative, "manifesto," came to mean a statement of purpose (whatever Yves St. Laurent might have meant when he attributed this name to a men's cologne). Frenay's statement is anything but clear, sometimes even when it is quite easy to understand. It would appear that, in 1973, when Frenay was himself attempting to appropriate the *gravitas* of another famous manifesto when he called it this, he had forgotten that doing so might just as easily diminish as glorify what he had set out to do. In any case, it seems that Frenay's later characterization of this document as a manifesto is hardly justified. So we have kept the title that he originally used, *National Liberation.* This title says it all and avoids anachronism, as well as possible misunderstanding.

8. Combat was a part of the earliest unified Resistance council, the MUR, and of the later CNR. Frenay himself became minister of veteran and deportee affairs in the Fourth Republic.

National Liberation

HENRI FRENAY

Since the defeat, men from all walks of life, united only by their shared love of the FATHERLAND, have gathered together to deliver France from foreign domination, to return to it its political and territorial integrity which its weapons failed to defend, to enable it to complete the much-needed NATIONAL REVOLUTION.

To insure the continued progress of the work undertaken, to rally to our cause all men of goodwill, it is necessary to state without ambiguity the aims of this movement and its exact position with regard to our government presided over by MARSHAL PÉTAIN.

The war and the defeat have prompted a broad examination of conscience that has given rise to a profound change in political institutions and the coming to power of an authoritarian Government led by a man for whom there is widespread respect.

The expression NATIONAL REVOLUTION is not too strong to characterize the legislative accomplishment of the Government during the past months. Despite the defeat, despite the mourning, despite the privations, the French People, with confidence in Marshal PÉTAIN, has for the first time in many years, started to hope again.

Is this hope justified?

Can the task of reform, undertaken so quickly, succeed under the present circumstances?

We do not think so, and here is why.

If this Revolution had been undertaken under peacetime conditions, when France was a free state with inviolate borders, it would doubtless have succeeded.

Spirit-duplicated text, five pages, found in Saint-Raphaël on or about May 20, 1941. Written in Sainte-Maxime during the summer of 1940, and subsequently edited by Frenay. This version was found in the Archives départementales du Var and transcribed by Jean-Marie Guillon. *Source:* ADV, 1 W 79, sent by the mayor of Sainte-Maxime to the prefect of the Var, May 1941.

In 1940, this is not the case, German troops occupy two-thirds of our country; the capital; the major industrial regions. Oversight commissions in place everywhere in the Free Zone are looking into our economic and military affairs. The press and all other organs of propaganda are either directed or controlled. The political police of the Reich has spread its espionage network over our territory. Every second of every day Germany is therefore aware of the situation in France from the three-fold point of view of the military, the economy and morale. *It can therefore monitor at every moment the stages of our recovery.*

Meanwhile, this revolution that is beginning will restore, in the words of Marshal Pétain himself, the three basic values: "Family, Work, Fatherland." That is to say that it is supposed to rebuild a unified France, patriotic and STRONG.

If we follow through with this undertaking, we will see an improvement in French prosperity and moral values at the same time that, as a result of a continuing war effort, the German forces will be dwindling. What is more, the position of France, although defeated, will be better than that of the victorious Germany.

Can we honestly hope that the Führer will allow this Revolution to happen at the risk that the fruit of his victory will one day vanish under his own eyes? We believe that this is an illusion; peace, like war, consists of a balance of forces. Germany, which is stronger in war, will continue to be stronger in peace.

To sum it up: the much-needed Revolution will not happen as long as Germany is in a position to dictate its will to us. In chronological order, this Revolution can only take place after NATIONAL LIBERATION, once the *Boche* is booted out of France altogether.

We are deeply committed to Marshal Pétain's project. We support the great reforms that have been undertaken in their entirety. We are moved by a desire to see them last, and we welcome further reforms to complete this effort. It is to this end that we are forming the

National Liberation Movement

Since the meeting in Montoire, the Government has committed itself to a policy of collaboration with the conqueror. For our part, our wish is to drive him out of France.

Does this mean that we are breaking with the Marshal?

Nothing could be further from the truth. These two positions are easily reconcilable; better still, they actually complete each other.

On the morning of June 25, FRANCE, whose army could no longer defend it, had its shoulders to the mat. Three months later, Germany was inviting us to collaborate with it. We can expect to get nothing out of refusing, except perhaps for even harsher measures than the ones we are now enduring; our men organized into groups of workers, the burden of occupation even heavier, restrictions even more severe, and all of France occupied. Such a stance would doubtless have been more noble, but it would have entailed heavy consequences.

This collaboration that has been strongly urged upon us benefited the Reich. Thanks to it, the Reich had its hands free to continue the struggle against England. This collaboration could benefit us as well. In fact, it will benefit us.

This necessary evil has enabled us to keep a part of our freedom, in order to bring about a national renewal. Most importantly, it has gained us a little time. The National Liberation movement will take full advantage of that. This is why we once again support the Government which endorsed it.

The Government must maintain an attitude that is dictated by circumstance. Were it to so much as wish to do otherwise in word or in deeds, the entire country would suffer the consequences. The most difficult thing for the Marshal to do at this time is to accept this constraint, that is full of dignity. This acceptance was implicit in the first words he spoke when he took power:

"I am offering my own self as a gift to France, to lessen its misfortune."

But WE, the people of France, we never promised nor did we sign anything. We understand the politics of our Government, and we know that it cannot do anything else. But what the Government cannot say, we want to SHOUT:

The enemy of today is the same as the enemy of yesterday. If our weapons have given way in front of his, we will not surrender our souls.

Victory hasn't changed Germany. It remains a country that celebrates the idolatrous cult of strength and blood. It is the godless country that just shut the Strasbourg cathedral in order to turn it into a museum. It is the country whose lord and master has broken his word at every turn, whose promises we cannot possibly believe. It is the land of terror, from which free speech has been banished forever.

The complete victory of Germany would mean not just granting his every demand, but the material and moral subjugation that all of his honchos have counted on and prepared for. Hitler's threats and grand schemes, Rosenberg's and Dietrich's, are still fresh in our memory. They are warnings to us, and they remain entirely in force despite the hopes that people are trying to soothe us with today.

Meanwhile, the war is going on under our very eyes. We cannot remain indifferent to it. Our destiny depends on its outcome. The attitude and behavior of our movement must be those that will allow France to have a voice in the future peace, and have its voice be heard. Some people hope that France will one day be the arbiter between two countries that are worn out by struggle. We think that is a dangerous delusion. We have already said, if Germany is weakened, it will further weaken France. Our country will have no role to play in this scenario. To the victor will go the spoils, however weakened the winner is by the struggle.

We must make up our own minds and answer this question immediately. In the victory of one or the other of the two great nations now at war, which will be the best for France—or at least the least damaging?

There will be no sitting on the fence. We have to decide. If we think that a German victory would be the best for France, then we should get over the bitterness of our defeat, and we should help Germany. But everything that we know about Germany suggests otherwise.

Therefore we turn to England.

It is she that we want to help.

In committing ourselves to this course of action, we are not fooling ourselves. We are not choosing among benefits, but between drawbacks. We have our military defeat to thank for this painful choice.

The Movement for National Liberation doesn't have any particular sympathy for the British. It is not unaware of the harm that England has done to our Country in the course of her history and even in the recent past. It does not forget the Peace of 1918, that we lost because of her, nor the painful events of Mers-el-Kébir and of Dakar. But it doesn't forget either that England is not occupying France with its soldiers, that it never plotted to cut our territory up in little pieces, nor our subjugation.

Between two evils, we have chosen the lesser, which is, according to us, England's victory. We have decided to collaborate in it.

In this collaboration, we are keeping our freedom of action in its entirety. The Movement for National Liberation is a fundamentally French movement. We will never act as the mercenaries of England. We will accept neither orders from her, nor subsidies. Everyone who decides to serve in our ranks, and those who are already with us, will be true French people. Jews will not have the honor of joining us unless they already fought for us in one of the two last wars. The money that will be needed for our activity will be French money. We will not ask for a shilling from Great Britain.

Thanks to which, on the day when we have beaten Germany together, we will not be hired help in the eyes of the English, but free men who will have received nothing and gave their utmost. The authentically French voice that we will make heard will have to be listened to because we will have earned it, and because we want it to be heard.

To a France whose defenses were shattered, the Movement for National Liberation will offer the resurgence of its heart and soul. It will have transformed our temporary material defeat into a total victory thanks to the spirit that guides it. As equals in the matter, France and England will force their terms of peace upon Germany. The Europe of tomorrow will not be built without us.

+ + +

Once Peace has been restored, our movement will not consider its work to be finished. We will doubtless have accomplished the harder part. But this will not be our final task.

It is probable, if not certain, that following the collapse of National Socialist Germany, there will be a rising tide of Communism, which might threaten France, if not in fact all of the western world.

The defeat of the Communist will be our second task.

Our men, disciplined, commanded and armed, will form the rampart against which the Communist tide will come crashing down. We will defeat the enemy within just as we will have defeated the enemy from without.

That is when we will be able to undertake the National Revolution, the success of which we do not believe in under the current circumstances. Our movement, which will have paid its dues in blood, will form the kernel around which people of goodwill shall cluster.

We pray to God to grant Marshal PÉTAIN a long enough life that we can fall in behind him and follow him in the path that he will show us.

+ + +

Men of France, we are committing ourselves to a long and difficult path, but it is also a straight path. We have laid out our plans before you. There is not a single one of them that you cannot support, not one that runs against your conscience. If you join us, we will ask everything of you, your work, your money, and perhaps your life. In exchange we will offer you nothing but the profound, even exalting, joy of working together for the resurrection of your fatherland.

There are men among us who will not be here on the day of victory. It's not because we don't believe it will happen, but because we are going to have to fight for it. Think it over.

If we are speaking frankly about this with you now, it is because we have no room for people who are lukewarm or wishy-washy. They can step aside.

We will win without them, and for them.

Instructions for People who want to join the Movement for National Liberation

Until further notice, the principal missions for people who intend to join are as follows:

1st—Recruit others

2nd—Establish means of being in touch

1st—RECRUITMENT

(1) Whom to recruit?

French people of long standing, excluding foreigners, even if they have been naturalized.

Jews, if they really fought in either of the last two wars. Exclude members of the PPF[1] who consider collaboration not as an unavoidable evil but as a political path toward the future.

How to recruit?

The movement must remain a secret movement for the time being, because if the German police found out its existence, it would require us to disband.

Consequently, before revealing to anyone the existence and the goals of the movement, it is necessary to study the candidate carefully, and it is imperative to establish with the utmost certainty, in a prior conversation, that the individual wishes for an English victory, that s/he is the enemy of Communism, of Freemasons,[2] and of international finance. One must be certain, moreover, of their discretion. In no case should one try to convince someone who is not already of our opinion. That will be the job of our propaganda agents. Everyone must be aware that sooner or later informers will try to join our group. In order to limit the damage caused by betrayal, the recruiter must be the only person in our movement known to the new recruit.

In both zones, the occupied and the free, we need propaganda and intelli-

1. The Parti populaire français, founded by Jacques Doriot, a former Communist turned fascist. The PPF was one of the two principal parties of collaborationist France, the other being the Rassemblement national populaire (RNP). (See glossary.)

2. Freemasonry is a philosophical movement that was targeted for eradication by Vichy along with Jews and Communists. (See glossary.)

gence-gathering people. In the occupied zone we also need people for active engagement.

Recruitment must be carried out with an eye to furnishing us with the personnel we need for each of these three roles. All of our active members should therefore look for new recruits starting with people in their own circle of acquaintances and family members. This kind of recruitment can be carried out quickly, because everyone knows the discretion and the way of thinking of their friends. It should be done not only in the city where the recruiter lives, but anywhere that he knows where to find friends we can count on.

Once this is done, recruitment is not over. Another more difficult kind must begin. It is necessary to search out people who can render specific services to our movement. Wealthy people, management types, from civil administration and government ministries, key industrialists who can provide invaluable information on German economic activity in FRANCE, etc. . . .

We must also keep in mind that propaganda must reach every stratum of society. Consequently, we must try to recruit people from all walks of life: Bourgeoisie, army, civil service, farming, factory workers, etc. . . . Keep in mind that women can be excellent propaganda agents.

2nd—IDENTIFY MEANS OF LIAISON

Until such time as the movement has the financial means to have specialized agents, it will be necessary to use whatever means are at the disposal of our membership. A traveling salesman who makes a regular route must let the person who recruited him know about it. The same goes for businessmen who have many branch offices, postal workers who are assigned to mail trains, airplane pilots, etc. . . .

Members should *look for and report* in the following manner whatever liaison services they can provide:

Point of departure:

Point of arrival:

Day and time of departure (or at what intervals):

Means of transportation (train, car, airplane, etc.):

This information should be communicated by word of mouth from one person to the next right on up to the Direction of the Movement.

WE WERE TERRORISTS

Editor's Introduction

Germaine Tillion was probably unique in having brought together people of extremely varied backgrounds to constitute one of the first resister networks in occupied France. She was not alone in having an immediate urge "to do something" in the wake of the Armistice. In both the occupied and the southern zones, there were people whose revulsion at the surrender, and aversion to the regime that formed around Marshal Pétain in Vichy, made them instant candidates for resistance. Jean Garcin, a twenty-three-year-old resident in the department of the Vaucluse in the Southeast, came from a family of *notables* who were industrialists, republicans but decidedly to the left of center politically, adherents of the mainstream political party known as Radical Socialists. The Radicals had been the moderates in the 1936 Popular Front coalition, less far to the left than the Socialists (the SFIO, Section française de l'internationale ouvrière, or French Section of the Workers' International), and much less so than the Communists. The Radical Socialists were the party of Edouard Daladier, the Bull of the Vaucluse, who had been head of government in the years immediately after the Popular Front. Daladier represented France at the meeting with Hitler in Munich in September 1938. Garcin's father had received him at table in the family home when Jean was still considered too young to sit among the elders.

The father, Robert Garcin, was mayor of the town of Vaucluse, now known as Fontaine-de-Vaucluse, in the French department of the same name. Robert's brother, Voltaire, was mayor of Châteauneuf-de-Gadagne. Their father, Jean's grandfather Siffrein, had founded the family paper mill and started this committed republican family in Le Thor in the middle of the nineteenth century. One can readily imagine the exceptional passion for social justice that led the patriarch to name his first-born son "Voltaire," after the Benefactor of Ferney, who was perhaps the single most revered historical idol of the Third Republic. The younger son, Jean's father Robert, would die in Buchenwald for his own opposition to Vichy and the Third Reich.

Jean's upbringing had bestowed on him strong republican values. He says so in the text presented here even more eloquently than does this brief family history. Among these values was certainly an obligation to obey the law.[1] Vichy counted on this traditional discipline from all French citizens, even as it set about dismantling the Republic. The regime's first acts were to abrogate the Constitution and to start promulgating new laws as only it saw fit. Patriotism for the committed republican meant being a responsible citizen in the broadest sense. And Garcin was truly patriotic, a quality that was rarely lacking among the men and women who became resisters of the first hour. But what exactly did this mean in the summer of 1940, and what could a responsible citizen do when confronted with a government that no longer respected the values of the Republic? This is a question they asked themselves, a core dilemma that is frequently evoked in the literature of resistant memory. What makes Garcin exceptional was that he could immediately see that his true civic duty lay in opposing the newly proclaimed French State.

Still, it was not easy for him to embark upon the path of resistance, even if he could see that the Vichy regime was breaking the republican covenant. There was also the tide of public opinion to overcome. Garcin cites this obstacle as well. What did this mean? People in the Vaucluse in the summer of 1940 were overwhelmingly in favor of supporting "the Marshal," as he was called, in his effort to save France. And it is safe to say that most people in France, of whatever party, had not wanted a war at all. For the most part they dreaded the prolonged bloodletting that had characterized the Great War. And no one, except Hitler himself, perhaps, thought that the French Army would collapse right away. Confronted with a humiliating defeat in a month-long war, the population was at least momentarily united, if only in their shock.

If ever something could be said to have added insult to injury, it was the terms of the Armistice for the French people. The Armistice put in place a burdensome occupation, with shaming provisions that no one liked, on the left or the right. The defeat also put in place a new French state, *l'État français,* that would be known by the name of the spa town where the government settled itself: Vichy. This had not happened as the result of an electoral process, with clear objectives put forward, debated, and accepted by the people. The exact nature of the new regime had to be understood by what it proceeded to do. It

1. The meaning of the terms *républicain* and *libéral* in contemporary French are almost exactly the opposite of the American usage. *Républicain* means having a strong commitment to the Republic, to the Declaration of the Rights of Man of 1789, and the rule of law under a constitution. (The Republic was determined to be "irrevocable" under laws passed in 1875.) Being a *libéral* today means having a primary commitment to free-market economics.

began immediately to govern by decree; the new laws Vichy promulgated were not "passed" in any sense of that term. Elected officials all across France began to be removed from office if they were Socialists of any stripe, and in October all Jews were summarily barred from public office, as well as from teaching, law, and medicine. In the meantime, public allegiance was conferred on one man, Philippe Pétain, the hero of Verdun, widely viewed as the savior of the nation.

As Vichy rolled out its anti-parliamentary National Revolution in the weeks that followed the signing of the Armistice, the argument was increasingly made by supporters of the new regime, and by Vichy itself, that it was the bickering between parties, and the leftist coalition government of 1936–37, called the Popular Front, that had weakened the country.[2] The parliamentary system itself was blamed for allowing France to be entrapped in a war that had been brought on by unspecified powerful banking interests and a number of foreign powers, Britain preeminent among them. Waves of propaganda reinforced these ideas, and allegiance to the commander-in-chief who had led the nation to victory in World War I was exploited to ensure consensus. Dissent could only be seen as unpatriotic. "*Soyons français!*" (Let's be French!) was the order of the day. This particular Vichy slogan hid the fact that what Vichy was doing was not what most people had prided themselves on as being distinctly French for the past half-century. It implied pulling together as one, and it was intended to foster acquiescence to Vichy's every move. In short, Vichy called upon people to behave as good republicans, even though that mode of government was decidedly over. A slogan such as this could easily be endorsed, and was, even by newspapers that had supported continuing the fight against the Germans right up until the day the Armistice was signed. The majority of French people had been opposed to war, this much is certain. And, once the battle had been lost, it was easy for many of them to adopt the political process itself as a scapegoat. This position was especially attractive to people who opposed the republican form of government to begin with, among them royalists, Maurassians,[3] and even right-of-center republicans who all blamed the drift to war, rightly or wrongly, on the Popular Front. By supporting Vichy

2. Significant defunding of the military in fact dated from the administrations of 1932 to 1934, when Pétain was minister of defense, well before the Popular Front came to power. The Popular Front was also criticized for its short-lived military support of the Spanish Republicans.

3. Followers of Charles Maurras (1868–1952), the extreme right-wing ideologue of integral nationalism and founder of Action française. (See glossary.)

and its new National Revolution, their shame in that loss was diminished, if not relieved entirely.

French men and women of these persuasions rarely, if ever, began to contemplate resisting until 1942 or 1943, and some not until after Liberation. Henri Frenay was something of an exception, and none of these categories applies to the case of Jean Garcin, who was unquestionably a supporter of the Popular Front. Despite Vichy's repeated calls for national consensus and the willingness of the majority of French men and women to grant the Marshal what he asked for, Garcin was one of those who, as he says, "entered the Resistance out of sheer instinct and usually right away." This was partly due to the strength of his republican values, which he shared with Moulin and Tillion, and with many other resisters of the first hour. But it must also have helped Garcin enormously, in 1940, that these views were shared by his father and an extended, tightly knit southern French family, living and working together in a family business, in a town where the family enjoyed enormous respect for its political leadership.[4] Garcin mentions the importance of his family and the security of the house in which he lived, the Moulin Rouge, along with the respect and intimacy of the community in which it was situated, many times over.

Finally, there is the politics of age: Garcin mentions his youth as a factor, although he does not explain exactly what this means. Older people, in particular men who had fought in World War I, owed a strong allegiance to Pétain, and this older generation mostly supported him loyally until the very end. Their wives, and whatever other family members surrounded them, were under this same quasi-obligation to obey the Marshal. The defeat of the army in May–June 1940 brought undeserved shame on the younger generation. The removal of the defeated soldiers to Germany, almost 1.8 million of them, appears to have widened the effect of this generation gap. The wives and children of the POWs had little voice in the matter. Demobilized soldiers like Garcin who escaped deportation were in an uncomfortable position at best. He mentions the younger generation in the early chapters of his memoir, including Charles de Gaulle, who was not of the same generation as the old generals who surrounded the Marshal. And he mentions how shared youth

4. For a discussion of the nature of the French family in history, and of the patriarchal type of family that was the general rule in Provence in the first half of the twentieth century in particular, see *L'Invention de la France*, by Hervé Le Bras and Emmanuel Todd (Paris: Gallimard, 2012).

helped forge his bond with Barthélémy Rique,[5] whose importance in Garcin's move into resistance cannot be overstated.

In addition to his party orientation, his and his entourage's deep commitment to the Republic, and his age, it seems likely that Garcin's specific military training, and his personal disposition to taking committed, physical action (what he calls "*action immédiate*"), also helped him to make the actual decision to resist. These elements of his personal background also very certainly helped to define *how* he would ultimately resist, once he took the plunge. Garcin served for three years in the Seventh Engineering Division in Avignon, less than fifteen miles from his home. He was scheduled to be released from the military in July 1940. The collapse of the French Army would cut that short by exactly one month. He had been trained in the use of explosives, and in June 1940 he was in fact a corporal leading a small unit that was performing demolition work in the Maritime Alps near the Italian border. The purpose of their mission was to help interdict Mussolini's troops from entering France along the route that is now followed by the A8 Autoroute "La Provençale." As the *Débâcle* unfolded in the North, Garcin by his own admission purposefully misinterpreted orders to relocate his unit to Colmar, in Alsace, and directed them instead to Colmars, in the Alpes-de-Haute-Provence. This meant that, when subsequent orders to stand down were issued, he and his men were fortunate to find themselves still in the unoccupied zone, and they reported for demobilization in Saint-Maximin, in the Var. Garcin then went home to the Vaucluse, less than a hundred miles away.

All of this said, one might conclude that this is the story of someone who delighted in blowing things up and in refractory behavior in general. Nothing could be further from the case. Garcin's background, left of center to be sure, was deeply committed to lawful conduct in a highly structured society, to human rights and to the Republic that guarantees them. This spirit informs everything that he says and does. And this appears to be the greatest challenge to resister behavior in wartime France: the belief that the old marshal represented the continuity of France, and that it was not just somehow vaguely patriotic to support him, it was the civically responsible thing to do. Following this hurdle, if public opinion could be overcome, there might be a dignified and responsible way in which to express dissent.

When a minor Vichy official, a paper-supply inspector named Barthélémy

5. Barthélémy Rique, a civil servant working for Vichy, was the first to hook Garcin up with a group of resisters.

Rique, with whom Garcin had struck up an improbable friendship, initially broached the idea of resisting, the young Vauclusien jumped at the chance. There were certainly ways to "do something," even ways that did not immediately involve blowing up power pylons or railroad tracks, or providing armed protection for meetings and parachute drops. But Garcin himself says that he was never drawn to propaganda work. His first assignment was to do some recruiting of his own. The people he turned to first are a reflection of his practical disposition: Alphonse Bégou, the farrier smith in the town of Le Thor, and Jules Ten, the stonemason. Both were men of the left, one a quiet family man, the other an activist, albeit a nonaligned Communist. This recruiting was to be for the group known as Libération-Sud. Garcin would eventually lead his team into another movement, the *groupes francs*.[6] The three men appear to have shared a dislike for Vichy, the Germans still being far away to the north at this time. Together they began to conduct sabotage operations against power and transportation systems in the area east of Avignon.

Garcin was no ordinary artisan, and he seems to have had an aptitude for communication both up and down the social strata. It is perhaps not surprising, then, that he was soon selected by his superiors for leadership, although he would also refuse to be stuck shepherding *maquisards*[7] behind the lines, or to be saddled with pamphleteering, although he recognized its utility. The story he tells about his meeting the head of the Mouvements unis de la Résistance (MUR), Yvonne de Komornicka, also known as Capitaine Kléber, in Avignon early in 1943, is telling in this regard. It also says something about the interrelationship of these movements. Komornicka was known to him only by her *nom de guerre* at that time. It was Rique, presumably still his immediate superior in Libération, who took Garcin to meet this MUR official. After sizing him up and finding him suitable for the job, Yvonne appointed him to be the head of all the local groupes francs in the Vaucluse, and bestowed a new name

6. *Groupe franc* does not translate elegantly or accurately. A "free team" or a "nonaligned group" or a combination of these might be correct, but all seem clumsy. I have chosen not to translate this particular designation. (See glossary.)

7. *Maquisard,* a member of a *maquis*. The word became synonymous with the groups of men who fled the increasing demands for laborers to serve in Germany starting in late 1942. The Resistance harbored them, and many of them became resisters, but not all Resistance groups were maquis, and probably vice versa. I will also leave this word and its derivative untranslated. (See glossary.)

on him: "Bayard."[8] She offered him her hand to kiss. This somewhat *ancien régime* gesture of submission did not come easily to the young republican. But he knew what to do, and he executed "as best he could" what must surely have been his first-ever *baisemain*. He says he could barely confess to his mates back in Fontaine-de-Vaucluse that the commander who had promoted him was a woman. He did not tell them about kissing her hand.

Garcin does not say either when he moved from working with Libération to aligning himself with the groupes francs, but it was probably some time prior to this meeting. Clearly that did not mean he had distanced himself from his friend Barthélémy Rique. Libération-Sud itself was a movement that began to form primarily in Socialist and labor-union circles in Clermont Ferrand and Lyon in late 1940. (A similarly aligned group called Libération-Nord developed independently in the northern zone at about this time as well.) Like many early movements, Libération-Sud's first activity was principally focused on printing and distributing a newsletter, called Libération. Rique had clearly been working with them for some time when he invited Garcin to join. Garcin notes in passing that his leaders—Libération-Sud people presumably, although he doesn't specify which ones—frequently reached out to people from Franc-Tireur and Combat in Avignon at this time. Franc-Tireur was a Communist movement, and Combat was on the right in the spectrum of nascent resistant organizations.

If Garcin is being accurate with regard to dates and names, this must have been toward the end of 1941 when Henri Frenay's Mouvement de libération nationale fused with a group calling itself Liberté and they took on the new name of Combat. It was at this time, too, that Frenay called on regional leaders of his organization to encourage the formation of the largely independent groupes francs and instructed them to arm themselves through whatever means they could, including theft, and to engage in all manner of sabotage, and even to undertake the assassination of German soldiers. The groupes francs were thus to be paramilitary in culture, and only loosely under the direction of Combat's own *groupes de choc*, which is what the regular armed wing of Frenay's movement called itself in 1941. The groupes de choc would join together with the armed factions of several other groups to create the Armée secrète (AS) in 1942. Garcin's groupe franc did remain autonomous,

8. "Bayard" was the honorary name of Pierre de Terrail, a peerless French knight in the sixteenth century.

even from the AS, until the very end. His description of his group's equipping itself, largely by preying on the Chantiers de la jeunesse[9] in the nearby market town of Cavaillon in December 1941, fits well with this chronology.

Garcin says that it was a call from "the local leader of Combat to Libération," Paul Faraud, that led him to be invited to join the team that covered the parachute drop of Jean Moulin into the Alpilles hills southwest of Avignon on January 1, 1942. Is this when he actually migrated from Libération to the groupes francs? One can only guess. Whatever the case, he does not seem to think that the shift was worthy of note. This suggests that the groupes francs were actually formed from the bottom up, out of men from a number of movements, and not from the top down, or from within Frenay's right-wing military Mouvement de libération nationale/Combat.

That there were contacts between Libération, a Socialist movement that clearly welcomed Communists as well, and Combat, a right-wing resistant movement that emerged from the army of Vichy, in the Avignon of 1941, is also worthy of note. Nothing in what Garcin says could lead us to conclude that people from Francs-Tireurs, the earliest Communist resister groups, were seeking contact with Combat at this time, however. Moulin's mission, officially sanctioned by de Gaulle's Free French in London, was to try to organize all of these burgeoning resistant groups in the unoccupied southern zone into a single, coherent Resistance movement. Garcin, perhaps wishfully, and unquestionably in hindsight, says he thinks that groups working for the same goals should in fact be able to find common ground and work together, but he recognizes that this is not what happened. Is it possible that the mere fact of an individual's having been appointed to bring these groups together—any individual—actually discouraged such a union? Garcin subsequently talks about the period that followed Moulin's arrival on the scene as a time of intense negotiation that has since been dissected by scholars under the "looking-glass of their personal opinions," suggesting that he thinks the divergences that characterized these discussions have actually widened since the war. Be that as it may, says Garcin, "On November 27, 1942, eleven months after he had parachuted in, fifteen days after the Nazi invasion of the southern zone, Mou-

9. The Chantiers de la jeunesse (Youth Job Sites) was a Vichy-sponsored youth organization begun in July 1940 to accomplish public works and to give France's young people something to do in the wake of the crushing defeat of May that put an end to the draft and threw existing youth programs and summer camps into chaos.

lin was finally able to hold the first meeting of the United Movements of the Resistance (MUR)."

Such a meeting indeed took place. It was held in Collonges au Mont d'Or, a village on the Saône just north of Lyon, but at the time the group was still called the Comité de coordination de zone sud. The first meeting of the MUR is usually understood to have been two months later, in Miribel, seven miles to the east, on January 27, 1943. An account of the following six months could fill two chapters in even a brief history of the French Resistance. The first of these would certainly have to cover the first meeting of the Conseil national de la Résistance (CNR) in Paris on May 27. The second would be the disastrous June 15 meeting itself, when Moulin and a half-dozen of the top leaders of the Resistance came together in Caluire, the *commune* next door to Collonges. The entire group, including the doctor, Frédéric Dugoujon, in whose house the meeting was supposed to take place, and his patients, were arrested. It was to be the end for Moulin. Garcin was not there, and his book does not aim to provide a full explanation of what happened. He says that in May he was put on standby to cover an important meeting on the outskirts of Lyon, but that the confirmation never arrived. This must have been the Caluire meeting, however. Garcin says that it was one of the great regrets of the groupes francs that they had not been there, although he admits without a trace of irony that, had he been there, he might not have survived to write this memoir.

Garcin further regrets that all of these movements "didn't have much contact between each other," which he ascribes first and foremost to their clandestine culture: "Their different standing orders in fact absolutely ruled out any such contact. Added to which there were personal issues, different opinions about rank, function and responsibilities." He says this after having observed his own leaders in Avignon in 1941 attempting to reach out to leaders of other groups. And what this frank and loyal military man says is no doubt sincere. It seems likely, moreover, that in an environment where increasing aid, both financial and material, was being funneled from London to resistance groups, culminating in the delivery of weapons to support the Allied invasion, intensifying jealousy and the struggle for influence were causing these groups to compete as much as to cooperate, and that following the period in which the first resisters rallied to the cause, the groups they formed actually became more separate and their self-interest more distinct. That being said, Moulin's second mission, to unite the various movements of the Resistance in the North and the South, was successful as well, resulting in the first meeting of the CNR in Paris on May 27, 1943. It is proof of Moulin's good work that it did not collapse in the wake of his subsequent arrest.

Like most such resister accounts, Garcin's story bears the stamp of its regional origin. The urge to resist, "to do something" in the face of the German defeat of France, appears to have been widespread in the country, but the way in which it was felt, and especially the way that people fulfilled the urge, varied considerably from place to place. There are a few excellent reasons: France is and was a country of sharply perceived regional differences and, throughout the past three Republics, it has likewise been a country of many political parties—some say as many as there are voters. Superimposed on this fractured landscape is the map of German occupation. From June 1940 until November 1942, the German Army occupied only the northern half (or five-eighths) of the country, while the southern part was administered by the collaborationist regime located in Vichy. The first resisters in northern France immediately saw the Germans as their target. In the South, their counterparts often saw Vichy as their first target. Garcin was such a one, as he says in the opening chapter of his memoir. They hardly saw gray uniforms at all in the Vaucluse until the winter of 1942. During the early part of the war, Vichy may have been the seat of the government, but Lyon was the first city of the southern zone. Much of the early history of the Resistance takes place there. It is not surprising, then, that Garcin's cover identity—as a police inspector, no less—was provided by his Resistance colleagues through sympathetic employees in the police department in that city.

Within the southern zone there were further realities, regional demographics, economics, and history that influenced how people began to resist. To take just one example: in the southwest, around Toulouse, early resistance activity was shaped by a local need to help refugees from all over Europe to get out of France via Spain through the creation of an "underground funicular" over the Pyrenees. This meant establishing safe houses as well as finding and protecting reliable passers. Toulouse was also the center of the French aircraft industry, which became an early target for sabotage, and for this reason the British Intelligence Service and the SOE[10] were present there very early and

10. The British had two networks in wartime France. The Secret Intelligence Service is the name of the agency commonly known as MI6 (Military Intelligence section 6) and often in World War II as the IS. There was also Churchill's so-called "private army," the Special Operations Executive, or SOE, of which section F was France.

worked closely with the Resistance. If this were not enough, in the countryside around Toulouse there were tens of thousands of leftist and antifascist refugees from the Spanish Civil War, which had ended just one year prior to the Collapse of France. Some of these men were responsible for setting up one of the first Communist resistance movements in France, the Thirty-fifth Brigade of the Francs-Tireurs et Partisans.

In the southeast, where Jean Garcin lived, there were also refugees, but they were not from Spain so much as from the North, from Alsace and Lorraine, and from countries to the east. German, Austrian, Polish, and Czech artists and intellectuals; Communists, many of them Jews, were all looking to hide or, better, to escape from Europe altogether. They make a brief appearance in these pages when the Abbot Krebs, chaplain to the refugees from the annexed region of Lorraine, helped to implant Frenay's group Combat in the Vaucluse. The place where many of the refugees were heading was Marseilles, the so-called "trap door of Europe." We do not hear much about this in Garcin's text because escape through Marseilles had started to fall off following the winter of 1942, when the Germans occupied the southern zone and helped the Vichy police to blow up the part of the city where the last refugees were hiding.[11] Garcin was still working in the Vaucluse at this time. Starting in 1943, Allied operations in the Mediterranean made the southeast region accessible to aircraft coming from Sardinian and Corsican airstrips as well as the designation and operation of landing and parachute drop sites in the mountains of the Vaucluse. This helped bring Resistance operations there to new levels of intensity, with the reception of supplies destined for the Resistance, and with infiltration and extraction of pilots and intelligence agents. By the time Garcin took over the groupes francs in Marseilles, in late 1943 at the earliest, his job still entailed providing protection for high-level meetings, such as the operation described in his prologue, as well as assisting the growing British intelligence SOE network in the region. Garcin calls this network simply "Buckmaster," after Maurice Buckmaster, the British head of SOE operations in France. His network is still referred to in this way in the Vaucluse as one of the *sites d'aterrissage et de parachutages* of 1943 and 1944.

Over and beyond providing the testimony of a candid first resister, Garcin's description of his months at the head of Marseilles's groupes francs gives us

11. In the destruction of the quartier Saint-Jean, January 22–24, 1943, many refugees were rounded up, and some 1,642 were sent to deportation.

priceless insights from a man who came up through the ranks to lead a total of forty operations in the Army of Shadows. His discussion of how and when he moved from his first participation as a fledgling member of Libération-Sud into full clandestinity and his exposé of the basic rules of such work are invaluable, as is the description of his role as leader of the Marseilles group, including managing day-to-day operations and screening candidates for terrorism. For terrorists by all accounts they were. This is what both Vichy and the Nazis called them, seventy years ago, when they stood up and looked around and counted very few people around them, yet they proceeded with courage and caution in equal parts. And in the final analysis, if they were never in the majority in wartime France, they left a legacy of which the country can be extremely proud. On Bastille Day in 1942, as we now know, France was heading into its darkest hour. That afternoon Garcin bicycled into Avignon for a demonstration and silent march up the rue de la République. Demonstrations had been called for all over the country on the BBC broadcast *Les Français parlent aux français*. His group mates, Bégou and Ten, were both there, he says, but so were many people they had no idea were their supporters. They were not all resisters, in the strict sense of the word, but seeing them there, Garcin realized that there was in fact "a party of Resistance" in France. This must have been of inestimable value in overcoming the sense that public opinion was against them. They had a peaceful demonstration, confronted the authorities, then dispersed. He rode home that night reassured, strengthened in his conviction that what he was doing was right, for he had met some real Frenchmen.

Nous Étions des Terroristes was written a half-century after the war's end. It is nonetheless a historical document of the first order. Garcin speaks throughout in the first person, largely about his own experience, and when he talks about others and about events, it is also as an eyewitness, and he knew that many of the people he was writing about were still alive to correct him. There are in fact scores, if not hundreds, of such personal accounts of resister activities that were written and published, by small presses as well as large, in postwar France, the majority of them in the 1980s and 1990s, as the players retired from their postwar professions. (Garcin served as a public official, as mayor of Le Thor and as a regional council member, for most of the rest of his life.) Many of these were published in small print runs and are now out of print and will simply disappear, as have their authors. Jean Garcin's is one of the most candid and no-nonsense of these memoirs. His testimony of how he became involved in active opposition to the Vichy regime and to the Nazis is particularly clear. His description of the organizing of groupes francs, a loosely affiliated league of unaligned hit squads that emerged in 1941–42, is likewise highly evocative.

We Were Terrorists

JEAN GARCIN

To Robert Garcin, my father,
political prisoner, deportee No. 39554,
died in Buchenwald, March 24, 1944

The mill on the Calavon. For two long years a farmhouse filled with cicadas, a castle for swifts. Here, everything was like rushing water, now in laughter, now the fists of Youth. Today the old resister stumbles over its stones, most of them dead from frost, from solitude and from heat. These presages are in turn swallowed up by the silence of the flowers.

—René Char, August 10, 1945

Prologue

IZON-LA-BRUISSE, Spring 1994

Mistral, Gabriel
—died on the Field of Honor
Razzoli, Bruno
—died on the Field of Honor
Nouvenne, Jeannot
—died on the Field of Honor
Hoffmann, Pinchus
—died on the Field of Honor
Blanc, Georges
—died on the Field of Honor

The litany goes on. Thirty-six times the tired voice of Laurent Pascal, the only one who escaped the roundup, calls upon the survivors of a generation that is slowly disappearing, to remember the martyrs of the Maquis Ventoux.[1]

Here, fifty years ago, on the border between the Drôme and the Vaucluse, thirty-six young men fell, shot down by Vichy militia and Hitler's SS.

Shot in groups of four, they are now only names on a worn monument. Most of them carried no weapon and were still asleep when the barbarians stormed in.

Refusing Obligatory Work Service in Germany, eager to live, instinctively patriotic, they had found asylum in the desolate setting of abandoned farmhouses as well as the hope that they might one day take part in the liberation of their country.

I knew very little of them. By that time I was serving as regional chief of the *groupes francs*[2] of the Resistance. We had no direct contact with the *maquis*, but I remember that upon learning of the massacre, it was as if someone had stuck a dagger in my heart.

The doleful voice keeps calling out the names on the monument on the

Translation of *Nous Étions des Terroristes* (Avignon: Editions Barthélemy), 1996.

1. For *maquis*, see page 168, note 7, and glossary. The Ventoux is a region surrounding the highest mountain in Provence, Mont Ventoux, situated twenty miles northeast of Avignon.

2. See page 168, note 6, and glossary.

Monteau farm. It's cold, and the sky is gray. The weather, too, is dressed to mourn the massacre.

Once again the naming out of the dead, bounced off of the stone cliff that shelters the cemetery of Egalayes, freezes my blood.

The memory of one of the first commemorations, already too distant, comes back to me. We were many then. The standard-bearers who held the tri-colored flags at an incline during the minute of silence were still young men. The entire Resistance was there, all opinions stood side by side. I remember that the Prefect at the time wore the insignia of the Free French Forces. Gathered around us, the families, fathers, mothers, sisters and brothers, filled the space, sad but proud.

I cannot help trying to fill in the holes that a half-century has carved in our ranks. The silhouettes that have vanished in death parade by. Looking at the officiating dignitaries, I feel a kind of disconnect. At first glance, the Prefect of 1994 probably wasn't born yet on that day. . . .

Max Fisher is steadfast at his post. It's his job to give the usual speech. He does it with a depth of feeling that I share. If it were just the habitual gesture of an official looking at his watch, I doubtless would still have left more serene. . . .

My chauffeur, thirty-three years old last spring, remained in the car. I find him deeply engrossed in *Télé 7 Jours*.[3]

Yes, it's a sure thing. In ten years' time, maybe even less, Izon will only be an annoying date in a crowded prefectoral agenda.

Séderon, Buis-les-Baronnies, Malaucène, Carpentras, Cavaillon. . . . My TV viewer drives me back to my house at an unhurried speed. The pleasure of seeing a few of the old-timers gradually overtakes my feelings of melancholy and pessimism. I must have dozed off for a moment. This happens more and more often. We are stopped, blocked by a line of cars at the entrance to Cavaillon. I ask my driver what's up.

"Oh, it's just some young people. Today is Mardi Gras."

They come into view. It's a bunch of kids, thirteen or fourteen years old. Crudely made up, dressed in rags, they are taunting the people in cars. The blue, white and red medallion on my car earns us special treatment. Rice, flour, plaster and confetti are generously applied to our car. They razz us and slap the bodywork in rhythm. It isn't mean-spirited. They're good-natured, just trying to provoke us, carefree and fun-loving as one should be at their age. I

3. *Télé 7 Jours* is a French weekly television guide.

smile back. They applaud my sense of fair play and let us pass. And I cannot help thinking next that they doubtless know nothing of the Resistance! It is definitely an obsession with me. I promise myself to change the theme and think about something entirely different.

At this precise moment my eye catches the street sign with the name of the avenue we are on:

Yvon Darriès
Resister
Tortured and shot by the Nazis.
1921–1944

"Yvon Darriès . . . Les Trois Lucs . . ."

+ + +

I have arrived first. Via the tramway line that ends in the main square of Les Trois Lucs. I have business here.

Les Trois Lucs. At the time, this was the edge of the known world for most people from the Marseilles of the Old Port or the Canebière.

I find a real village square, a set straight out of a Pagnol movie. A few detached villas of the "My Dream" or "Enough 4 Me" variety, surrounding a few shops, the bakery, the butcher's shop, a dimly lit yard-goods store and a café with a snappy exterior, the Bar du Terminus. In the middle of the square, the celebrated terminus of the Réformés–Les Trois Lucs trolley line where I had just stepped down onto a tiny platform that barely emerged from the roughly joined cobblestones of the street.

I have no difficulty identifying the villa where the meeting will take place in a little while. It looks innocent enough with its pastel-colored shutters and poorly clipped boxwood hedge. It may still be there, in the same state, housing men and women who were not yet born when the plan of action for the Resistance in the entire southern zone of France was decided there on that first of December of 1943. . . .

Fifteen days earlier, during our monthly meeting in Paris, Duroc had informed me:

"You will have to provide protection for a meeting of the Nationals in Marseilles soon."

He hadn't said any more than that, and I hadn't asked any questions. That wasn't done, and for my own part, I thought that the less I knew the better it was. Just in case.

It was only two nights before, in a greasy spoon in the neighborhood of the Opera, that Paule, my liaison agent, had given me the date, the place, and the name of the villa that had been rented several months prior for whatever useful purpose.

The weather is beautiful. A winter sky that the mistral has cleared of unwanted clouds. Some men are leaving for work. Women enter and exit the shops whose windows appear better stocked in little signs announcing upcoming distributions and the tickets needed for them than in actual goods for sale.

It is so peaceful that it seems surreal at a time when the maquis is fighting for survival, when the cellars of the occupier and of the Militia shake with the screams of tortured patriots, and where, from west to east, millions of people are being snuffed out in death.

I decide to go have a cup of coffee, or of whatever is being used as a substitute for it at the moment. The proprietor of the Terminus, a short man with an eager face, serves it to me with a smile. Above the bar, leaning against the bottles, is a sign announcing a "day without," a day without alcohol. The toasted barley doesn't taste too bad, but the saccharine does nothing to improve it.

I put my cup down and look around the square. My men are there. The *gazogène*-equipped[4] Peugeot in which they arrived is now parked, its hood raised, not far from the villa. With much of his body deep inside the engine compartment, Peyrerol establishes his purpose for being there by repairing an imaginary breakdown. Yvon Darriès, the youngest in our group and a pharmacist's assistant in Cavaillon, where a street will one day bear his name, plays the part of an interested spectator.

Crillon, whose real name is Jules Ten, my friend and number-two man, is pacing up and down on the sidewalk across the street. As he is accustomed to, he is carrying a bag that doesn't detract in the slightest from his overall nondescript appearance. It is a burlap sack, what we locally call a *bourras*, which suggests he is on the lookout for some forage for his rabbits. To look at him you would think that, having found what he needed, he would be on the next tram home. Not a single one of us shows any interest whatsoever in a taxi, a tiny Simca with a gazogène twice its own size that pulls up in the square. Paule manages to squeeze out of it, followed by a large and muscular man wrapped in an overcoat with a fur collar. Both of them head for the villa

4. *Gazogène*, a system for extracting combustible gas to power motor vehicles from wood. It became popular in France during World War II. (See glossary.)

and disappear over the threshold without so much as a glance behind them. The Simca goes around the square and heads back down the avenue towards Marseilles, bumping over the tram tracks as it goes.

I pay for my coffee and go back out, passing the conductor and the motorman of the trolley that has just arrived. Two men have gotten off and are heading towards the villa. They pay no attention whatsoever to Crillon, and he returns this in kind.

I head towards a gate behind which I have decided I will station myself. I feel the café owner's eyes on my back, but I pay it no mind. He doubtless takes me for a business traveler making rounds, or an ordinary civil servant involved in the distribution of supplies, of which there are many.

So far I haven't recognized any of the men who have arrived. It is true that the partitioning of organizational structures within the Resistance neither facilitated nor encouraged forming social ties, and it was doubtless better that way. In addition to this general approach, it was in the nature of the groupes francs of which I was the departmental chief. We were autonomous and had few contacts with other organizations that sometimes—it was known to happen—found our manners disturbing to their routines, or to their wait-and-see outlook.[5]

The nature of our work, engaging in direct confrontations, sabotage, executions, and jobs that required a hands-on approach, called for special precautions.

This is why I really only knew two members of the national leadership at this date: Duroc, the number-two national man in the groupes francs, and Morlot, the regional chief, whom I would succeed when he left for Paris to take command of the groupes francs in the capital region. It was the same for the members of my own group who knew no one except me.

The last two guests to arrive at the villa are in fact Morlot and Duroc. One arrives on a bicycle, and the other gets out of a private car that pulls away immediately.

The next hour passes in utter tranquility. The comings and goings of housewives increase in frequency. A trolley arrives, sits idle for a few moments, then begins to get ready to head back into town. I watch the maneuver of the motorman as he flips his control stick around, causing a momentary flash of sparks, and prepares to drive back from the opposite side of his platform. The mood is serene. Today, one of my grandchildren would say that everything was cool.

5. *Attentisme* was an approach or strategy that emphasized the resisters' role as preparing to support an Allied invasion as opposed to engaging the enemy directly. (See glossary.)

The sun is already high up in the sky. It's December, but it is nonetheless quite warm out, and my warm-lined jacket is a little too heavy for me. Taking it off would mean exposing my weapon, an outdated automatic pistol that I had grown used to using, stuck under the belt of my pants. So I keep the coat on.

Peyrerol has placed a small pile of wrenches and screwdrivers on the ground beside him that Darriès is busy passing him. Like me, Crillon is growing warmer in the sun. I know him well. He is always in motion. Time must be dragging a bit for him.

Once again, everything is going along just as it should, uneventfully. These meetings are never very long. The participants have all grown accustomed to working in clandestine conditions. They have no desire to make them last any longer than necessary, and they do not waste words when they talk. In a few moments they will all come out and vanish into the surroundings.

Crillon and his two buddies will head back to Lagnes.[6] Paule and I will take a trolley back to the head of the line at the Church of the Réformés, from whence we will make our separate ways up to the St. Charles railroad station to catch a train for Toulon. I have to reestablish a contact there that was severed by some arrests.

I am deep in thought about this when a detachment of Militia members emerges from the Marseilles road, five men in uniform and beret, their weapons on shoulder straps. They don't seem in any particular hurry. Doubtless just a routine patrol, checking identity papers and permits to be operating any vehicles. My heart pounds a bit harder for a moment, then starts to calm. These investigations are numerous, and my fake/real ID card as a police inspector has already stood up to several inspections like this.

I glance over at Crillon. He is just as experienced as I am at this. He doesn't blink. I am more worried about my two guys with the car and a breakdown. I know them to be more hot-headed, more nervous. The Militia men head toward them, still in no hurry at all. The leader of the unit is out in front.

Peyrerol straightens up out of the engine compartment and turns to answer the officer. A conversation begins but I can't understand a single word. Darriès is listening to it with a faint smile on his face and one hand in the pocket of his leather jacket. The Militia leader makes a sign to his men and draws his side arm. Just by luck, no shots were fired, despite his repeated squeezing of the

6. Lagnes, a village in the Vaucluse near Isle-sur-la-Sorgue, location of the *mas du Chat*, where Garcin's original resisters' group lived and where an important maquis will be hidden after February 1943.

trigger. It was the last move he would ever make. Yvon Darriès shoots next, the Militia officer falls mortally wounded. All hell breaks loose for about twenty seconds. Hidden behind my gate I start shooting at the group of men. Across the square Crillon opens up with the Sten that he has pulled out of his bag.[7] Peyrerol slams the hood of the car down, jumps behind the wheel and starts the engine.

I must have fired three or four bullets, Crillon a whole clip. I hear screams. A woman is down over in front of the bakery, and she is screaming in fright. There are no more Militia men. They are all lying on the pavement.

Crillon runs over to the car and jumps in. Darriès climbs in beside the driver. The three of them know what they have to do now. They head for Allauch.[8]

Gradually, people begin to emerge from the shops and things start to calm down. As if out of respect for the dead, no one goes near the bodies of Darnand's men, poor fighters but proven traitors.[9]

During the confusion, I reach the terrace of the bar, and I step inside. The owner is pale. He is pouring himself a shot of Calvados, then he looks up at me and without a word serves me a small glass of it as well. Our eyes meet. I can see sheer terror in his look. I thank him and reach for my wallet. He stops me with a word.

"It's on me," he breathes.

I nod, looking out at the square where the entire population of Les Trois Lucs is now running around. Morlot and Duroc cross in front of the bar. Like a typical pair of rubberneckers they stop and look at the bodies lying on the ground, then they hurry off in the direction of la Valentine. Meanwhile, next to me, a man in butcher's garb is placing a phone call. He yells into the telephone that some men have just been shot in Les Trois Lucs. . . .

The meeting was held, the villa emptied out, my mission was done. The bell of the trolley car pulled me out of my thoughts. Faithful to their schedule, doubtless moderately moved by the death of the collaborators, and reluctant to answer the questions the police will soon be there to ask, the two employees of the Tramway Authority decided to act like nothing had happened at all.

I jump on board at the last moment. Except for Paule, who is sitting in the back, it is empty. A police car and a van pass us with their sirens blaring. I offer

7. *Note in French edition:* A British machine-pistol, extremely loud and inaccurate.

8. A village in the Etoile mountain range just east of Marseilles.

9. Joseph Darnand was a French Army officer who fought bravely in World War I, who became a far-right nationalist in the 1930s and later a paramilitary leader under Vichy. (See glossary.)

up a palliative comment to the conductor, who has seated himself not far from where I am. "If that's not a shame. . . ."

His look of sheer contempt is all the answer I get, a shrug of the shoulders that exudes indifference. There are still people who care. The bastards are in the minority.

A stunning proof of this happened four years later. I had returned to Les Trois Lucs. I had told my wife the story of this encounter, she herself was a resister alongside Chaban and Bourges Monory.[10] Passing through Marseilles one day, I was seized with the urge to revisit the scene. She loved the idea.

The cool shady terrace of the Bar du Terminus was inviting. The man whom I took to be the proprietor was still there. We told him what we wanted to drink. He took our order and then said something that mystified me completely:

"I have something for you," he said, turning to go back inside.

When he came back with our drinks he handed me the clip from an automatic pistol. I could have fallen off my chair.

"Here," he said, "I am returning it. . . . The last time you were here you forgot it."

This man had seen it all happen and could have described me, but he had said nothing. . . .

+ + +

It may seem like bravado, but I can honestly say that during those years, when death, or worse, was waiting for us around every corner, I never felt fear at all.

Perhaps it would be more accurate to say that I never consciously felt it. I did take care to analyze the risks that we underwent afterwards. But in the heat of the moment, never. In the same way I never really took stock of the details of what happened during action while it was going on, only later did I make an effort to recall them.

It was the case on that day. During the incident, I don't recall that I ever really looked at the faces of the Militia men. At that moment they were just so many targets that had to be hit.

10. Chaban and Bourges Monory [*sic*] were, respectively, Jacques Delmas (1915–2000), called "Chaban" in the Resistance, later known as Jacques Chaban-Delmas; and Maurice Bourgès-Maunory (1914–1993), both resisters in the Bordeaux area. They both later became well-known political figures.

It wasn't until I was in the train to Toulon that their faces came back to me with clarity. The leader, the oldest one, wore round intellectual glasses over a straight-laced stooping silhouette suggestive of a high degree of inbreeding. The others, one of whom had a striking case of juvenile acne, generally had nondescript features similar to the boys of the same age that were being received into our maquis and trained more or less rigorously for the fight to free the homeland. In fact, they were scarcely different from the three German sailors who, like me, were standing in the corridor of the train car, heading back to their ship after shore leave in Marseilles.

I was only twenty-six years old, but I felt like I was older than all of them—underfed warriors in training in the Ventoux, collaborators from Marseilles, or seasoned fighters of the German Navy. It was just that, if three years in the Resistance had not succeeded in taking away the appearance of the young bourgeois sportsman that I was, they had aged me appreciably. Doubtless too much, if one ponders the fact that killing young men like them, even if they were traitors, didn't trouble my conscience in the slightest, nor did it evoke any particular emotion.

It is time to tell the succession of events, and the strength of the ideas, that turned Jean Garcin, born on January 11, 1917, in Fontaine de Vaucluse,[11] into the head of the groupes francs of Region 2 of the Resistance and, for the Gestapo and the Militia, the terrorist Bayard.

11. *Note in French edition:* The village that is called Fontaine de Vaucluse today. [To avoid confusion with the name of the department, we will call it "Fontaine" henceforth.—Ed.]

My Friend, Can You Hear . . .[12]

CHAPTER ONE

> The National Assembly confers all powers on the Government of the Republic under the authority and the signature of Marshal Pétain, to promulgate by one or by a succession of acts, a new constitution for the French State. This constitution will guarantee the rights of Work, Family and Fatherland.
>
> —Law of July 10, 1940

How did one get into the Resistance?

The question has been asked a thousand times, and a thousand answers given. One could, of course, ask it in a different way. Then it might take on a universal quality and relate to many other revolts and not just the French Resistance. For what reasons does one choose to enter into open conflict with the law, which wouldn't be such a problem if at the same time one didn't also find oneself at odds with the overwhelming majority of public opinion?

Without pretending to give the definitive answer to a question that has already been debated in many historical studies yet is still asked, I think that one can distinguish two kinds of volunteers in the Resistance.

Some acted as a consequence of military circumstances or personal situations that they found themselves in. This group became more and more numerous and preponderant as the conflict wore on, with the hardening of Nazi-like restrictions imposed by the Vichy regime, the Service du travail obligatoire (STO),[13] and the horror of repression by the Gestapo and the Militia.

Events forced them onto the path of honor, and regardless of when this happened, they deserve our respect.

Others, fewer in number, entered the Resistance out of sheer instinct and usually right away. In order to make their actions coincide with their conception of democracy and of the Republic, out of hatred for nazism and fascism, often out of family tradition. They had read *Mein Kampf*,[14] or at least they knew

12. Taken from the opening line of the "Chant des Partisans," lyrics by Joseph Kessel, which became the hymn of the Resistance.

13. Obligatory Work Service, a draft instituted by Vichy early in 1943 to help France meet increasing demands for laborers to work in Germany. (See glossary.)

14. *My Struggle*, Adolf Hitler's 1925 autobiographical manifesto in which he declared his plans for Germany, for Europe, and for the Jews, among other matters. (See glossary.)

what was in it. They could already see the monster peeking out of Hitler's chancellor's costume. I was one of them.

For people like this it wasn't necessary to wait or to hope for some reaction from Marshal Pétain. Just reading the law of July 10, 1940, that 80 members of Parliament out of 636 had the good sense to vote against, was enough. I was one of them, but I take no credit for it whatsoever because my determination was written in my genes.

The Garcin family had come down from Savoy in 1845 following my ancestor and eponym Jean Garcin, a member of the papermakers' guild, and settled in the Moulin Rouge where I still live now, on account of the extraordinary generosity of the waters of the Sorgue. Cool and abundant, they are perfect for the making of paper.

We were able to create an industry there that was prosperous for a long time without ever abusively exploiting the labor it employed. In local popular tradition one said: *When one goes into the Moulin Rouge, it is until death. . . .* I myself never had to fire a single one of my workers. They lived all around us, the oldest among them used the "tu" form when talking to their bosses, my uncle Voltaire and my father Robert, and they used it with me as well.

My grandfather, Siffrein Garcin, was the mayor of Gadagne, and he left behind him the memory of having been jailed under the Moral Order of Mac-Mahon.[15] His son Voltaire (a freighted given name) was a Freemason and a Radical Socialist, and he followed his father as mayor and as member of the general council. My father, Robert, was elected mayor of Fontaine de Vaucluse in 1903 and remained in that post until he was removed by Vichy.

For these two men and on the occasion of my twentieth birthday, in 1936 came the Popular Front, which we saw not as impinging on our prerogatives and the ruin of our patrimony but as the dawn of bright tomorrows when all of France would join together in song, with social peace and equal opportunity for all.

This was a time when a bunch of famous figures would sometimes dine at the Moulin Rouge while I was holding down the far end of the table, Edouard Herriot, Léon Blum, Daladier, Marcel Cachin, Louis Gros, a deputy whom the

15. Gadagne is a town to the southwest of Fontaine. Patrice de MacMahon (1808–1893) was a distinguished French soldier and statesman of Irish descent. The Moral Order was a coalition of rightist parties in the early Third Republic that aimed to prepare the nation for a third restoration of the monarchy. It has become a synonym for "reactionary" in leftist parlance.

Vaucluse is still proud to count among the number of those who dared to say "no" to Pétain.[16]

We shared their beliefs and the conception that they held of honor at the time.

I was a student at the engineering school in Grenoble,[17] and at the end of 1937 I had just been elected president of the Leftist students' association, when I was called up and enlisted in the Seventh Engineering Division in Avignon. I was supposed to be in uniform for three years.

I don't recall the exact date of my demobilization, but it must have been in July of 1940. Corporal first class and a specialist in the use of explosives for destruction (a skill that proved useful to me in years to follow), I had carried out my last assignment, to destroy the Garavan viaduct, on the Italian border, the day after Mussolini's Italy entered the war.

The operation was a complete success, and I had then to lead the squad that I was commanding to rejoin the rest of our outfit, which by this time had been moved to Alsace. I was handed marching orders for Colmar. No specified department or itinerary.

This was in mid-June. Everywhere around us French troops were falling back in disorder, leaving hundreds of thousands of prisoners behind them.

This was doubtless the fate that we were heading towards. At the head of my team of sappers, I headed with utmost determination for Colmars. Yes, Colmars, with an "s," and in the southern Alps. . . .

It was not very difficult to rejoin the demobilization center of the regiment in Saint Maximin after the Armistice. I was demobilized there in mid-July, but not before I had approved several leaves for myself, during which I went back to the Moulin Rouge, where we heard over the wireless about the latest

16. Edouard Herriot (1872–1953), a Radical Socialist, three times prime minister and long-time mayor of Lyon; Léon Blum (1872–1950), a Socialist, three times prime minister and head of state during the Popular Front of 1937–38; Edouard Daladier (1872–1950), a Radical Socialist, three times prime minister, head of government at the time of the Munich Accords and when war was declared in September 1939; Marcel Cachin (1869–1958), a Communist, senator, and deputy as well as long-time editor of the newspaper *l'Humanité;* Louis Gros (1873–1963), a Socialist, senator, and deputy, mayor of Avignon whom Vichy removed from office but who reclaimed his seat at the Liberation, on August 26, 1944.

17. Possibly the Institut d'électrotechnique de Grenoble, an ancestor of today's Institut polytechnique de Grenoble.

disasters of that period. But like just about every other Frenchman at the time, I did not hear the Appeal of General de Gaulle.[18]

Once we knew about it, and it had been not only reported on but re-broadcast by the BBC, most people shrugged their shoulders and asked themselves with contempt just who this unknown little general was who had the presumptuousness to think differently than the venerated marshal who had been sent to them by Heaven above. People made fun of the grandiloquence of the speech itself, and of the stiff tone of voice in which it had been delivered.

It wasn't like that at all at the Moulin Rouge. It was a proud and solitary voice that rose over a chorus of bleating sheep. The voice felt good. Even my mother, the daughter of an officer and precisely because of it especially antimilitaristic, appreciated the way the speech sounded. According to her way of thinking it made better sense to listen to a young general with only two stars, and those of a temporary commission at that, than to a senile old man with seven.

The theory of the "man sent from on high" had never been a Garcin family favorite, as well one might suspect. The Marshal who embodied it, the ambassador of France to his friend Franco, was already held in dubious regard around our house even before the war. Knowing that he had been granted full powers disgusted us, and we expected the very worst.

It didn't take long. On the 17th of July, only a week after what some were calling his investiture and that we called a putsch, he promulgated a text that filled us with bitterness. This law made it illegal to hire anyone for a public service position, including people who were undeniably born French, if their father was not himself born a Frenchman. . . . France, the safe haven of Liberty itself, was already closing the doors upon its very self. And this without anyone, not even the German conquerors, having asked the new regime to do any such thing. Xenophobia and its odious partner, racism, became official. And this was only the start. The October 18th statute on the Jews was already in the pipeline. The months of the summer of 1940 seemed the longest of the entire war because our morale was at its lowest. Where could we turn to find hope?

18. *L'Appel du 18 juin*, broadcast by General Charles de Gaulle from London over the BBC, was a call to the French people not to accept capitulation. It was the start of official French opposition to the German occupation. A repeat performance was broadcast on June 22, 1940, and was heard by more people than the first.

The United States would only enter the war a full year later, and the USSR would still be the ally of Nazi Germany for many months to come.

There remained England which was not backing down, but whose modest military resources did not appear sufficient to stop a likely debarkation and the onslaught of panzers that would follow. We had our own country's collapse on our minds and the millions of our men who had been made prisoners in a short few weeks. . . .

Only the energy of Winston Churchill was capable of raising some hopes.[19] I remember being struck by some words from one of his speeches:

> There are no hopeless situations, there are only men who have given up hope. I can only promise you blood and tears. . . .

But would the courage of a people inspired by their leader be enough to turn a catastrophic situation around?

Like others whom I did not know yet, I thought so, but this arose out of blind optimism and incantation. Outside of my family and the company of a few close friends, I was very much alone.

Distracted by the start-up of rationing, and afflicted by the absence of the prisoners of war, the population allowed itself to drift into a kind of lethargy that was fueled principally by fatalism, if not by darkest pessimism. Once the worst was over, I felt pretty sure that the former group at least could be counted on to find their way back to their old opinions and to the wish to live together in a republic.

Then there were the odious creatures whom the war had muzzled, supporters of the extreme right, men we called *cagoulards*, who now reared their heads again.[20]

Blaming democracy for a military defeat that, deep inside, suited their purposes just fine, they denounced the governments of the Popular Front

19. *Note in French edition:* I had the honor to meet this great man in Fontaine de Vaucluse where he stayed with us for several days. He spent the time painting. I reminded him of his words and told him how they had given us hope. He smiled.

20. Cagoulards were members of the French fascist league La Cagoule (the Hood) that rose to prominence in the early 1930s, whose activity had culminated in the February 1934 violence at the pont de la Concorde.

in particular and excoriated (with what disdain!) everyone who had supported them.

Appointed by Vichy to replace duly elected officials as heads of municipal councils, they were actually pleased to see the regional councils dissolved and applauded anti-Semitic measures. They pummeled the elected officials of the Third Republic with their sarcasm and their accusations, then proclaimed their utter indignation, and soon initiated steps to actually prosecute them.

I had but little professional contact with those people. In day-to-day life it was even less complicated: we didn't talk to each other. . . . It was only in among a very small group of family and friends that, being unable to find better, we discussed the news that reached us.

From the very first days of the Occupation in the northern zone and the installation of the Vichy regime, radio had been obliged to get in step. It only broadcast what it was allowed to by the Propagandastaffel. I still recall a little ditty that was often heard over the BBC:

> RADIO PARIS MENT, RADIO PARIS MENT . . . RADIO PARIS EST ALLEMAND
> (Radio Paris lies, Radio Paris lies . . . Radio Paris is German.)

It didn't take long for people to realize this. We listened most of the time to a Swiss broadcaster, Radio Sottens. Afterwards, despite efforts to garble the broadcasts, it was the BBC that had a daily broadcast hosted by free Frenchmen: Pierre Dac and Maurice Schuman, along with Pierre Holmes, the so-called voice of the free French, citizen of Isle-sur-la-Sorgue, and so many others who, little by little, reached England.

The news hour was sacred. Without having to take measures to insure clandestine listening which were soon to become necessary, we gathered around the set. Then came the commentaries, angry outbursts and protests. . . . As the weeks went by, a dark cloak fell over all of the France of the Rights of Man. Consider the following list of events as evidence in the matter:

—July 11	Pétain adopts the title of Chief of State
—July 13	Albert Lebrun's mandate as President of the Republic is summarily terminated
—July 22	Law approved permits revoking naturalization
—July 30	Creation of the Youth Work Program
—August 13	Secret societies are banned

—August 29	Creation of the Legion of Veterans
—September 15	Blum, Reynaud, Daladier and Mandel imprisoned[21]
—September 27	German order against Jews in the occupied zone
—October 3	Law governing the status of Jews
—October 24	Pétain and Hitler shake hands in Montoire
—October 30	In a speech, Pétain declares: "Starting today I am choosing the road of collaboration."

It was on that day, the 30th of October 1940, after listening to the Marshal's speech, that I heard the verb "to resist" used for the very first time in the sense that it will retain forever in glory.

My father had just turned off the radio. He couldn't stand the sound of the second stanza of the Marseillaise. It had become the only part of our national anthem that was allowed to be performed. The first stanza was too warlike, and the Germans didn't like it. Vichy chose the last. The one that Rouget de Lisle dedicated to "the children." I am not making this up. It had the advantage of having funereal overtones, and we needed to become accustomed to thinking of ourselves as beaten. This is why Vichy chose it.

From the depths of his armchair, my uncle Voltaire, whose dominant traits did not include being mute, said nothing, refusing to open the usual discussion. It was so uncharacteristic in fact that we were all speechless, waiting for him to speak. When he did, it was to utter a single sentence:

No! It's no longer possible. We must Resist!

CHAPTER TWO

> It is with honor, and to preserve French unity—a unity that is ten centuries old—in constructive engagement with the movement toward a new European order, that starting today I am choosing the road of collaboration. . . . this collaboration must be sincere. It must be free of any aggressive intent. . . .
>
> —Marshal Pétain, October 30, 1940

21. For Blum and Daladier, see note 16, above. Paul Reynaud (1878–1966) was several times a minister, including minister of finance under Daladier. He was the penultimate prime minister in the Third Republic. Georges Mandel (1885–1944) served in many posts in the Third Republic and was minister of the interior at the time of the Collapse of France. All four men opposed the surrender of France to Germany.

Yes. There was no longer any other way to go. It was necessary to Resist, but how? With whom and with what?

These were questions to which there was no clear answer. Sharing ideas doesn't necessarily mean actually working together, conspiring and risking jail and persecution together.

The preexisting social divisions, membership in parties that existed before, positions that were adopted over the course of a number of crucial years, 1934 and 1936, allowed us to know, roughly speaking, who was who. But that only amounted to a lot of talk.

Talk played its part. No place was exempt from it, no family or just friendly gathering, no Sunday game of *boules*, no apéritif at the local bistro or class dinner where we didn't let it be known how we felt or how much we hoped to see the object of our disapproval, this French State, stumble and then disappear. In point of fact it was a struggle that had been going on for nearly two centuries, which pitted the red clan against the white. The saber and the aspergillum on one side, social progress and solidarity on the other.

Our motto, Liberty, Equality, Fraternity, had been removed from the front of buildings. Work, Family, and Fatherland, respectable ideas enlisted in a truly lame cause, had replaced it, and this we absolutely could not put up with.

By then the embryo of a Popular Front was taking shape around the Garcin brothers. Without the Communists, whose party had been outlawed at the start of hostilities as a result of the Germano-Soviet pact.

We talked, we tried to convince as many of the undecided people who were impressed and stymied by the Marshal's war record and particularly by calls to remember Verdun.

Thinking back on it, I can now write that the little group of opponents of which we were the hardened core—that included the restaurant owner Philippe, a pummeled veteran of the '14 to '18 war, Gassin, who was the secretary over at the Town Hall, the butcher Clément, and the garage man, Roquebrune—was better suited to carrying out effective propaganda against the Vichy regime than starting to bring the fight to the Germans. They were far away, and only occupied a part of France. The German soldier was only a conqueror by force of arms that hid the true face of Nazism, the cruelty of which was still unknown to us. The real enemy was Vichy.

These months of winter '40–'41 were spent like this, the chrysalis of a Resistance, a kind of expectancy tinged with faint hope, since England had not yet been invaded and was standing up to an unprecedented aerial assault.

Our thoughts went out to the Free French, who counted the sub-Saharan colonies in their camp and whose administrative bodies were gradually declaring their allegiance.

+ + +

Paradoxically, I owe it to the Vichy regime that I finally met an organized resister (if one could really be said to be one at this time). His name was Barthélémy Rique, alias Casimir.

There was definitely suspicion in the Garcin family the day he showed up at the Moulin Rouge and in Fontaine. He was in fact sent by Vichy to oversee the paper-manufacturing business and to set prices. The restrictions which German demands for raw materials imposed on France had caused a complicated maze of regulations to spring up. So you can imagine the reaction that the unwelcome arrival of this kind of civil servant might have caused.

But the ice was broken right away. The man was young, likable, and showed an openness of mind that charmed us right away. On his second visit, it became clear that this civil servant sent by Vichy had drunk from the same well as we. That he belonged to the same generation as we sealed the deal. We formed a close friendship that the years have scarcely altered.

One can easily imagine that our young man's banter was not limited to the close reading of Vichy economic circulars. If politics quickly became the central subject, the means to influence them wasn't on the day's agenda.

Not at first. I remember well the tipping point that marked my joining the Resistance. It must have been in the spring of '41. We were coming back from a walk near the Moulin Rouge. Casimir was smoking one of his Gauloises, and I was pulling on my pipe with my usual application. It was not yet time to head in for lunch, so we sat down on the wall of the little bridge. There was a long moment when all we could hear was the rushing sound of the Sorgue. Barthélemy was looking at me and I definitely knew that something big was coming. I was completely unaware of his clandestine activities, but I greeted his words with no surprise.

—Would you be all right with the idea of joining an organization?

I understood right away that he wasn't talking about a stamp-collecting club or a ping-pong team. I simply nodded my head, yes. He likewise was not surprised either. The course my life was to take was decided on that day.

I don't recall talking about this openly with my mother or my father. I was twenty-four years old and I must have found it humiliating to check with them like a kid. They figured it out right away, and their blessing, although not formally bestowed, was quick to follow.

I used the van from the mill that had been equipped with a gazogène to attend my first meeting, which Casimir had called at the Million garage in Orange. A handshake took the place of a formal contract on signing up. Some instructions regarding security, the choice of an alias (I was to be known as Gamma for several months), and I belonged to the movement known as Libération.

Gustave Collion, a calm but no-nonsense forty-year-old, was the departmental leader of the group. He was known as Lassia. His number-two man was Francis Million. In the Resistance we called him Michel.

Neither of them was new on the scene. Before the war broke out they were both proponents of radical thought in the northern Vaucluse, and my parents had met them often.

Since we had few funds and supplies to work with at that time, our instructions were simple. We were supposed to recruit trustworthy men and organize a Secret Army with the goal of fighting the Vichy regime, and to be ready to engage in military action when the moment came.

In hindsight I can write that we were for the most part a gathering of people of goodwill. We would keep each other informed, and some of us wrote and distributed tracts and slogans. Our leaders would try to reach out to other organizations such as Franc-Tireur, which Albert Benaroy led at the time, or with Combat, both of which were well organized in Avignon and in the southern Vaucluse.

Within Libération, Barthélémy Rique was responsible for recruiting people for the Secret Army by reaching out to men who might be able to fight effectively, as he had done with me. Then we were supposed to form ourselves into groups, and this is what I set about to do.

+ + +

If I had to summarize this period that saw the coming together and the organization of the French Resistance in the Unoccupied Zone, without any real contact with London and the Gaullist movement, I would use a simple analogy. It was the period of the oil slick. Every new recruit in turn contacted one or several like-minded people, and so on.

The essential criterion lay in the area of political opinion, and it was by no means without risk. One had to move ahead with small steps and carefully gather information about the political evolution of targeted individuals.

This is because Pétainism and its grassroots organization, the French Legion of Veterans,[22] that counted several million Frenchmen among its members, had led many former leftists to abandon their previous views.

It was necessary, for starters, to exclude from consideration all but those people whose youth and experience provided some guarantee that they could possibly be of real use to the organization.

One of the very first people whom I thought of was Alphonse Bégou. He was about thirty-five years old and married. He was the farrier smith of Le Thor, in Provençal *lou manescau.*[23]

Outwardly, he appeared to be a quiet father, and he was solidly built, but he turned out to be possessed of a truly prodigious calm and unflinching courage. Working with me in the groupes francs, he was to become Captain Balkan.

A village blacksmith's shop is an excellent place to meet people. In a time when horses were coming back into use, it was never empty and one could go there just as one went to the local pub. Bégou knew everything, he saw everybody in the neighborhood, he could pass messages, repair weapons if needed, or let drop a damning crack about the regime for the benefit of his permanent audience at the forge if he wanted to. The same could be said about his courageous wife, Fonfonette.

I stopped by often enough, and his opinions—a mix of Radical Socialism and Communism—were well known to me. I hasten to add that his aversion to the regime of the Soviets never prevented him from working in close harmony with sworn Communists when it came to smashing the *Boches* and Vichy militiamen.

I had no difficulty drawing him into an adventure that he and I lived through together right up until the Liberation.

My second target was Jules Ten, who later became Captain Crillon in the groupes francs. Born in 1910, he was thirty-one years old at the time. He was a strongman in every sense of the term. Never tired, never discouraged, always ready for action, this taciturn stonemason from Lagnes proved himself to be a charismatic leader and an incomparable commander of men. He was a Com-

22. La Légion française des combattants was formed by an act of law in Vichy in August 1940. All previously existing veterans' groups in France were subsumed into it. At its peak in 1942 it might have counted two million members.

23. A farrier smith is a blacksmith who is competent to make horses' iron shoes and to nail them in place.

munist, and his antipathy for the Vichy regime and for the Nazis left no room for doubt.

We only knew each other by sight. We might have encountered each other on the soccer field when the feisty team from Lagnes met mine, the team from Fontaine de Vaucluse that was in every way its equal in sportsmanship.

I had let Louis Gassin, the secretary over at the Town Hall, know what I was doing. He was a man who had worked for the mayor, that is to say, my father, for ages. So he was aware that I was on the lookout for good people.

—You ought to go see Jules Ten over in Lagnes, he said to me one day.

—Really?

—We talked a bit the other day at the market over in Isle sur la Sorgue. . . . He said the right kind of things. . . .

He said *the right kind of things*. Coming from the mouth of this staunch Provençal republican, this was tantamount to bestowing the Legion of Honor on him in front of the entire regiment.

I met Jules Ten on a small job site where he was building a wall for an enclosure. I didn't beat around the bush. He might not get on board, but I knew I could count on him to keep his mouth shut.

—I'd like to talk with you about politics.

He sent his helper, a boy who was maybe fifteen years old, to fetch a bottle of water. I explained to him very quickly what I had in mind.

—Damn, he said. I've been waiting for this for a long time.

We shook hands and he got back to work. Later, he was to be the man with the burlap sack, the man with the Sten gun, whom the Germans would look for in vain.

Balkan and Crillon also recruited others in turn. They made no mistakes. We did not yet know that there would one day be groupes francs or the United Movements of the Resistance,[24] and the role that we would play in them, but hope made us feel like we were coming alive.

CHAPTER THREE

> To the Soldiers, Sailors and Airmen, and to the People of France, July 14, 1941, marks the celebration of National Faith and Hope for all of us. Of Faith, be-

24. The MUR, Mouvements unis de la Résistance, was the first coalition of Resistance groups that would be organized by Jean Moulin in late 1942. (See glossary.)

> cause never, despite the tears shed by all of France, never have we believed more strongly in her and in her destiny. Of Hope, because we can see on the distant horizon all of the signs of Victory. Soldiers, Sailors, Airmen, Frenchmen, my dear companions! Let us be steadfast, pure and true. At the end of our ordeal there is the greatest glory in all the world, that of men who never gave in.
>
> —Message of General de Gaulle, July 14, 1941

Everyone knows that memory is selective. Today, as I stir my memories of the period, roughly from the spring of 1941 until the end of 1942, I have some difficulty remembering the details of what we did.

Military events were so important then, the USSR's entry into the war, then that of the US, that they tend to overshadow the modest beginnings of our clandestine activity.

Secondly, the often dramatic intensity of what we did in the period that followed, after the creation of the groupes francs, skews our sense of perspective and has led to a certain neglect of the prior episode. It cannot be dismissed as the time of a wait-and-see game, however.

We were not active in the propaganda game, distributing tracts and writing graffiti and other inscriptions on walls in cities and villages. Other people did this quite well. It was at this time that we first saw bloom the V for victory adorned with a cross of Lorraine.

An official report of the National Police that I have in front of me in fact deplores the proliferation of these signs that the Resistance was alive and well. The diligent captain who wrote it includes a handsome bouquet of such clandestine scribblings to his higher-ups. It is dated February 1941. In it one can read the contents of a tract that was widely distributed in the mailboxes of residents of Orange:

> *FRENCHMEN!*
>
> If you want to remain worthy of the name and wish to see the father land reborn, strong and FREE . . .
>
> If you want to reclaim the ground under your feet and be able to live upon it in Peace:
>
> Place all of your trust in DE GAULLE

Help in every way you can and fight with him
FOR YOUR OWN GOOD.

And, continues the meticulous policeman, this was not all. In bright red paint on the walls of the town one could also read:

FREE FRANCE FIRST!
FRANCE WILL WIN!
FREE FRANCE WILL TRIUMPH!

And:

A PEOPLE THAT DOESN'T DEFEND ITSELF IS NOT WORTHY OF LIVING!

He goes on to deplore the fact that an investigation into the origin of these provocations, particularly in stationery stores, had turned up nothing. . . .

Perhaps the captain would have found out more if he had come to the Moulin Rouge or to Fontaine to conduct his investigation. My uncle and my father never hesitated to supply paper to organizations that were engaged in resistance, including Communists, if they asked them for it. It is true that the person Vichy had charged with overseeing production was a certain Barthélémy Rique, whom I had come to know by the name of Casimir.

These signs of a simmering spirit of resistance, still lacking in structure and sometimes entirely the work of individuals, never failed to move me. These tracts, these slogans, in chalk or in paint, very often coming from outside of our movement, made us aware that others besides us, moved by the same will, were working for the same cause.

For my little group, without wishing to underestimate the value of propaganda, it was only one way of arriving at our ultimate goal. Getting weapons and fighting. That was the only course of action that interested us. We were young, and we wanted to rip into the forces of the Vichy regime, as we were soon to demonstrate. We had some personal firearms, automatic pistols or ancient revolvers, dug out of drawers of night tables or from under piles of bedsheets in family wardrobes. But we didn't have sleeping bags, clothes, shoes and tools, everything that is needed in order to mobilize and to start living a clandestine life.

We had no idea at that time what life in the maquis was going to be like. But Vichy's politics and the presence in the government or very close to it of men like Laval, Déat, de Brinon, Darquier de Pellepoix and Doriot[25] gave us ample reason to imagine a growing repression that would oblige us to take the plunge into full-time life in the shadows.

So we found ourselves pretty much in the state of mind of a community of squirrels as winter approaches, one that they sense will be long and hard at that. We had to stock up on necessities. Which is to say we had to steal and stash whatever we could. Of all the involuntary suppliers of the Resistance, the Chantiers de la jeunesse were without a doubt the most trusted, the best stocked and the most appreciated. At the time when Resistance groups were forming, one could almost believe that the Chantiers had been created in order to be broken into and robbed or held up at gunpoint. Let us say that their leaders preferred the latter approach because it made them look less bad. . . .

The Chantiers were numerous in our part of the country. Their headquarters was in Cavaillon, and the young people who took part in them lived all around, in the Trou du rat in Robion or in la Laine, an old abandoned factory at the foot of the Carpentras aqueduct in Fontaine. This is where Jules Ten began to clean them out, starting around the end of December of 1941.

The booty from his raids, all acquired without striking a blow, was stored in a former iron mine not far from *lou mas dou Cat,* otherwise known as the farm of le Chat.

The young people who fulfilled their national service in this way were led by nice young officers who were bored to death doing insignificant forestry projects. I ran into them often at the café and sometimes, too, at their camp when they invited us there. They were very close to agreeing with us about the National Revolution and the paternalist slogans of Vichy.

The day after one of these "revolutionary reappropriations," as our modern leftists would call them, the captain only seemed mildly indignant about it. He was describing what had happened quite calmly when Ten, who had heard we were there talking, walked up and joined the conversation. He ordered the

25. This is a list of some of the most notorious collaborators in Vichy: Pierre Laval (1883–1945), the number-two man in Vichy, twice minister of foreign affairs and Pétain's designated successor; Marcel Déat (1894–1955), a Socialist who founded the RNP and was minister of labor; Fernand de Brinon (1885–1947), Vichy's ambassador to the German occupation authority in Paris; Darquier de Pellepoix (1897–1980), director of the Office for Jewish Affairs; and Jacques Doriot (1898–1945), a Communist who founded the PPF. (See glossary.)

next round of *pastis*.[26] Nothing in the officer's attitude suggested that any of us were acquainted.

Apart from this kind of action, we were also engaged in sabotage. We spent our nights unbolting train rails, blowing up electric power pylons with charges of antique perchlorate explosives or dynamite that Pierre Bascou, the owner of the limestone quarry over in Le Coustellet, generously provided us.

I told this story not long ago to a friend of mine who is a died-in-the-wool Resistance history buff and he was surprised. He pointed out that at this time we probably hadn't any instruction as to what to do because the region wasn't actually occupied and the targets we hit were of little strategic value. This was all quite true, we acted entirely on our own pure and youthful initiative. I could only tell him the truth:

—We were just exploring what we could do. We wanted something to happen. . . . We were young. . . . Standing at parade rest was not our style. . . .

To truly understand the situation of a resister at this time, one first has to realize that each movement was totally unaware of what was happening inside every other group. Their members were all unknown to us, even though we were all still living out in the open.

It was sometimes quite funny, and mistaken assumptions were the order of the day. As witness a completely benign summons I received in 1941 from Ferdinand Bec, the Chief Advocate of the court in Avignon. The man was entirely on the level, had an excellent reputation, was a schoolmate of my uncle Voltaire at the lycée Mistral and always looked out for the business interests of the Moulin Rouge and of the paper mill in Fontaine de Vaucluse. The only flaw in the picture was that he belonged to the political right, however moderate he was, and in consequence of this he held the position of president of the Special Delegation.[27] And because of this he had been appointed mayor of Avignon by Vichy when the elected mayor, senator Louis Gros, was stripped of his office because he was a Socialist.

I could hardly refuse to honor a perfectly reasonable invitation to meet with him. He received me at his private home in the rue Pontmartin with warmth and conviviality. I was unable to grant what he wanted from me, how-

26. *Pastis* is an anisette liqueur that is extremely popular in southern France.

27. *La délégation spéciale*, a special administrative task force, usually consisting of three to five people, that is convened when extreme circumstances leave a municipality or a regional government without leadership. It is delegated to appoint a mayor or to make any other interim administrative decisions as may be deemed necessary.

ever, and I used the vaguest of pretexts, though not without firmness, to reject his offer.

He wanted to offer the young industrialist and veteran that I was the position of president of the Legion, an odd kind of single party expressly formed to glorify Vichy! If he hadn't been propped up against his austere legal bookshelves, so imposing behind his desk, I might have decided to laugh!

This story is indicative of the confusion that now reigned in minds that usually thought more clearly. This man, who ran a city that was the administrative seat of its department, with sixty thousand inhabitants at the time, who was a gifted lawyer, could—because of the circumstances—imagine that a member of a family with a distinguished republican record would serve without difficulty under the banner of an old soldier, the head of an increasingly fascist state, who was intent on burying that very Republic. . . . It's a little as if, the day after Franco came to power, someone had invited la Passionaria to join the Phalange.[28]

Back at the Moulin Rouge, my uncle Voltaire thought he could detect in this bizarre initiative some tortuous political maneuver, I cannot recall exactly what. I preferred to see it as the product of a tragic naïveté. The aura of the Marshal was so compelling at the time that the barrister Bec simply could not imagine that a young factory owner of his acquaintance might not be susceptible to its attraction.

As resisters, I was aware and proud, we were only outsiders in a France that was fast asleep in the cult of the providential father. It wasn't wildly reassuring. Fortunately, this was only a passing delusion.

+ + +

On July 14, 1942, we became aware of the importance of what I might call the party of the Resistance, in opposition to the proclaimed and assumed unanimity of good citizens who favored Vichy.

The radio broadcast of Free France had called on everyone to demonstrate on that day in all of the cities in France. In the course of the week prior, tracts put out by all of the various movements had picked up and were echoing the call. I left Vaucluse alone on my bicycle at 4 p.m. heading for Avignon.

28. La Passionaria was Dolores Ibárruri (1895–1989), a Spanish/Basque journalist, public speaker, and singer. A member of the Spanish Communist Party during the Spanish Civil War, she had to flee Spain after Franco's rise to power. La Phalange: the Spanish Nationalist (Fascist) militia.

The stepping-off point that had been circulated in whispers was to be the courtyard in front of the railroad station, from which point the participants would parade up to the place de l'Horloge via the rue de la République.

The moment I arrived I was surprised by the size of the crowd. We were more numerous than I had ever imagined. I found Ten, who had come directly from his place, and Fofon Bégou (Alphonse), who was there with three of his friends from Le Thor. We were not armed, because it was supposed to be a peaceful and a silent demonstration.

This was not the last of my pleasant surprises. Among these men and women I recognized a lot of faces of people whom I had never suspected to have such a public attachment to democracy and such a hostility to Pétain. Elbow to elbow, here were anonymous shopkeepers together with doctors and lawyers. . . . I saw solid community leaders I could identify. We felt less alone.

Our slow procession up to the place de l'Horloge and the City Hall was carried out with calm determination. The thin cordon of good-natured policemen posted to stop us at the level of the former army barracks that is now the city's administrative complex gave way immediately without violence.

Not wanting to be seen together any more than necessary, our little group then melted into the crowd. Myself, I looked like a peaceful young man with his bicycle at hand. I use the word "crowd" on purpose, by the way, although it is not my own. The prefect himself used it in his report on the events to Vichy.

Things degenerated rapidly on the place de l'Horloge. From inside the headquarters of the Legion, which was located on the first floor of a building on the edge of the square, a response emerged that was as ragtag as the individuals that made it up. Over a loudspeaker, these sorry individuals announced to the public that a train car had just arrived at the station filled with chocolates from England intended for the Jews and the Gaullists. . . . What a sense of humor on the eve of the Vel d'Hiv roundup![29]

There were whistles and shouts. Some people began to sing the first stanza of the Marseillaise. Then we witnessed the unimaginable: the authorities sent in units of the SOL, the Service d'ordre légionnaire, the sinister predecessor of Darnand's Militia, to drive everyone out of the square. The national anthem was that unbearable to them!

29. *Note in French edition:* The Vélodrome d'Hiver in Paris. [This is where 13,000 Jews, including 4,000 children, arrested all over Paris, were held in an indoor bicycle stadium on July 17, 1942, before being dispersed into transit camps and ultimately deported east—Ed.]

The dispersal happened with no further incidents. All of which may seem very tame today, in the light of what we know happened over the next two years, but on that day I pedaled my bicycle back home to my family with satisfaction in my heart. I had met some real Frenchmen!

CHAPTER FOUR

> I want the Germans to win.
>
> —Pierre Laval, June 22, 1942

> In the light of the extraordinary circumstances, the Marshal, who will continue as head of the State, to embody French sovereignty and the continuity of the fatherland, has decided to confer upon President Laval the powers of a head of government, to allow him to confront swiftly, at any hour and in any place, the difficulties that France is going through.
>
> —Marshal Pétain, November 17, 1942

In the night of December 31, 1941, an agent of General de Gaulle named Rex parachuted into the Provençal countryside. He was charged with the task of linking up all of the different Resistance organizations in the Unoccupied Zone. It was a mission whose purpose and necessity we agreed with. That man was Jean Moulin.

A request that was made by Paul Faraud, then the departmental head of Combat, to Libération, led me to be a witness to his landing. In fact, I was asked to take part in the security team to meet three agents from London. Leading a swat team was a mission that resonated with me. I wasn't told any more than this, and I didn't ask.

The assignment that involved me was set for a late afternoon at a farmhouse that I had no trouble finding. The farmer who lived there didn't ask me a single question, and his numerous family members didn't seem at all surprised by my presence. That night, after a dinner where the conversation never ventured beyond matters of food shortages and the weather, a man I had never met before came to get me. Together we made our way to a stone hut where he posted me. Hours passed alone and in silence. I understood that I was not alone on duty out there, but I saw no one and I didn't perceive any friendly or suspicious activity. My automatic pistol was loaded, and I waited.

Around one or two in the morning, I finally could hear the rumbling of the Whitley[30] that was approaching. Next I followed the slow progress of three parachutes in the silence of the winter night. They disappeared behind the dark rows of cypress trees that limited my view in the darkness around me. After what seemed like a very long hour, the same anonymous resister came to tell me I could go. He let me know that *everything worked out just fine.* I slept in the barn of the farmhouse where we had met. After a hearty breakfast that was served without chit-chat, I had nothing to keep me from heading home at the wheel of the gazogène truck. I crossed the river via the bridge at Bonpas,[31] where checkpoints were frequent, without being stopped or running into any trouble.

I didn't find out until much later that the person who had parachuted was called Rex, and that he was the boss of all of us. So, even if only very slightly, I had participated in an event that will forever define the history of the French Resistance. The north wind, our mistral, that pushed the parachutes a bit too far south, and doubtless also the usual problems of pilot error prevented me from actually meeting Jean Moulin.

It was not the only opportunity I had to work next to him. In May of 1943, when I was in Paris for one of my meetings with my direct superior, Duroc, he asked me to stand by for a mission that he described as very important, to serve as security for a high-level meeting. It was supposed to take place in a suburb of Lyon at a place and a date that would be communicated to me in due course.

The confirmation never arrived, and on the following 21st of June, in Caluire, on the immediate outskirts of Lyon, Moulin was arrested along with the principal leaders of the Resistance.

Despite all our standing orders and the usual rules, no protective measures had been taken. Had someone proposed to assure the protection of the meeting by a group of their own choosing and then desisted?

On that day the Nazis arrested men who were exposed and unarmed. They knew it, and they weren't a large group.

One of the great regrets of the groupes francs is that they were not there that day. Perhaps I wouldn't be here to tell the story, but Moulin would not have been led to his death like a beast to the slaughter. I have an idea as to

30. A model AW 38 twin-engined British bomber manufactured by the Armstrong Whitworth aircraft company.

31. This is the pont de Noves, over the Durance River, seven miles south of Avignon.

who was responsible. What am I saying, an idea? A certainty. We shall have occasion to come back to this.[32]

+ + +

Jean Moulin's mission was to bring together all of the different resistant organizations. With the irrefutable logic that hindsight affords us, today this seems like it simply had to happen. How can one help imagining that a group of individuals, motivated by the same ideals, mobilized by the same enemies, Vichy and the Nazis, would be able to understand each other, and join up?

In the real world of the time and of the circumstances, things were decidedly less simple. We have already said that these organizations didn't have much contact with each other. Their different standing orders in fact absolutely ruled out any such contact. Added to which there were personal issues, different opinions about rank, function and responsibilities. The new organization had to have a strict hierarchy in order to ensure its smooth operation. Some people were going to have to defer to others, which it is easy to see was not going to appeal to everyone.

So it took Moulin a while to bring about the union of the three principal movements, the only ones on the ground not counting the intelligence networks set up by the British, like Buckmaster, that kept their legitimate autonomy.

On November 27, 1942, eleven months after he had parachuted in, fifteen days after the Nazi invasion of the southern zone, Moulin was finally able to hold the first meeting of the United Movements of the Resistance (MUR).[33]

It was held in Lyon, in the presence of General Delestraint, whom de Gaulle had named as commander of the Secret Army. Frenay represented Combat; Lévy, Franc-Tireur; and d'Astier de la Vigerie, Libération. All three agreed to join their organizations into one. The MUR was born.

There was one important group missing, it has to be said. This was the Francs-Tireurs Partisans Français (FTPF), a group that had a largely Commu-

32. In chapter 9, pages 85–87, of his book, Garcin will argue that the arrest of a resister in Marseilles, one Jean Multon, also known as "Lunel," was the likely source of the information that led to Moulin's arrest, torture, and death in German custody during the summer of 1943. For a detailed recent analysis of most of the arguments regarding this key event, see Jacques Gelin's *L'Affaire Jean Moulin: Trahison ou complot?* (Paris: Gallimard, 2013).

33. This was in fact a meeting of the coordinating committee that laid the groundwork for the first meeting of the MUR proper, which was held in January 1943.

nist majority. They were no less present on the ground, had paid their dues in blood, and were fighting courageously on their own, specializing in hitting individual targets and in railroad sabotage.

+ + +

It seems to me unnecessary to revisit all of the discussions, quite often over-the-top, that the local hierarchies engaged in in the run-up to the meeting in Lyon. It is well known enough to be left to the specialists who have dissected it under the looking-glass of their personal opinions.[34]

The Resistance was flourishing in the Vaucluse. The three movements that were about to link up were all represented there, as was the FTPF, and the Front National, which was headed by Dr. Georges Pons.[35]

The men of action strongly resented the need for this union which would be good for everyone and would furnish the means needed to carry on the armed struggle that we hoped would be widespread as well as effective. For us, an attack group that was already up and running, looking for arms and explosives, the union would mean a clarification and a simplification of our relationship with London. And, along with precise instructions, general objectives and appropriate weaponry.

Jean Moulin had held one of the innumerable preliminary meetings leading up to the wedding itself in Avignon. The security and the discretion involved were so great that I didn't even find out it had actually happened until several months had gone by. It was held in November, at the Hotel IV, in the rue Bancasse, whose proprietor, Teyssier, was one of our friends. Libération was represented by Collion and Dr. Klotz, also known as Boyer, our departmental leader. Cucumel and Faraud were there representing Combat. I didn't learn of the role that I was to play inside the MUR until later, when I happened to be visiting Yvonne de Komornicka.

Barthélémy Rique called me, it must have been the end of 1942 or the beginning of 1943. He informed me of the structure of the MUR and of the

34. It seems likely that Garcin is thinking about studies by Jean-Pierre Azéma and Henri Michel. The more recent work by Olivier Wieviorka, *Histoire de la Résistance*, also discusses this moment in some detail.

35. *Note in French edition:* A political party that was founded by the Communist Resistance organizations, or that was close to the Communists. [This group has no connection with the contemporary party of the same name.—Ed.]

naming of its departmental head, Kléber, at the meeting which he had called at his house in Orange, where he was still living with his family. He didn't tell me much more than this, and I didn't get tangled up asking a lot of questions. We would see well enough. The pseudonym of Kléber evoked an authentic warrior and had a nice ring about it. It suggested we were going to see action, and talking about it with Ten and Bégou, I recall we were happy about how things were going.

On the appointed day, Casimir took me to the entrance of a villa off of the Sixte-Isnard boulevard, at number 4 rue des Chalets in Avignon, and I still do not know if he was hiding the news from me for fun or not. A girl, seventeen years old, gracious and attractive, answered the door. She recognized Casimir and said she would go and fetch her mother.

The mother didn't make us wait long. She was a pretty woman, forty years old at most, with ebony black hair. She looked us straight in the eyes. She shook hands with each of us, then looked me up and down, weighing me, to be more precise, with an eye that was clearly used to authority but was friendly all the same.

I was already under a spell that was to last close to fifty years.

This woman had a real presence, it was unmistakable. But being a good man of the South I could only imagine one thing, that she was the wife of this Kléber fellow whom I had come to meet, and to follow his orders. . . .

That's when Casimir pushed my astonishment to the top:

—So, Jean. Meet Kléber.

+ + +

It was not out of the blue that Yvonne de Komornicka was chosen to head the MUR in the department of the Vaucluse. She had already proven herself.

Starting in 1940, in Nancy, where she lived with her three daughters, she set up an escape network for prisoners of war. They mostly came from camps in occupied Lorraine, and her network helped them to reach the Unoccupied Zone in the South via the Jura, the regions of the Arbois, and Bugey. That kind of activity couldn't go on in such a sensitive area close to the border indefinitely.

Informed that she was on the verge of being arrested, she fled from Lorraine and wound up in Avignon, where a number of her compatriots, expelled by the Reich when it annexed their province, had already taken refuge. Among this group, there was a man, a real one, the abbot Krebs, the chaplain of the

Lorraine refugees, an outspoken proponent of Gaullism, patriot and man of courage. He was in touch with Frenay, and he was the founder of Combat in the Vaucluse.

We know how many priests were involved in the Resistance. We are also aware of the actions of a number of bishops in the defense of those minorities that the Nazis had plans to wipe out entirely. The Vaucluse was not lucky enough to have such a man in the episcopal seat. Monsignor Llobet, the archbishop of the city, could not condone the actions, admittedly way ahead of their time, of the abbot Krebs. He was thrown out of the diocese, and it fell quite naturally to his assistant, Yvonne de Komornicka, to succeed him.

After her arrest in 1943 and her deportation to Ravensbrück, Paul Faraud took over. Faraud was the former mayor who was turned out by Vichy, a veteran of the 1914–18 war, an officer in the reserves, and a resister from the very first hours of the occupation.

We met, that day, in the villa where her flock of young ladies served us a drink that wanted to be called tea but was in fact just a tisane.

Kléber had seated herself on a kind of *cathedra* with cupboards where she ruled over us, and from whence emanated orders and directives. Including, among other matters, those that interested me first and foremost, the creation inside the MUR of a number of groupes francs charged with immediate action, from acts of sabotage to the protection of other organizational activities.

I didn't dare to simply propose my services on the spot as a volunteer. The training that I had received in my regiment of engineers as well as in the field since the start of the war, my small but very real contributions to date, entitled me to do so, but I didn't dare.

What relief I felt, as she wound up her discussion of this topic, when she officially appointed and renamed me in a decisive tone of voice:

—You will be the leader of the groupes francs, and your name shall be Bayard!

Our visit ended with a hand extended at a height that precluded any idea of shaking it. Kissing hands was never my forte, but I did my best.

+ + +

I had an appointment that same evening with Jules Ten and Alphonse Bégou. They knew that the unification had been decided on and that we were going to have to work within the new organization.

We drank an artisanal pastis that didn't owe anything at all to the chemists of the house of Pernod and Sons. They would never have approved of the strong taste of marc from the cooperative in Le Thor.

—So? asked Bégou. Who is the new boss?

I took my time answering. In our southern latitudes, there are certain truths that can be difficult to spell out.

—He is called Kléber, I offered judiciously.

—Kléber is great, Ten said, approvingly. What's he like?

In a cowardly way, I preferred to answer him in Provençal.

—*Es oune fume. . . .*[36]

They looked at each other. They doubtless thought that I had gone crazy.

Yes, she's a woman, I repeated myself in a tone that would discourage any wisecracks.

—Well, what of it? She's a woman. . . . So? said Bégou in a forced voice. That's okay!

Ten didn't say anything. He settled for finishing his glass to the very last drop, and left it at that. For my part, I confess I did not tell them anything about kissing Kléber's hand.

CHAPTER FIVE

> Germany is contributing to the reduction of unemployment in France by giving workers who reside there the chance to work in Germany. It is right to collaborate loyally with German services in their effort to recruit willing laborers.
>
> —Vichy directive to all prefects, March 29, 1943

The Nazis thought they could bring the USSR down in a few months. Their first successes encouraged them to believe in their dream of being invincible warriors. As of the following winter, 1941–42, their dream had flown out the window. The vastness of Russia had played its part. It was to go on for a while.

Hitler has to revise his plans for industry. He needs a lot of men and women to turn out shells, to melt steel, to get ready, to assemble planes and tanks. . . . The supply line toward the eastern front is like the bottomless barrel of the Danaids.

36. *Note in French edition:* In Provençal: "She's a woman."

Up until now the Germans had made do with volunteers. There weren't all that many of them. In March of 1942 only 14,000 French workers went to work in the weapons factories of the Reich. The number is laughable when you think that Belgium sent 122,000 during the same period, Holland 134,000, and tiny Denmark 63,000.

Clearly volunteer help won't cut it. So they would have to increase propaganda advertising it. With Vichy's help, of course, and they join in with no shame. In Lille there will be a publicity bus painted in the color scheme of the National Revolution encouraging volunteers to the strains of "Marshal, Here we are!" In truth, a pretty sorry business.

First there was "The Relief,"[37] three skilled workers toward the freedom of one French P.O.W.

It will also fail, despite the efforts of the evil Laval, who wrote to von Ribbentrop on May 12, 1942, the following lines that hardly need any explication:

> . . . I want the French people, in the greatest possible numbers, to fill the vacancies in your factories created by those workers who are leaving for the eastern front. The French are rooted in their native soil, but I know that they are ready to leave it for a task whose national and historical importance has been explained to them. I will do my utmost to this end, and I beg you to help me by providing a psychological terrain which will facilitate my work. . . .

As a psychological aid, Hitler will call out of obscure anonymity one of his fanatics from the very start, the Gauleiter,[38] Fritz Sauckel, whom he appoints as of March 1942:

> General Plenipotentiary for Labor Deployment

He is an impulsive brute whose name will be forever linked to deportation for an entire generation of Europeans. He has no illusions about relying on

37. La Relève, of May–June, 1942, was a plan put forward by Laval in response to F. Sauckel's call for 250,000 French workers in May 1942. The demands would increase in size, and the Vichy regime's response would only become more coercive. In February 1943, Vichy began to draft young French men and women under a program called the Service du travail obligatoire (STO).

38. A Gauleiter was the leader of a regional branch of the Nazi Party.

volunteerism and the relief effort that is quickly denounced by radio from London as a fool's deal, and by the Resistance with their slogan:

ENOUGH PRISONERS!
ENOUGH HOSTAGES!

Sauckel demands 500,000 skilled workers from Laval. The head of the government waffles a bit, and then, as he often does with Nazi decrees, he capitulates. This will result in the Law of September 4, 1942, *concerning the use and future purpose of the workforce.*

This text obliges all men aged 18 to 50, and all unmarried women between 21 and 35 years of age, to undertake such work as the government judges useful in the greater interest of the nation.

The French people generally know how to read between the lines. And, if they don't know how to, the Resistance is there to help them.

Combat calls for civil mobilization of the nation against *mobilization for slavery.* The Francs-Tireurs et Partisans accuse Laval of being *a slave trader. . . .* For its part, Libération calls on workers and bosses to introduce errors into official paperwork so as to *clog up the vast administrative machine that Vichy has created.*

It is not yet the great departure toward the maquis, but we were getting closer. Already, the day after this scheme organized by the traitors who governed us, some people started receiving their convocation to leave for Germany. . . .

Myself, I received a form to fill out. . . . It was time to take the plunge.

+ + +

It was on that October day in 1942 that my real life as a resister began. With the overriding obligation to respect certain rules, neglect of which could result in torture and death.

I never broke them and, doubtless, I owe it to this that I made it through that war without experiencing the worst. I owe it equally to the organization of the groupes francs, which I will soon come back to.

These rules of life that I adopted for myself, and that I would pound into our new recruits' heads, were basically quite simple:

—Modify your physical appearance as much as possible. Myself, I began wearing a pair of glasses with clear nonprescription lenses, and I grew a moustache.

—Attract no attention, by wearing classic clothing. I favored a sport jacket and a plain raincoat.

—Don't adopt habits. I never slept in the same place for more than a few days. I never let myself frequent a restaurant or a café.

—Break off all connection with prior life. This was certainly the hardest part. I didn't see my father or mother again after the day when I decided to take the leap. My father never came back from Buchenwald, and I didn't see my mother or my uncle until the Liberation, although I passed very close to home quite often.

—Take on an entire new identity, of course. Mine was one that was provided for me a little later on, and it really made my work a lot easier. I became police inspector Jean Rigaud, an identity with a supreme bonus attached to it: the police department in Lyon, which I was supposed to be working for, included a number of patriots who twice confirmed the authenticity of my existence when I was stopped, once in Marseilles and once in Paris, and a telephone inquiry made. . . .

—Speak as little as possible, and know even less.

—Don't trust anyone except your own men, your immediate superiors, and your chosen go-betweens.

—And, in case all of that isn't enough, carry a loaded weapon, with a chambered round.

I was not the only one to have "taken the plunge." There were many for whom the requirement to register or being called to appear for service drove them to leave their home or their factory. They weren't yet resisters, just defiant people for whom the idea of forced labor (it was nothing other), in Germany or anywhere else was simply not acceptable.

They left their homes, went to live with friends, or headed for the nearest mountainside. It became necessary to take care of them, to find ways for them to survive, find false papers for them, all of which were things that my grandfather, a former mayor, and my mother, set about doing without delay.

It was in response to this that woodcutters' camps were created. These were not yet maquis even, but they were going to become ones. It was Marcellin, a timber farmer in Lioux, in the Vaucluse mountains, who made this possible by hiring them. Plenty of men wanted to sign on. We took them in a truck that was perfectly in order, thanks to our friend Pierre Bascou, and in this way they dropped out of sight.

I might as well say that feeding these men was not easy, and that with enforcement immediately making itself felt, the maintenance of this system depended more on acrobatics and good luck than on a healthy organization. I must also say that a clandestine existence did not agree with everyone in this little world. Some even went so far as to complain about not getting any chocolate. . . .

It was difficult to continue in this manner. I got the name and address of the man I needed to speak to from one of my contacts in the MUR.

This was Colonel Beyne, of the group Combat. A tax-collector in Sault, he organized a resistance group in the wild and wooded Ventoux mountain countryside starting in 1941.

Beyne was solidly built, corpulent even, jovial, and he inspired confidence. His name will be forever linked with that of the Ventoux maquis, which he commanded right up to the Liberation. A veteran of Verdun, the Republic that he helped to restore made him a grand officer of the Legion of Honor.

I met him for the first time at the close of 1942 in Sault. Free of any occupation troops and already protecting a brigade of the *gendarmerie* that was at the very least accommodating. I want to salute the *gendarmerie nationale* at this time for, in the overwhelming majority of cases, having known how to ignore the patriots and for often taking part in the skirmishes alongside us at the Liberation.

The village behaved like it was a freed commune already. Our conversation, in the company of Max Fisher, his adjutant, a nice Parisian fellow, took place in the main square, out in the sun, peace and quiet, and even a kind of euphoria. We had no idea what was to come, which explains how we could feel that way.

He agreed in principle to expand his contingent by forty of my woodcutters. They would bunk in abandoned farmhouses with his men who were taking basic military training on the slopes of the Ventoux, and they would be supplied by Bascou, Fleury Mitifiot from Cavaillon, and la Maguette from Plan de Saumane.

Why should I hide the fact that some of my recruits did not find themselves housed in the comfort to which they were accustomed? Beyne made everybody who stayed sign unequivocal military articles. Some people refused. . . . I didn't stick around to find out what else was in store for them. Beyne invited me to remain as part of his staff. I declined. My temperament led me to want to take part in action. This suited me better than waiting around for a widespread insurrection.

+ + +

So, some weeks later, I was in fact named to direct the activity of all of the groupes francs in the Vaucluse. Yvonne de Komornicka introduced me to the head of Region 2, my immediate commander.[39] He was Charles Gonard, also known as Morlot in the Resistance. A cold, dry man, I nonetheless maintained good relations with him. Our involvement was never tinged by actual enthusiasm, however.

I think that he must have decided very early on exactly what I was capable of doing for him, since soon afterward he asked me to take over, in addition to the Vaucluse, the command of the groupes francs in the Bouches-du-Rhône and in particular of Marseilles. It was only after his departure for Paris that I took command of Region 2, which corresponded to the contemporary region of PACA,[40] and the river bank of the Rhone valley in the department of the Gard.

My being named for the Vaucluse was not a problem at all for me. My group was already in place. It's time to say a word or two about them.

Besides Bégou-Balkan and Ten-Crillon, whom you are already familiar with, our little team consisted of a bunch of guys who were ready for action, and who had proved it a number of times already.

There was Yvon Darriès, a pharmacist's assistant, whose determination was easily equal to the feeling of warmth that he inspired in people; René Peyrerol, champion automobile racer and true mechanical genius; Jacques Robert, with the fashionable manner of a man of the world; Jean Pécout, a successful farmer from Lagnes; and others, without forgetting Oscar, one of the bravest and most committed of the lot. Maneo Nutti, also known as Oscar, was born in Italy, from whence his family, pursued by the fascists, was driven. No sooner were they settled in France than they had to confront the same hideous beast. . . . He showed that he was not a man who would make peace with them lightly.

The average age hovered around twenty-five. Only Bégou was a grown man. He was pushing forty, but he went at everything with the strength of the young. For every operation we planned they were all ready, willing and able.

They went underground, some sooner, some later. Bégou never went. He remained *lou Manescau,* the farrier smith of Le Thor, a peaceful and jovial

39. The former southern zone of France was divided into six regions, each designated by a number, while the former northern zone was divided into six zones, each designated by a letter.

40. *Note in French edition:* The current administrative region of Provence-Alpes-Côte d'Azur.

citizen who appeared to mind his own business. And if he had to put some distance between himself and his family for a few days during the Liberation, it was only because of his own one-time slip-up.

The Germans, who were still fighting in Marseilles and Toulon, were evacuating their heavy materiel via the railroad. Over tracks that were our territory, like a true Buckmaster, Fofon Bégou had noted the presence of one of their convoys that was standing in the station at Le Thor.

A day and a half later, it is Sunday noon. The streets are packed with people. Everyone is talking about what was going on, people are debating this and that, when all of a sudden three fighter bombers appear with British insignia on them, flying at a low altitude. They bank into a turn and head back towards the village. It doesn't occur to anyone to seek shelter. Why would anyone bomb Le Thor?

It is then that it dawns on Bégou. If the planes are there at all, it is not because of some intervention of the Holy Ghost, and that it is in fact because of him that they are there!

—Hide! They're here to bomb the railroad station!

The English pilots were very accurate. No one among the population was hurt, but such an accurate prediction of what was about to happen, and indeed such keen insight into Allied strategy in the first place, could easily have made some ill-intentioned souls wonder. That night, and for several days afterwards, Alphonse Bégou did not sleep in his own bed. It was nonetheless quite uncommon behavior for the man.

+ + +

I was, and I still am, very proud of the groupe franc team that I formed in the Vaucluse. To command the one in Marseilles, as Morlot ordered me to do, was more of a problem for me. They were men I did not know, with whom I was going to have to take some serious risks and whom I was going to have to ask to take yet others. How would they feel about my stepping in as their leader? Must I also add that the pressure Morlot appeared to be under when he placed me in charge of them was disturbing as well?

It was at the so-called Temple of Beer, in the Allée Léon Gambetta, that Morlot finally introduced me to Levis, once we had gone through the rigmarole of our clandestine practice, ascertaining that we had not been tailed, identification of all possible suspects, determining the manner of initiating the contact. Levis had been the head of the Marseilles groupe franc up until then.

I was seated across from a graceful and willowy young man, possessed of a definite yet discreet elegance. He was a student, or at least he appeared to be, twenty-two or twenty-three years old, and he had a smile that would never lead one to suspect he had a thorough knowledge of weapons, grenades and explosives.

I can't remember what we were drinking that day, but unbeknownst to us it was a cup of friendship. Our close understanding never knew a bad day. Daring almost to the point of trying the impossible, organized and always ready to take command, during real firefights and at Liberation, he was a man who could be counted on, and I weigh my words well.

Once contact had been made, as our protocol required, Morlot disappeared. We smiled as we ordered another round. For better or for worse, we were both in the same pickle.

Like me, he hadn't waited for two years, as the unpopularity of Vichy and the Nazi occupation of the southern zone grew, to become involved in resisting. In 1941—and he only twenty at the time—this young man from the Lozère[41] tried to join the Free French forces by going through Spain. There he got to know the guards in Franco's prisons before they turned him over to Vichy.

Our ideas were in complete harmony. Jean Comte—that was his real name—favored direct action. Like me, he only saw propaganda, an essential part of resister activity at the time to be sure, as a way to make underground acts of war known to the general population, and to explain their necessity.

Direct action first and foremost! This perfectly sums up the meaning that we were determined to give to our resistance to Vichy and to the occupier. It was also at the root of the difficulties that clouded our relations with the other sections of the MUR and their Directorate.

People from the Secret Army, from propaganda, from infiltration of the public services or social agencies frequently saw the smooth operation of their activities disturbed by reactions, reprisals, and the tightening of repression that our violent engagements, sabotage and executions provoked from militiamen, Vichy cops, and other Nazis.

However, there never was a real head-to-head with the Directorate, but how many times did they urge us to have more patience, to calm down. . . .

Out of this difference of points of view emerged a situation that served our purposes in a number of ways. We would become a quasi-independent organ-

41. Lozère is the department of France just to the north of the Languedoc-Roussillon region, 250 kilometers northwest of Marseilles.

ism in the larger body of the Resistance, with little or no connection to other units of the MUR. In addition to relative freedom of action, this autonomy also granted us security, which resulted in our having relatively few losses and arrests. This was not true, as the *affaire Flora* showed, in other sectors of the Resistance.[42]

+ + +

Levis quickly brought me up to speed regarding his team, which posed no particular problems. The larger-scale operations that the MUR assigned to us required us to make many changes, but in fact even this was never a source of real difficulties. Levis showed me their drop boxes, their meeting places, and their safe houses. Over the next months we made many improvements in all of this.

The Hotel du Caire, just off of the Old Harbor, provided me with a much appreciated place to stay. Lucien, the proprietor, and his wife did a great job of acting like they didn't know what I was really involved in. Without ever once mentioning it to me, they never asked me to fill out a police hotel registration card, all the while pointing out that it was easy to get anywhere in the neighborhood directly via the rooftops. Discreet people.

Reputed to be hot, the neighborhood of the Opera, as it was called, was perfect for my purposes, and I held my meetings there often. The preferred place to go to ground in Marseilles, and the rule of silence had become its dominant faith. The French gestapists were also well represented there, which afforded clandestines like us an additional bonus. Document controls were actually less frequent there than elsewhere.

We also had other places to meet up. These were mainly the larger cafés along the Canebière, each of which corresponded to a different day of the week: Monday was the Café Riche, Tuesday the next one along, going up the avenue, and so on. . . .

Our corporate headquarters, if I can call it that, was without a doubt the AGEM [Association générale des étudiants de Marseille], the local office of the

42. The Flora report was written by Ernst Duncker, also known as Delage, an SIPO-SD (German Reich's Security Police, a division of the Security Service) agent in Marseilles, submitted to the Gestapo in May 1943. It named 241 resisters by name and group, including Jean Multon, and did enormous damage at that time, including in all probability leading indirectly to the arrest of Jean Moulin in Caluire in June.

students' association in Marseilles. It occupied an entire building in the Allées de Meillan. It was a kind of a caravansary where a lot of people came and went all the time; there were lots of games and laughter, an ambiance that suited us perfectly. Just one example of the kind of thing that went on, one day I saw, stacked in a room on the fourth floor that was used for administration of the center, several hundred kilos of explosives. . . .

So this wasn't what preoccupied us for the most part. What took up most of our time was recruitment.

As Madeleine Baudoin (also known as Marianne Bardini) explains extremely well in her book *Histoire des Groupes Francs des Bouches-du-Rhône*, if the Secret Army could muster five regiments—on paper, anyway—it was a lot harder to find volunteers for direct action. They had to be ready to undertake dangerous jobs, cut themselves off as we had done from our prior lives and live in total secrecy, be available day and night, and be in good shape as well as militarily and technically competent. Just being willing was not enough.

In our organization's interest and in their own, we had to test the applicants by giving them a challenge. In order to do this, I myself used a method that proved very effective.

A volunteer would be introduced to me. An interview process had already determined that the basic requirements were met. The patriotism, the spirit of resistance[43] (these two were not always in the same proportion), goodwill and intelligence, were in no way lacking. I would then make a meeting time with him in the neighborhood of the Opera where low dives and whorehouses and nightclubs were plentiful. Entirely by chance as we visited these spots that were popular with the troops of the occupier, I would pick a target, some isolated and passably drunk teuton Feldwebel [staff sergeant], packing a visible sidearm, usually an automatic, highly visible in its holster.

Observing his departure from the table of a sidewalk café across the street or at the corner of the street, I would explain to our candidate that our mission was none other than to procure a weapon for him. What would be more natural than to take that weapon from the enemy? It would be enough to knock him out.

I used this technique five times. One of the boys abandoned me imme-

43. The expression "l'esprit de Résistance" had by 1995 taken on a widely accepted meaning in resister parlance. Not coincidentally, this is the title of a book published in that same year about the Resistance by Serge Ravanel. In his introduction, Ravanel says that this spirit "conveyed a certain ethic in society, with primacy placed on the common good, and a reaffirmation of the Rights of Man . . . a spirit of youth, devotion and responsibility."

diately. He had doubtless formed a different idea of what the groupes francs were all about. Two others excused themselves upon taking a good look at the unfortunate conscript staggering along the sidewalk towards his barracks. The other two carried out their work very neatly with a swiftness and an understanding of the German body-type that did them proud. They were accepted based on this "written exam," and had no need to sit for an oral.

We never tried to go for big numbers, but the quality of men mattered. It was best to do our assigned jobs with the fewest men possible. Levis's team needed men, however, even if it meant I had to get men to come down from the Vaucluse, which I did many times in the days to come.

The two pillars of this team were called Templier—an accomplished forger of false identification papers, but also as cold-blooded and decisive an individual as you could ask for, whom we shall have occasion to talk about during the episode of the escape of a Buckmaster,[44] Claude Lemaire—and Rudy—a toucan of a man with all of the faults and qualities of a happy hotspur.

We will never say enough good about, or celebrate the essential work undertaken by, our liaison agents. They were young women who gave up living peaceful lives to do dangerous things in the service of the agents to whom they were assigned. They provided the sharp-eyed mistrustfulness of a bodyguard with the devotion of a mother duck or a wife. . . .

Yvonne de Komornicka had assigned Paule Algoud to me, and we worked together until Liberation. She was a very brave and savvy young woman. About thirty years old, she could take incredible risks, for example disguising herself as a waitress to go into a police station and pass a message to one of my men, Tibère, who had been arrested a few hours earlier. . . .

Madeleine Baudoin, or Marianne Bardini, was my liaison agent with Levis. She was both brilliant and elegant, a woman you could scarcely fault for anything except her inability to remain still. It was often difficult to keep her from coming into the field and taking part in missions. This is how she got a serious gunshot wound in May 1944. Need I add that she had barely recovered when she got back out there beside us?

44. A Buckmaster: an agent of the British SOE, Section F (France), which was commanded by Maurice Buckmaster. One of the principal activities of all Resistance groups, from the very start of the war until the end, was to help British intelligence operatives in France, including escaping from the country when their work was done. (See glossary.)

Afterword

Jean Garcin's text continues to tell, in the same straightforward and unassuming manner, of the life of a Resistance leader, with episodes of direct action to enliven the narrative, to be sure, but with more and more of the recollections of a man called upon to coordinate groups among themselves, and in particular about the functioning of the MUR,[1] the organization that Garcin began to liaise with starting in 1943. Garcin had begun his participation in acts of resistance as a demolition expert, and he was part of a *groupe franc,* an unaligned band of men who saw themselves first and foremost as opposed to Vichy, undertaking operations on its own, and after that in the service of movements that were more politically aligned in the later years of the Occupation. But Garcin always wanted to be involved in what he called immediate action, performing acts of sabotage or standing guard while higher-ups held meetings. And as the episode that begins his account attests, standing guard was by no means without its risks. Despite his efforts to remain a fighter and to avoid being assigned to propaganda-related activities, or to the care and management of the swelling numbers of younger men dodging compulsory work service in Germany following February 1943, Garcin was promoted from chief of all such unaligned action groups in the department of the Vaucluse to become leader of the groupes francs for the entire region, including the city of Marseilles. Among the subjects he touches on is an account of the local fallout from a disastrous Gestapo counterintelligence (anti-Resistance) operation known as Flora, which began in Marseilles but had repercussions throughout the entire country. And linked to this are his reflections regarding the betrayal of Jean Moulin and the Caluire group in June 1943, and he does not pull his punches in this hotly contested case.

Despite having already engaged in acts of sabotage, and having been an armed guard for resistance operations such as the parachute drop of Moulin into the Alpilles west of Saint-Andiol on January 1, 1942, in chapter 5 Garcin

1. Mouvements unis de la Résistance, the first coalition set up by Jean Moulin in the southern zone, first convened in January 1943. (See glossary.)

says he only became a real resister in October of that year. This should be considered in partial response to a question that students often ask, "What did it mean to become a resister?" October 1942 was when Garcin first took on a clandestine identity and ceased all contact with his former life, including with his mother. In Garcin's estimation, it was not just taking up arms and harassing Vichy or, following November 1942, the Germans, that made him a resister. The psychological burden of going underground, adopting a new identity altogether, and sticking to it, night and day, week after week, was enormous. This alone qualified as a turning point that no single act of sabotage or support for the opposition could equal. It was also at this time that the Resistance began to be truly organized and that Garcin truly became part of a larger chain of command. For someone like him who may have valued his freedom to act above anything else, this must also have been an equally large personal sacrifice.

A bit farther along he recalls: "Simple disrupters of the political order in 1940–41, resolute and actively in opposition in 1942, in the spring of 1943 we became terrorists."[2] This use of the "T" word here, which in today's world might seem surprising, is absolutely correct. The Germans and Vichy saw people like Garcin as terrorists, and they actually used this very word to try to turn public opinion against resisters. Garcin is proud of having been considered a terrorist by the fascists. He must also be using the word with some sense of irony. Writing in the early 1990s, before the post-2001 "War on Terror," Garcin was not aware of the degree to which this word would again become stigmatized. But by the 1990s the world had already seen the Lod Airport massacre (1972), the *Achille Lauro* hijacking (1985), and further years of escalating violence, and the word "terrorist" was being widely used to denote "a person who uses violence to frighten people in order to promote a political outcome." Garcin was certainly aware of this possible meaning of the word, and I can easily imagine that he thought it to be a bitter irony that he and his fellow resisters could also be seen in this way. But to this day we also recognize that, if that political outcome means restoring the freedom of a people or of a homeland, then the terrorist may also be perceived as a freedom fighter, a patriot, and a hero, as indeed Garcin was. His usage here at the very least invites reflection on how language changes. I feel certain that Garcin would not have supported killing innocent people in airports or in editorial boardrooms; hence my contention that he is using this word

2. Garcin, *Nous Etions des Terroristes,* 73.

both with pride and with a sense of the irony that this pride entails. The Resistance was usually very careful not to injure the innocent, and their greatest fear was not of being killed themselves, but of sparking reprisals against their fellow citizens. All of which is to say that Garcin's memoir and the other texts in this collection must be carefully read through the filter of history. The more one knows about what happened in France not only during the war but in the decades since, the better they will understand all of these sources, but the texts will probably reward readers at just about any level of study.

The first quarter of Garcin's memoir and the three preceding documents in this collection all show how people first became involved in resistance activities in France. My interest in seeking out such accounts sprang from a desire to help students of this period understand both when and how the Resistance began. These four texts are rich in detail about the rhythm of daily life during this gray and darkening early period of the Occupation. The further one follows this history, the more particular the concerns appear, focus on the enemy sharpens, political positions harden, and yet the difficulties of organizing the Resistance in France become more occult and harder to define. A companion volume containing newsletters and propaganda produced by these early movements will one day help complete this picture of the early days of the French Resistance. In addition, I would like to offer some antidote here to a belief, held mainly outside of France, that there was little real resistance to the Nazi invader in France, and certainly not until after Germany's eventual defeat became a real hope following the Battle of Stalingrad. This belief is as much a myth as is the one that holds that resistance was widespread and its reassuring corollary that really only a minority of French men and women collaborated with the invader and the illegitimate regime in Vichy.

All of these simplifications of the story are flawed. The documents presented here will certainly help put the first of them to rest, the version that fails to credit French men and women with resisting the Germans and Vichy from the very outset. None of our four resisters could be accused of taking an *attentiste*, or wait-and-see, attitude toward engaging in acts of resistance.[3] The idea that there was little real resistance to the Nazis, like the more generous but still condescending notion that the contribution of the Resistance was perhaps real, but insignificant as well as tardy, may be the odd child of the

3. For *attentisme*, see the glossary.

equally questionable view usually associated with Charles de Gaulle that the Resistance was immediate, widespread, and effective. De Gaulle's writing of his version of this history begins with his pronouncement at the Paris Hôtel de Ville during the Liberation that the city was "standing up to liberate itself" and "knew how to do it on its own."[4] De Gaulle was referring to a Resistance-led insurrection that had succeeded in liberating a number of police stations, including the main Prefecture building on the Île de la Cité in downtown Paris, in the days just before the Allied forces entered the city on August 25, 1944. So, true perhaps, but no one can deny that France was liberated by an Allied army that had fought its way to Paris from Normandy. The obvious exaggeration at that moment, as well as subsequent morale-boosting statements about the Resistance by General de Gaulle, and others since, have doubtless encouraged a generation or two of pundits and France-bashers to certify that the Resistance never really amounted to anything at all.

In fact, through the preceding four years, de Gaulle had rather cautiously encouraged the Resistance to organize, all the while doing his best to keep the brakes on their taking what Garcin would call "immediate action." He repeatedly reminded the resisters of the danger of reprisals against the innocent and explicitly warned them not to engage in *fanfarronades,* or "showy" acts. This warning certainly did not extend to well-directed acts of intelligence gathering, nor would it even rule out carefully planned acts of sabotage. The existence of a well-organized army of interior resisters, and a proven connection to it, would serve de Gaulle well in his struggle for leadership of the Free French in 1943. That he foresaw this eventuality in 1941 seems unlikely, but he certainly knew it in 1944. But de Gaulle was a military man, and it makes good sense, in addition to raising a real army abroad, that he would want to encourage the formation of a competent interior force, to be ready to assist behind the lines when the real army of liberation, an Allied army that would include French units, launched an invasion. That moment had clearly come, but it had only come after that real army of liberation had assaulted the occupier and fought nearly two hard months to reach the capital. So de Gaulle's statements at the Hôtel de Ville could possibly be considered as somewhat ironic, in addition to their certainly being characterized as illusory hype. It is doubtful that General de Gaulle intended his words to be taken in either

4. He goes on to repeat this conception of what had happened in the same speech: "Paris liberated! Liberated by itself," and alluding to the help of several French armies, indeed to the help of all of France, but never mentioning the Allies.

way. Hannah Arendt's observations about the pervasiveness of lies in modern political speech spring readily to mind.[5]

Such provocations have led some otherwise level-headed observers to seek yet other reasons to scoff. It is also quite possible that the strong presence of leftists, including Communists of varied alignments, in the ranks of the Resistance led and still lead some to want to minimize the role played by the Resistance in the liberation of France as World War II turned into the Cold War. (This attitude surely colored the way similar stories were spun out of events in Italy, Greece, and possibly in other theaters as well.) Lastly, skepticism about the contribution of the Resistance may also have been sparked by the perception of how quickly France was defeated in May and June 1940. The astonishing text by Jean Moulin presented here, though it will do nothing to change that history, will perhaps add some much-needed nuance to our understanding of the Collapse of the Third Republic, as well as furnishing us with a fascinating look into the heart of a Frenchman who was among the first to be detained and mistreated by the Nazis, and who three years later would die at their hands.

A few words comparing these four texts come to mind that would have been out of place in introducing them individually. Moulin's account in *First Fight* is certainly different from the three others in that it tells of how he chose to resist even before there was an Armistice, before Vichy even. His first act of insubordination was against the Third Republic, when he decided to remain at his post and began rallying people to get the situation in Chartres under some kind of control. He told his staff that the order for all *affectés spéciaux* to withdraw had been conveyed, and that they could decide for themselves what to do, but he was staying.[6] This decision probably called for as much independent moral judgment as anything that came after, but it was not an opportunity that was offered to every one of our four witnesses. Moulin was a trained civil servant and an exceptional one, to judge by his record. Like Garcin, and probably Tillion as well, he was a strong believer in the Republic and its order in general. He notes that the French military commanders he encounters found his decision to stay to be unusual as well. It may be debatable whether his refusal to leave his post constituted an act of resistance, but his refusal to speak to a local man whom he had suspected of being a fifth-columnist

5. Hannah Arendt, "Lying in Politics: Reflections on the Pentagon Papers," *New York Review of Books*, November 18, 1971, in her *Crises of the Republic* (see bibliography).

6. See pages 38–43 herein.

when he shows up in the company of a German officer clearly anticipates the strategy of silence that would find widespread adherents in occupied France. Suffice it to say that Moulin repeatedly shows a propensity for independent thought and prescient action.

What happened next is more complex, but it is also different from anything the other three were, or could have been, called upon to do. This was Moulin's refusal to sign a Wehrmacht affidavit implicating some retreating Senegalese French soldiers in the slaughter of a number of people at a farm in a nearby hamlet called la Taye. Here the fundamental difference from the other accounts, and from his insubordination of the days leading up to this moment, is that to all extents and purposes the war was over when he was ordered to appear before the German general to sign an affidavit. Between his appearance in uniform before the Prefecture on June 17 to meet the arriving German Army and 6:00 p.m. when he is ordered to appear at the German headquarters to sign a document, he notes that word was spreading that France had capitulated. He says no more about it than this, although he was writing down this version of the events some nine months later. He does not acknowledge having listened to a broadcast announcement. And here begins the story of his detainment by the Wehrmacht, and the rapid escalation of physical abuse aimed at getting him to sign a document defaming Senegalese units of the French Army. It soon becomes clear that, beyond his being ordered to affirm an unproven and manifestly racist allegation that would dishonor his country's army, by signing their affidavit he would also be acting against his own conscience. He says a number of times over the following twenty-four hours: "I wonder how long I can hold out." And at the end of his ordeal he makes it quite clear that he was doing this for the honor of France: "My duty is clearly spelled out. The Boches will learn that a Frenchman is capable of falling on his sword."[7] This despite the knowledge that the government had already capitulated. In this exercise of his duty, to the honor of France and of his own personal integrity, Moulin became a resister.

Jean Moulin survived this first encounter with the enemy, as his story makes clear. He continued as prefect in Chartres until November 1940, when he was stripped of his duties by the government in Vichy. He was already engaged in networking with other resisters by this time. After this date he moved into full-time resistance activity, traveling about the country meeting with people of similar conviction, including our third early resister, Henri

7. Page 80 herein.

Frenay. Moulin met him in Marseilles during their respective recruitment and networking activities in August 1941.[8]

Frenay had been a soldier, and it was as a soldier that he had presented himself for service in the new French state's limited armed forces in the summer of 1940. Given his training in German language and culture, it is perhaps not surprising that he was assigned to service in military intelligence. No sooner had he done this, however, then he began to contemplate earnestly how best to resist the Nazi occupier. Whatever one concludes about his political outlook or his personal style, Frenay began resisting in August 1940 when he decided to set down the first draft of the document included here. Readers may be surprised to learn that he saw resistance as leading to a France in which Marshal Pétain would still be the head of state, and the National Revolution espoused by Vichy would be brought to fruition. While both Moulin and Frenay began their resistance activities while serving Vichy (Moulin in the northern, occupied zone, and Frenay in the southern, so-called "Free Zone"), their outlooks were diametrically opposed from the very start. Understanding this makes much of what happened in their later relations much clearer, from their struggle over military leadership in the Resistance of 1943, and their strained dealings regarding funding, to Frenay's ultimate denunciation of Moulin as a crypto-Communist on national television in 1977.[9]

Likewise a resister of the very first hour, Germaine Tillion had had no experience of political or military service whatsoever when she realized that terrible things had happened in her beloved country that she had not expected, and that she had "to do something." Wanting "to do something" has since become something of a cliché for the motivation that prompted many of these early resisters to act. Ironically, as a student of human societies among the French peasantry and then in the Aurès Mountains of Algeria—and ultimately as one of the definitive chroniclers of daily life in the Nazi concentration camp system—Tillion admits to having been out of touch with the contemporary realities of her native land in the late 1930s. Her text makes reference to her first acts of resistance, which included joining up with retired officers of the

8. Frenay tells the story of their meeting in *La Nuit finira*, 157–60.

9. This was on *Les Dossiers de l'Écran*, October 11, 1977, "Les Grandes Figures de la Résistance: Jean Moulin," a telefilm by Henri Calef. For a short documentary on this important moment in the deciphering of the history of the Resistance, see www.youtube.com/watch?v=37Kt6mX7vBQ. Frenay may have been confusing Moulin with his one-time boss Pierre Cot, who was definitively exposed as a Soviet agent in 1990.

French colonial army to start helping refugees get out of the northern zone, where she lived. She says in an interview that she got in touch with them following her inquiry as to what she could do at an office of the French Red Cross in July 1940.[10] She then brought the two colonels, Hauët and de la Rochère, with her into the group of resisters she encountered when she returned to work as an anthropologist at the musée de l'Homme in Paris in fall 1940.

Her mother's role in all of this cannot be determined from our text, but it appears to have been considerable. Emilie Tillion was already recognized as an author, with particular competence in art and archaeology. She took an active role in recruiting writers in and around Paris for inclusion in the group's newsletter, *Résistance.* This meant physically passing documents, and laboriously retyping them onto mimeograph, or worse, spirit-applicator stencils in this pre-internet, pre-fax, pre-copier world. Emilie ultimately died in the Ravensbrück concentration camp for her involvement in the Resistance. The poignant complicity of these two women in the earliest acts of resistance underscores the importance of personal relationships in these emerging structures. Germaine also wrote a number of tracts at this time. The musée de l'Homme group alone consisted of several dozen people, including Emilie, and according to Tillion's account, they largely came together by word of mouth, from one acquaintance to another. Her dismissal as superfluous of the idea that their group even had a name suggests that, in this first hour, it was not yet about ideologies, or parties, at all. She points this out herself, saying they had people of just about every stripe, except for there being no Communists. In autumn 1940, that is not surprising.[11] Nor does she say that they would not have admitted Communists if individuals had met the other criteria, meaning first and foremost that one or more of the others already knew and trusted them. It was above all a group of good people who mostly knew each other already in one context or another. Beyond that, resisting was simply something that had to be done.

The same appears to have been the case in Jean Garcin's experience. His story resembles all three of the others in a variety of compelling ways. Like Moulin, he was originally of a Radical Party[12] family from the southeast. He was not a professional civil servant like Moulin, yet, but they were both

10. *Sisters in Resistance,* a documentary film by Maia Wechsler (2000).

11. Page 121 herein.

12. See Radical Socialist Party in glossary.

fervent believers in the Republic. Like Frenay, he was a soldier, albeit a non-commissioned one. Garcin's decision not to lead his men north to Colmar in Alsace in June 1940 resulted in their being demobilized in the South. How fortunate this was to be he could not have realized. Like Frenay, who also escaped at this time, he could not have known that the German Army was going to remove over 1.8 million French soldiers to Germany and put them to work there for the Grand Reich for the next five years. What Garcin did shows precisely the same kind of initiative that Frenay took when he left his unit in Alsace and headed for home, and as Moulin when he refused to leave his post in Chartres in front of the German advance. But, very much unlike Frenay, from the outset Garcin saw his first enemy as Vichy, and unlike all three of the others he was immediately drawn in by his urge to take immediate action rather than to be an organizer. That being said, he then tells in pretty much the same words as Tillion how one person spoke to him, leading him to speak to two others, carefully determining in each case that they shared the same outlook. In Garcin's case, like Tillion, once he was in a small group, he was introduced to a leader in a larger group, and began to represent *that* group to an organization that united other groups. Garcin and Tillion both networked *up* into the Resistance. Frenay and Moulin began as leaders, and proceeded to network *down*. But the first links were always forged between acquaintances, if not close friends.

Frenay's manifesto stands apart from the other three documents in one major regard: it was intended to guide other like-minded individuals in making their first contacts. One evening in December 1940, he took it to see his old friend and German studies mentor, Berty Albrecht. He tells the story in his memoir, *La Nuit finira*. She says how happy she was to receive a letter from him, that she is reassured by what he tells her he wants to do. There were so few people around that she felt had any spine at all: "I am happy to know that you are a 'rebel.'"

Then, after a moment's hesitation:

> —But Henri, you are even younger at heart than you are in years. Have you really thought how crazy what you are doing is, and what dangers you will encounter, because war is not a game: *Jetzt ist es kein Kriegspiel,* she said in German, *aber ein grausamer Krieg.*[13]

13. "Now it is no war game but a horrible war."

Frenay assured her that he knew what he was doing, and she appears to have believed him, and this must in part be a tribute to her prior mentoring of the young man.

> She smiled; then, putting on Grock's accent,[14] she said:
>
> —You want me to work for you?
>
> Thus began a trusting collaboration between the two of us in the Resistance, of the many moments of complete attention to what we were doing that nothing could get in the middle of, except for prison, and the death that she herself chose.[15]

Thus, even this call to arms that Frenay first hammered out alone in his room finds its earliest audience among people he knew personally. For indeed, as he says in the manifesto, recruiters must "look for new recruits starting with people in their own circle of acquaintances and family members."[16] It was the fastest and the safest way to build an organization under the circumstances at hand. In most other respects Frenay's text is unique, in its continued allegiance to Pétain, perhaps excusable at this early hour, and in its stated awareness of just how perfidious Hitler was, and how evil National Socialism. He had read Hitler when he was a student of German in Strasbourg. Frenay's anti-Communism is clear and intransigent. His military background may explain somewhat his failure to embrace the Jews as equals in the struggle, both in his written word and in practice. The text included here speaks for itself in this regard. In practice, there would be no (active) Communists in Combat. There were, however, to be a number of distinguished Jewish members.

Bearing in mind the formal and the substantive differences between these texts, and the different points of view of their authors, the tenor of these voices seems remarkably similar. The similarity lies in a shared feeling, an unspoken assumption that France is not just a physical territory but an ideal that has been aggressed. The authors' urge to "do something" arises out of a shared conviction that they still support that ideal and that they have a moral obligation to continue doing so. They may have shared other feelings as well, but it would not be wrong to say that this first thing that they have in common is "patriotism."

14. Grock was a famous clown who performed using fifteen languages and as many musical instruments.

15. Frenay, *La Nuit finira*, 61–62.

16. Page 159 herein.

The word comes up fairly often in Moulin's account, but it is almost entirely absent from the other three. Tillion uses the word only once, when she cites the "unwavering patriotism" of her colleagues. Of course, she was writing a decade after the battle had been won, and it may be that this made her less inclined to invoke it as a motivation. But she is also recalling a period right after the Armistice when people of her milieu were in deep shock over what had just transpired, and while they were doubtless moved by love of country, the summer of 1940 was not the time for proud flag-waving. As she says: "The Armistice caused an almost immediate split across all of French society, and this split could be perceived in every milieu."[17] She later recalls how Pétain's speech marks the changing point in her political consciousness. Frenay uses the word "patriotic" only once to characterize once-free France: "unified France, patriotic and STRONG."[18] That he does not invoke patriotism more explicitly seems all the more astonishing since he was clearly planning to seek adherents among the traditional right wing, starting in the military. Garcin, writing fifty years later as a retired politician, uses the word rather more frequently, often to honor people who served the cause. Of course, many people in the general population would have embraced the idea that they were patriots while supporting Vichy.

And there is every indication that support for Vichy, or at least for Marshal Pétain, was massive in the early months of the Occupation. Hard statistics about this and about the numbers of people in opposition to the new regime at that time are hard to come by. The documents we are looking at here bring very little new light to the discussion of how many resisters there were at the beginning, or at any other time, and I see no reason to change the total number of 200,000, plus or minus some pretenders and some undeclared, that I cited at the outset. The present volume does not purport to be a quantitative study of the Resistance, but I can and do recommend the Centre d'histoire de la Résistance et de la Déportation de Lyon (CHRD) for anyone who wants to pursue this line of study.[19] Just who was counted, and who was counted *as what*, are just two of many questions that one might ask of all of these numbers. For example, Jean Garcin was introduced to his first contact in the Resistance by a Vichy official, Barthélémy Rique.

17. Page 120 herein.

18. Page 154 herein.

19. The Centre d'histoire de la Résistance et de la Déportation de Lyon has a very accessible Web site with useful resources for the student and the teacher.

These four documents make it possible for English-speaking students to see the story in new and comparative human detail. Taken together, and thanks to their breadth of origin, they allow us to say with certainty that something that would later be called the French Resistance indeed began here, in the summer of 1940, and that patriotism was undoubtedly one of the motivating sentiments. But apart from these things, which are hitherto far from uncontested, what do these accounts tell us that we want to know? Germaine Tillion's article begins with two questions, "What were the people who fought in the Resistance thinking?" and "What did they hope for following victory?" The second of these is certainly of interest, and not at all surprising given the period in which she was writing. By asking this question, she draws attention to specific moral choices that she felt needed to be made in 1958, as much as to those that resisters might have imagined in 1940.

Allusions to what the people who fought for France in World War II hoped for there after the war crop up frequently in accounts of the Resistance, as well as in memoirs by people who served with the Free French in London, and this would be a worthwhile subject to look at in detail, but it might not be the best question to ask of a group of first resisters. Frenay's document is the most explicit about the France to come, as befits a political tract, while the other three do not address it directly at all. Moulin, Tillion, and Garcin, however, would all probably endorse a return to republican democracy. When he wrote *National Liberation*, Frenay hoped for a return to a free and independent France, of course, but one that would be led by Pétain in the pursuit of the National Revolution proposed by Vichy. But no one in Vichy ever spelled out what this revolution would entail, and there is little specificity to Frenay's imaginings, either, apart from the certainty that it would include severely repressing Communism.

"What were these people thinking?" is a question often asked by students of the Occupation, and we can fairly ask it of all four of these resisters. As we look for answers, though, we must bear in mind that these *were* early resisters, and in this they are different from those who joined the struggle after June 1941 (Barbarossa) or even November 1942 (Operation Torch). They are likewise distinct from the young men who fled from the mandatory work order of 1943, as they are different from the opportunists who sat on the fence until 1944 even, and from those who served Vichy for longer than Jean Moulin did and with even greater devotion than Henri Frenay, but who later became very real resisters. And while two out of the four are highly personal accounts, one is a recruiting document and one a scholarly article. But they all address the thought processes that led otherwise law-abiding citizens to decide to break with the civil authority in their country.

Moulin's response to what happened while he was assigned to prefectoral duty in Chartres is replete with references to what he was thinking. His decision to stand his ground in the face of the government's retreat was based on considerable experience in public service. His initial response to his Wehrmacht inquisitors was likewise both considered and deliberate. Up to that point, at least, his responses were dictated by his sense of professionalism and duty, even when he decided to act counter to his government's orders. His confrontation with the Germans on June 17 took place after he had become aware that France had capitulated, although he hardly acknowledges the fact. Once physical abuse began, however, the situation could be said to have changed even further. The abuse clearly went beyond psychological coercion, as the officers began to strike him and then hit him with their guns. He could have given in at this point, however reluctantly: an extorted signature could be seen as meaningless in any case. But he thought that it would have brought dishonor to France and to himself. He chose to behave this way, even if it was not entirely a rational choice.

Tillion answers her own first question without reference to a prior understanding of what her responsibility to any political agenda or as a citizen might be: she had grown out of touch with the political realities in her country. Her decision to become more cognizant of those realities was a response to the indignity inflicted on the country and on herself by the surrender and the Armistice. She felt she had "to do something." There is a sense that her political education really began with this decision, and the immediate result was that she began to resist, and in order to do this she immediately began to network. I believe that this is how political activism often begins. It is certain that this is where it began for most people in France in the 1940s. Frenay and Garcin both appear to have been somewhat more familiar with national politics and had less of a leap to make, although clearly nothing had prepared either of them for this kind of work. Frenay's text shows with particular clarity his sense of the danger Hitler and Nazism posed, and the specific threat to what he saw as French values at the moment when he decided that he had to act.[20] In both of their cases, this realization was immediately followed by an acceptance of the need to recruit and organize. As for her own networking, Tillion says it was entirely limited to interactions among her own friends. She points out as well

20. Page 155 herein.

that they never doubted at the time that what they were doing was supported by "a considerable segment of French opinion," though at the same time they must have known that there were a lot of people who did not agree with them. But there were many others still on the fence, and she says it was her hope that their example would inspire the undecided to join them.

In Garcin's words, "It was the period of the oil slick. Every new recruit in turn contacted one or several like-minded people, and so on."[21] Both Garcin and Tillion stress the sentiment that the individuals they brought in were all "people of goodwill," and they both mention how dangerous they knew the situation was and what care they were obliged to exercise, so there can be no doubt that they were without illusions as to how many people disagreed with what they were doing in these early months of the Occupation. Frenay, who worked for the first four or five months of the Vichy regime in the eponymous spa town itself, says, "It is imperative to establish with the utmost certainty, in a prior conversation, that the individual wishes for an English victory, that s/he is the enemy of Communism, of Freemasons, and of international finance."[22] Because he knows that there are many people around who will disagree with what they are doing, everything had to be done with thought and afterthought. But in both of their texts the reason for doing these things remains a scarcely defined sense of an affront to France, where they as individuals have been constrained by the country's collapse and by the occupier. As Garcin says, "We wanted something to happen."[23]

But I believe that the answer to the question "What were they thinking?" has to be, to some degree, that they were not just thinking. They were feeling. Does this mean they were behaving irrationally? Probably. Emmanuel d'Astier de la Vigerie—who began resisting as early as September 1940—famously quipped that in order to be a resister of the first hour one had to be a bit crazy.[24] The early resisters were listening to their hearts. That is a talent that not everybody has, or if we do, certainly not to the same degree. In Moulin's refusal to quit his post, there was undoubtedly reasoning going on: "My intention is to maintain those civil services that are still in place around me for

21. Page 197 herein.

22. Page 158 herein.

23. Page 203 herein.

24. Interview in *The Sorrow and the Pity*, a 1969 documentary film by Marcel Ophüls. D'Astier became the leader of Libération-Sud, one of the largest and best-known Resistance organizations in the southern zone.

as long as possible." He also said that he was aware that if he fled, it would encourage others to do the same. Did he think that discouraging people from fleeing would change the outcome of the military confrontation? Probably not. But he saw that the mass exodus of civilians was taking place in fear, causing considerable discomfort and ever-heightening anxiety. Much of Chartres had long since fled. Moulin was clearly concerned for the people on the road. He also talked with fleeing French troops. He was certainly assessing the situation, to better know how to act, but one cannot miss his feeling of camaraderie, and of support for their fight. As with his staff employees and the Chartrains who stayed behind, he seems to share in the experience of all of the people with whom he interacted.

The story behind each of these texts involves the author's identifying with the community at large, against the occupier, against the French government that is false or at best captive. Tillion and her two colonels reached out to people of goodwill similar to their own. They were all sensitive to the same indignity in the Collapse, and they shared the same feelings of powerlessness and disgust. Perhaps the people who read her article in 1958 would also identify with their quite righteous indignation and find a similarly shared sympathy for the struggle of the Algerian people. In Vichy, Frenay realized immediately that the Germans were aiming at nothing less than a total victory in the end, and that Vichy was powerless to stop it under the terms of the Armistice. There was little Pétain could do to change it, either. But individual citizens could act. By coming together, they could do what Vichy could not. In his own way, Garcin was motivated by indignation at what Vichy represented—and by a glimpse of the monster peeking out of Hitler's uniform, for he too had read *Mein Kampf.* He cites "instinct" and "family tradition" as being as important as any reasoned political argument in the actions of early resisters like himself.[25]

What lies behind all of these stories of first resisters is an awareness of the role of community, if not actual friendship, in what they did; something more than duty, however defined, or the reasoned application of an opposing political position, was at work in their coming together. Certainly this sense of community came partly out of a concern for confidentiality, for security, but it left its mark on the organizations that were formed in this way. Security was not a concern at all for Jean Moulin when he acted contrary to orders as a prefect before the Germans arrived. He was simply trying to help people who

25. Page 188 herein.

were mostly not from his conscription—mostly, but not all, French people, even. The victims themselves were united by their desperate situation. And Moulin was bound to them by altruism more than by duty, certainly more than by his job description, which would have had him retreat from the advancing front. In Tillion's and Garcin's memories of their early organizing, the importance of friendship is particularly evident. Even Frenay, who was already aiming to create an organization for national liberation, saw the need to work from people close at hand outward in order to build the movement he envisioned. In the last analysis, the most striking characteristic of all of these accounts of early resistance is not related to what the protagonists were thinking as much as to what they were feeling. We do not have to conclude that they were behaving foolishly in order to accept that their greatest strength really lay in empathy.

TIMELINE, 1939–1945

YEAR	INTERNATIONAL EVENTS	FRANCE	RESISTANCE
1939	—Sept. 1: German Army invades Poland. —Sept. 3: Great Britain declares war on Germany. —Sept. 17: Soviet Army invades Poland.	—Sept. 1: French Army mobilizes. —Sept. 3: Declares war on Germany.	
1940	—May 10: German Army invades Belgium and the Netherlands. —May 13: German Army enters France. —June 10: Italy declares war on France.	—June 10: French government leaves Paris. —June 14: German Army enters Paris. —June 17: Prime Minister Pétain calls for armistice. —June 18: De Gaulle's first call to armed resistance. —June 24: signing of the Armistice at Rethondes. —July 10: National Assembly grants full powers to Marshal Pétain.	—June 14: Jean Moulin decides to disobey orders to evacuate. —June 17–18: Moulin detained by German Army in Chartres. —July–Aug.: G. Tillion and Colonels de la Rochère and Hauët begin work.

YEAR	INTERNATIONAL EVENTS	FRANCE	RESISTANCE
1940		—Oct.: First roundups of undesirables, mostly foreign born. —Dec. 13–14: Laval out as PM, replaced by Flandin.	—Aug.: H. Frenay drafts MLN in St. Maximin. —Sept.: The musée de l'Homme group gathering in Paris. —Nov.: Jean Moulin suspended from functions as prefect. —Dec.: First issue of the newsletter *Résistance* appears in Paris.
1941	—June 22: German Army attacks USSR. —Dec. 5: Red Army counterattacks in front of Moscow. —Dec. 7: US enters the war.	—Feb. 9: New cabinet in Vichy; Darlan comes in. —Mar.: General Office on Jewish Questions (CGQJ) is formed. —Oct. 22: Guy Môquet and 47 others executed in reprisal for Lt. Hotz.	—Jan.–Feb.: The musée de l'Homme group is penetrated. Nine arrested. —Spring: Jean Garcin enters resistance group in the Vaucluse. Moulin surveying resistance activities. —Aug. 21: First assassination of a German officer by a resister (Col. Fabien) in Paris. —Oct. 20: Lt. Karl Hotz assassinated by resisters in Nantes.

YEAR	INTERNATIONAL EVENTS	FRANCE	RESISTANCE
1942	—Jan. 20: Wannsee Conference near Berlin launches the Nazis' "Final Solution" of the "Jewish problem."		—Jan. 1: Jean Moulin parachutes into France, near les Baux.
		—Apr. 18: Laval back as president of the council and head of three ministries.	
	—June 4: R. Heydrich succumbs to his wounds in Prague.		—July 14: Widespread demonstrations organized by Resistance.
		—July 17: *Vel' d'Hiv* roundup in Paris.	—Aug. 13: Germaine Tillion arrested in Paris.
	—Oct. 4: Start of the Battle of Stalingrad. —Nov. 8: Anglo-American forces land in North Africa (Torch).		
		—Nov. 11: Occupation of the southern zone by the German Army.	
1943		—Jan. 30: Creation of la Milice under J. Darnand.	
	—Feb. 2: German capitulation at Stalingrad.	—Feb. 16: Mobilization of the first classes of youth in the Obligatory Work Service (STO).	
			—May 27: First convening of the National Council of the Resistance. —June 1: Foundation of the French Committee for National Liberation.

YEAR	INTERNATIONAL EVENTS	FRANCE	RESISTANCE
1943	—July 10: Allied landing in Sicily. —Sept. 8: Italy capitulates.	— Sept. 9–early Oct.: Uprising and liberation of Corsica.	—June 23: Arrest of Jean Moulin and others near Lyon. —Aug.–Dec.: Twelve to eighteen parachute drop zones operating in the Vaucluse.
1944	—June 4: Allied forces enter Rome.	—June 6: Allied forces land in Normandy. —Aug. 13–24: Active resistance in Paris before its liberation (Aug. 25). —Sept.: Vichy leaders evacuated to Schloss Sigmarigen, Germany. —Épuration trials and executions begin and go on until 1949–50.	—July–Aug.: Resistance groups openly attack the retreating Germans; many casualties.
1945	—Apr. 28: Mussolini executed. — May 8: Nazi Germany capitulates.		

GLOSSARY of PLACES, PEOPLE, ORGANIZATIONS, and TERMS

Abraham, Marcel (1898–1955). Paris-based teacher, writer, and resister.

Abwehr. The military intelligence division of the German Army.

Albrecht, Berty (1893–1943). Born in Marseilles, died in Fresnes Prison, outside Paris. Resister, close associate of Henri Frenay in the MLN and Combat.

AS (Armée secrète). The armed division inside the Resistance, following the creation of the Conseil national de la Résistance in May 1943.

Attentisme. With reference to resisting, this "wait-and-see" approach was opposed to taking direct action (*action directe*). These contrasting strategies were hotly debated in the last two years of the war. *Attentisme* was a strategy that favored collecting intelligence and preparing to support an invasion by a qualified armed force, but not engaging the enemy. This corresponded to the tactics endorsed by de Gaulle's Free French bureau in London. Advocates of this strategy argued that a moderate approach to resistance would also avoid provoking German retaliation upon the innocent.

Aveline, Claude (1901–1992). Pen name of Eugen Avtsine, writer, poet, publisher, and resister.

Barbarossa (Operation Barbarossa). The name given to the German Army's plan to attack the Soviet Union, which began on June 22, 1941.

Baril, Louis. Colonel in the French Army, head of the intelligence service (Deuxième Bureau) of the French Army in World War II.

BCRA (Bureau central de renseignements et d'action). The intelligence wing of de Gaulle's Free French office in London, directed by Andre Dewavrin, known as "Col. Passy."

Bellanger, Claude (1910–1978). French journalist. Was an active resister.

Berliet. A line of Citroën trucks.

Besnard, Pierre. A member of the Chartres City Council in 1940.

Béziers. A city five miles inland from the Mediterranean in the department of the Hérault, roughly halfway between Montpellier and Narbonne.

Blaise. A river in central France, tributary of the Eure.

Blum, Léon (1872–1950). French politician of the 1920s and 1930s, three times prime minister, including during the Popular Front. Spent World War II under arrest, was briefly tried in the High Court at Riom, but the case against him was dismissed.

Bolshevik Revolution. The Marxist revolution in Russia in 1917 that overthrew the Tsar and led to the formation of the Soviet Union.

Buchenwald. German concentration camp, opened in 1937, where many French non-Jewish resisters were sent in World War II.

Buckmaster, Maurice (1902–1992). British intelligence officer in charge of Section F (the French section) of the Special Operations Executive (SOE) in World War II. His name became synonymous with "British secret agent."

Calavon. River in the Vaucluse, southern France, tributary of the Durance.

Caluire. Small town just north of Lyon, France, where Jean Moulin was arrested in June 1943.

Cassou, Jean (1897–1986). Art critic, poet, novelist. He wrote for the newsletter *Résistance.* Served a year for acts of resistance, but got out and continued to work in the southern zone until the end of the war.

Cavaillon. City in the Vaucluse department in southern France.

CDLR (Ceux de la Résistance). Important resistance group in the northern zone, which began as a group within Combat, went dormant, and later returned under the leadership of Jacques Lecompte-Boinet.

CGT (Confédération générale du travail). The General Confederation of Labor, France's largest congress of labor unions from 1895 to this day.

Chartres. City in the Eure-et-Loir department of France, sixty miles southwest of Paris.

Châteaubriant. Town in northwest France where the Germans executed twenty-seven French prisoners on October 22, 1941, in reprisal for the assassination of Lt. Karl Hotz in Nantes.

Châteaudun. Town in France, twenty-five miles from Chartres.

CNR (Conseil national de la Résistance). The unified organization of resistance groups brought together for the first time by Jean Moulin in Paris, in May 1943.

Collapse (*la Débâcle*). The defeat and surrender of France in World War II. A more precise translation of *Débâcle* in this instance might be "rout."

Combat. The name adopted by the National Liberation Movement founded by Henri Frenay for its resistance groups in 1941, following its merger with the group Liberté.

Cot, Pierre (1895–1977). French politician of the 1930s, serving three times as minister of aviation. He moved steadily left during his career, and became a Soviet agent at some point. He taught at Yale University during most of World War II.

Daladier, Edouard (1884–1970). French politician of the 1930s, three times prime minister, including at the time of the Munich Accords, when he represented France.

Darnand, Joseph (1897–1945). French Army officer, fought bravely in World War I, became a far-right nationalist in the 1930s and later head of state security in Vichy. Darnand was named chief of the militia at the end of 1942, a post that he held until the end of the war. He was executed by the French in 1945.

d'Astier de la Vigerie, Emmanuel (1900–1969). Began resistance activity in September 1940. A co-founder with Daniel Mayer of the left-leaning resister organization Libération-Sud.

Déat, Marcel (1894–1955). A Socialist who founded the RNP and was minister of labor.

Débâcle. *See* Collapse. Literally more like "rout." Also frequently called "*la Pagaille*" in literature of the period.

de Brinon, Fernand (1885–1947). Vichy's ambassador to the German Occupation authority in Paris.

de Froment, Pierre (1913–2006). Lieutenant in French Army and a colleague of Henri Frenay. One of the founders of *Les Petites Ailes de France,* an early Resistance newsletter.

de la Rochère, Col. Charles (1870–1944). Retired officer in the French colonial army, began working with Paul Hauët and Germaine Tillion in the summer of 1940.

de Lipkowski, Henri (1897–1944). Industrialist, member of the Libération-Vengeance group. He died in deportation to Buchenwald.

Département. A French administrative district. Such districts are not sovereign states, nor do they correspond with historical regions or feudal fiefdoms. Each has a prefect named from Paris in the district seat and a number of subprefects in smaller towns.

de Pellepoix, Darquier (1897–1980). Second director of the Office for Jewish Affairs, Vichy government office in Paris.

de Torquat. Commandant of the Seventh Regiment of Dragoons, a unit of the French Army that passed through Chartres during the Collapse.

Deuxième Bureau. The intelligence service of the French Army.

Devillers, Henri. A French soldier captured in 1940 who gained his freedom as a POW by becoming a double-agent. He penetrated the Combat group and was caught by the intelligence service of Vichy and executed in 1942.

Doriot, Jacques (1898–1945). Though initially a Communist, Doriot became a fascist and founded the PPF.

d'Orves, Honoré Estienne (1901–1941). Naval officer regarded as the first martyr of Free France. Sent on a mission by London to set up spying networks in and around Nantes, where he was arrested by the Gestapo. Tried and executed in Paris, August 1941.

Dreux. City in France, twenty miles from Chartres.

Duclos, Jacques. One of the top leaders of the French Communist Party, he held many public offices from 1926 until 1969.

du Tillet, Colonel. Commander of the subdivision of the French Army stationed in the Eure-et-Loir department in 1940.

École des surintendantes d'usine. School for Factory Supervisors, a state school in Paris that trained women to be social workers. It was founded in 1917 to help reintegrate veterans into the workplace following World War I. The school became a hotbed of early resister activity in 1941, in part thanks to the efforts of Berty Albrecht.

Épuration. Literally "purification," the period beginning in 1944 when the French settled grievances resulting from the war on a community level, as well as later when they tried thousands of collaborators in front of national tribunals. The punishments meted out ranged from public shaming to summary execution (in cases settled in the streets) to fines, stripping people of their right to work, or of their citizenship, to execution (in cases tried before special magistrates).

Exodus, *Exode*. Literally "flight," term used to describe the mass exodus from northern France and the Low Countries, and then from Paris, in front of the advancing German Army, June 1940.

Fawtier, Robert (1885–1966). A professor and a resister, he survived deportation to the Mauthausen concentration camp. A medievalist by training, he was a colleague of Tillion at the Comité d'histoire de la Deuxième Guerre mondiale.

Feldkommandant, Feldkommandantur. A sector or city military commander in the German army and his headquarters, respectively.

Feldwebel. A staff sergeant in the German army.

Fifth-columnist. A term used to designate a member of a group working to undermine the security or the morale of a people, usually in the interest of a foreign country.

Flora. An operation conducted by the Gestapo in France in 1942–43. It was responsible for many arrests of high-level resisters in May–June 1943.

FN (Front National). "National Front" is the name given to the section of the French Communist Party devoted to active resistance. (This has no connection with the current right-wing party of the same name.)

Free French (France libre, France combattante, Forces françaises libres, FFL). The group of men and women who formed around General Charles de Gaulle in London in 1940, who subsequently moved to Algiers in June 1943. It changed its name to France combattante in 1942, then dissolved into the Forces françaises libres in August 1943.

Freemasonry. A philosophical movement with roots in the eighteenth-century Enlightenment. In France it is seen as a guardian of the free-thinking, rationalist spirit of the French Revolution. Freemasons are known as defenders of the Declaration of the Rights of Man and champions of secular government. It was targeted for eradication by Vichy along with Jews and Communists.

Frenay, Henri (1905–1988). A French soldier who escaped surrender to the Germans in June 1940, first to serve in the intelligence service of the army of the Vichy regime, then to found and lead the Mouvement de libération nationale resistance group that ultimately became Combat.

French Communist Party. *See* PCF (Parti communiste français).

FTP (Franc-Tireur; Francs-Tireurs et Partisans); also Francs-Tireurs Partisans Français (FTPF). Literally "free-shooters," irregular Communist militias formed locally, first within MOI and subsequently by the French Communist Party's Front National. "Et Partisans" was added in homage to similar groups of Spanish Republicans.

Garcin, Jean (1917–2006). A soldier trained in demolition work, resister, later became a local mayor, member of the Regional Council of the Vaucluse (later PACA), author of *We Were Terrorists.*

Garcin, Robert (1898–1944). Mayor of Fontaine de Vaucluse, resister, father of Jean, died in Buchenwald concentration camp.

Gauleiter. A German regional governor.

Gazogène. A system for extracting combustible gas from wood, popular in France during World War II. The wood-gas generator allowed cars and trucks to get a hundred miles per gallon of gas. The generators can be seen as black canisters outside the driver's door or on the roofs of cars and trucks starting in late 1940.

German Communist Party (Kommunistische Partei Deutschlands, KPD). Founded in 1918 and outlawed in 1933, the day following Hitler's accession to office as chancellor. It suffered heavily in the first round of persecution in Germany.

Gestapo. Short for Geheime Staatspolizei or State Secret Police, a department of the National Socialist Party Security Service.

Grock. Stage name of one of the most famous clowns of the prewar era, Charles Adrien Wettach (1880–1959), remembered for his use of over a dozen languages and as many musical instruments. He was especially famous for his German accent.

Groupe franc. "Free group" or "unaligned squad." These were teams of resisters that specialized in armed operations (*coups de main*) and sabotage. *Franc* harks back to a designation in army circles of independent armed groups of volunteers. The German equivalent is Freikorps; English, free corps.

Guédon, Robert (1902–1978). Army officer and associate of Henri Frenay. Founder of the Mouvement de libération nationale in the northern sector.

Guéry Institution. A parochial (diocesan) Catholic school in Chartres.

Hauët, Col. Paul (1866–1945). Retired officer in the French colonial army, began working with Germaine Tillion and Charles de la Rochère in the summer of 1940.

Hotz, Karl. A lieutenant in the German Army, he was shot in the back by a group of Communist resisters in Nantes, October 20, 1941.

IS. Intelligence Service, another name for MI6, the British military intelligence office concerned with overseas operations.

Izon-la-Bruisse. Town in the Drôme Provençale where the *maquis du Ventoux* was martyred by the Gestapo in February 1944.

Jeunesses laïques et républicaines. An early twentieth-century French student organization dedicated to promoting understanding of republican values.

Komintern (Comintern). Also known as the Third International, it was a congress of Communist parties founded by Lenin in 1919 and dissolved by Stalin in 1943. Its purpose was to foster Communist revolution in the world outside of the Soviet Union.

Kommandantur. A local headquarters of the German army.

Lejards, Monsignor. A bishop at the Chartres Cathedral in 1940.

Les Éditions de Minuit. A French publishing house founded during the Occupation to print resistance literature.

Libération (Libération-Sud and Libération-Nord). Two distinct groups of left-oriented resisters, initially formed late in 1940, by Emmanuel d'Astier de la Vigerie and Daniel Mayer in the South and Christian Pineau in the North. They were both aligned from the start with the Socialist Party (SFIO).

Luisant. A French town, now a southern suburb of Chartres.

Lyon. France's third-largest city today. An important manufacturing center and the most important city in the southern zone in World War II.

Maquis. A place where many young French men hid from the draft of laborers to work in Germany from late 1942 until 1944. These men were called *maquisards*, from the French expression *prendre le maquis*, meaning "to head for the hills." (*Le maquis* literally means a scrub forest, or outback.) Resistance groups helped hide them, and many maquisards subsequently joined up. The word *maquis* is not truly synonymous with "the Resistance," though frequently is used as if it were.

Marceau, Gen. François (1769–1796). Heroic general of the French Revolution, rose from the ranks because of his strong belief in the Republic.

Marseillaise, la. The French national anthem. Singing it was restricted under Vichy because of its warlike sentiments toward invaders.

Marseilles. The second-largest city in France today. This Mediterranean port was the trap door of Europe through which many refugees escaped fascism in World War II.

Maurras, Charles (1868–1952). French right-wing political thinker, nationalist, Catholic, anti-Semite, director of the movement Action française and its newsletter.

Mein Kampf (My Struggle). Book by Adolf Hitler, written 1924–25, presenting his views on the defeat of Germany in World War I, the Versailles Peace Treaty, and his plans for settlement of Germany's grievances. The book includes an explicit anti-Semitic agenda, as well as a call to reunite territories taken from Germany under the Versailles Accords.

MLN (Mouvement de libération nationale). The first name for Henri Frenay's resistance organization. Later became Combat.

MOI (Main d'oeuvre immigrée). First organized by the General Confederation of Piecework Labor, a splinter group of the larger CGT in the 1920s, and taken over by the French Communist Party in the 1930s. The MOI provided a structure in which to organize immigrant workers while keeping them separate from the voting membership of the party. Communist resistance movements began within these groups as early as 1941, often calling themselves Francs-Tireurs et Partisans.

Molotov, Vyacheslav (1890–1976). A Soviet politician and diplomat, he negotiated a treaty of nonaggression with Nazi Germany (the Molotov–von Ribbentrop Pact) in August 1939 that divided Poland between the two great powers and cleared the way for the German invasion of Poland at the start of World War II.

Montpellier. France's eighth-largest city, six miles from the Mediterranean Sea, in southern France.

Môquet, Guy (1924–1941). A high-school student and member of the Jeunesses communistes, imprisoned for his political activism. Shot along with forty-seven others in reprisal for the assassination of Lt. Karl Hotz.

Moulin, Jean (1905–1943). A French civil servant, prefect of the department of the Eure-et-Loir at the time of the Collapse, he was turned out of office by Vichy in November 1940. He began organizing resistance efforts in the year that followed, and in fall 1941 he traveled to London, where, using the code name "Rex," he was appointed as emissary of the Free French to resisters in the southern zone.

MUR (Mouvements unis de la Résistance). The first coalition of three resistance movements, Combat, Libération-Sud, and Franc-Tireur, organized by Jean Moulin in autumn 1942. The first plenary meeting was held near Lyon on January 26, 1943.

Nacht und Nebel (Night and Fog). The term used in a directive from Hitler on December 7, 1941, stating that anyone accused of threatening the security of the Reich would disappear into "Night and Fog" in the Nazi penitentiary system.

Nantes. France's sixth-largest city, on the Atlantic coast in western France.

National Council of the Resistance. *See* CNR (Conseil national de la Résistance).

Nogent-le-Rotrou. Town in France, thirty miles from Chartres.

Orange. Town in the south of France, fifteen miles north of Avignon.

Panthéon. A building in Paris that serves as a national memorial and mausoleum for France's greatest heroes, including Jean Moulin and Germaine Tillion.

PCF (Parti communiste français). The Soviet-aligned French Communist Party was banished from politics on September 3, 1939, because the Hitler-Stalin Pact made it an ally of Germany. It was made illegal soon thereafter, but it came back somewhat during the early years of Vichy. Once Operation Barbarossa ended the alliance between Hitler and Stalin, the PCF took a full place at the table with other Resistance groups, and it would be a very powerful player in French politics in postwar years.

Phoney War (*la drôle de guerre*). The period between the declaration of war on Nazi Germany by Britain and France (September 3, 1939) and the German attack on Belgium and Holland, followed by the invasion of France (May 10, 1940).

PPF (Parti populaire français). Founded in 1936, the French Popular Party survived until the end of World War II. It was formed by a splinter group that separated from the French Communist Party, and it went on to become France's leading fascist party in 1942–44 under the leadership of Jacques Doriot.

Président du conseil. This office was tantamount to prime minister or president in the French Third Republic, in which the head of government was not elected by popular vote but was designated by a president whose role was simply one of oversight rather than being executive.

Propagandastaffel. The unit of the German Reich's Ministry of Education and Propaganda that was charged with censorship in occupied France.

Radical Socialist Party (Parti républicain, radical, et radical-socialiste). One of the oldest parties in French politics, it is a centrist party that was very strong during the Third Republic. Often referred to simply as the Parti Radical, its name was never reduced to an acronym. It saw itself as particularly attached to rule of law under a secular state (*républicainisme*). It staunchly upheld the right to private property, but it was antimonarchist and anticlerical, so it could, and did, side with either the right or the left in coalitions.

Ravensbrück. A town sixty miles north of Berlin where a Nazi concentration camp for women was situated. Many French women resisters were sent there.

RNP (Rassemblement national populaire). The National People's Rally was one of the major political parties of Vichy; it existed for just three years, from 1941 to 1944. It was collaborationist as well as explicitly racist, but saw itself as Socialist and an advocate of labor. It was led by Marcel Déat.

Sarkozy, Nicolas. A center-right president of France, 2007–12.

Sauckel, Fritz (Ernst Friedrich Christoph Sauckel, 1894–1946). The governor of Thuringia, who was German minister of labor beginning in 1942. Sauckel directed the vast labor recruitment efforts of the Nazi regime, including the management of millions of slave workers.

SD (Sicherheitsdienst). Literally, the Security Service (of the National Socialist Party). By 1940 this intelligence service had been subsumed into the Reichssicherheitshauptamt (RSHA) as one of its seven departments, another one of which was the Gestapo.

SFIO (Section française de l'Internationale ouvrière). The French Section of the Workers' International. A French political party from 1905 until 1969, when it officially became the Parti socialiste. It espoused a more moderate path to redistribution of wealth than the Communists, and saw itself as reformist rather than revolutionary in terms of its methodology. Usually antiwar, it supported the declaration of war on Germany.

SOE (Special Operations Executive). Sometimes called "Churchill's private army," a corps of behind-the-line fighters sent to the Continent by the British to engage in intelligence and sabotage. The French section was headed by Maurice Buckmaster, and French resisters often referred to its operatives as "Buckmasters." Not to be confused with the IS (the Intelligence Service, or MI6).

SOL (Service d'ordre légionnaire). A militia organization within the Légion française des combattants (the French Veterans' Legion), created by Joseph Darnand, head of state security in Vichy.

Spanish Civil War. A conflict between the constitutional Republic of Spain and a rebellious faction within the army from 1936 until 1939. Following the victory of a leftist/anarchist coalition in the polls, army units around the country and in Spanish Morocco revolted. The renegade generals were soon commanded by General Francisco Franco, who became the dictator of Spain until the late 1970s. The fascist powers (Italy and Germany) supported the generals while the western democracies largely abandoned the Spanish Republic, which fought hard but lost the war.

Stalingrad. City in the USSR (Volgograd in today's Russian Federation) on the Volga River, where the Red Army decisively defeated the Sixth German Army in February 1943.

STO (Service du travail obligatoire). Obligatory Work Service was a Vichy program to conscript and send French men and women to work in Germany. The successor of a voluntary 1942 Vichy program called the Relève that was sold to the population as a way to help bring prisoners-of-war home, the STO was decreed into law in February 1943; it ultimately was credited with sending a half-million workers to Germany.

Third Republic. The government of France from 1870 until 1940. Its Constitution was drafted in 1875. Although the Constitution specified that the democratic form of government could not be abrogated by law, the Third Republic ended when a majority in its last Parliament voted full powers to Marshal Pétain following France's defeat by Nazi Germany in June 1940.

Thorez, Paul. One of the top leaders of the French Communist Party before, during, and after World War II. He fled to Moscow during the Phoney War, where he remained for the entire war.

Tillion, Germaine (1907–2008). French anthropologist who became a resister in the summer of 1940, and later joined the musée de l'Homme group along with her mother, Emilie. They worked on the newsletter *Résistance* in the winter of 1940–41. Both women were later arrested and deported to Ravensbrück, where Emilie died in March 1945.

Torch (Operation Torch). The Allied invasion of North Africa, starting on November 8, 1942. One immediate result of this action in France was the Nazis' decision to occupy the southern zone of the country as of November 22, 1942.

Verdun. Town in northern France, scene of one of the bloodiest battles of World War I.

Vichy. Town in central France where the collaborationist government under Marshal Pétain installed itself from June 1940 until September 1944.

Vidon, Maurice. Mayor of Chartres, 1925–29.

Vildé, Boris (1908–1942). French anthropologist at the musée de l'Homme in Paris. The resistance network the Groupe du musée de l'Homme formed around Vildé and Anatole Lewitsky in autumn 1940.

Viollette, Maurice. Mayor of Dreux, 1908–58.

von Ribbentrop, Joachim. A German aristocrat, early confidant of Hitler. He became foreign minister and in August 1939 negotiated a pact of nonaggression with his Soviet counterpart, V. Molotov, which led directly to Germany's invasion of Poland.

Wehrmacht. The old Prussian name for the German Army.

BIBLIOGRAPHY

FRANCE IN WORLD WAR II

Aron, Raymond. *De l'armistice à l'insurrection nationale*. Paris: Gallimard, 1945.

Aron, Robert. *Histoire de l'Épuration*. Vols. 1–3. Paris: Fayard, 1967–75.

Aron, Robert, and Georgette Elgey. *Histoire de Vichy 1940–1944*. Paris, Fayard, 1954.

Aron, Robert, and E. Ganrier-Rizet. *Histoire de la Libération de la France*. Paris, Fayard, 1959.

Azéma, Jean-Pierre. *1940, l'année noire: De la débandade au trauma*. Paris: Fayard, 2010.

Bloch, Marc. *Strange Defeat*. New York: Norton, 1999.

Bracher, Julia, ed. *Riom 1942—Le procès*. Paris: Omnibus, 2002.

Corpet, Oliver, and Claire Paulhan. *Collaboration and Resistance, French Literary Life under the Occupation*. New York: Five Ties, 2009.

Duke, David. *Paris at War*. Cambridge, MA: Harvard University Press, 2015.

Fogg, Shannon. *The Politics of Everyday Life in Vichy France*. New York: Cambridge University Press, 2009.

Glass, Charles. *Americans in Paris*. New York: Harper Collins, 2006.

Jackson, Julian. *The Fall of France*. London: Oxford University Press, 2003.

———. *France: The Dark Years, 1940–1944*. London: Oxford University Press, 2001.

Joly, Laurent. *Vichy dans la "solution finale": Histoire du commissariat général aux Questions juives, 1941–1944*. Paris: Grasset, 2006.

Koestler, Arthur. *Scum of the Earth*. London: Eland, 2006.

Marrus, Michael, and Robert Paxton. *Vichy France and the Jews*. New York: Basic Books, 1981.

Mencherini, Robert. *Provence–Auschwitz, de l'internement des étrangers à la déportation des juifs, 1939–1944*. Aix-en-Provence: Publications de l'Université de Provence, 2007.

Riding, Alan. *And the Show Went On: Cultural Life in Nazi-Occupied Paris*. New York: Knopf, 2010.

Rousso, Henry. *The Vichy Syndrome*. Cambridge, MA: Harvard University Press, 1991.

Ryan, Donna. *The Holocaust & the Jews of Marseille*. Urbana: University of Illinois Press, 1996.

Sadosky, Louis. *Berlin, 1942*. Paris: Centre National de la Recherche Scientifique Editions, 2009.

Sapiro, Gisele. *La Guerre des écrivains, 1940–1953*. Paris: Fayard, 1999.

———. *La Responsabilité de l'écrivain*. Paris: Seuil, 2011.

Shirer, William. *The Collapse of the Third Republic*. New York: Simon and Shuster, 1969.

Spotts, Frederic. *The Shameful Peace: How French Artists and Intellectuals Survived the Nazi Occupation*. New Haven: Yale University Press, 2008.

Vinen, Richard. *The Unfree French: Life under the Occupation*. New Haven, CT: Yale University Press, 2006.

THE RESISTANCE

Aubrac, Lucie. *Outwitting the Gestapo.* Lincoln: University of Nebraska Press, 1993.

Baudouin, Madeleine. *Histoire des Groupes-Francs (MUR) des Bouches du Rhone de septembre 1943 à la Libération.* Paris: Presses Universitaires de France, 1962.

Bénédite, Daniel. *La Filière Marseillaise.* Paris: Clancier-Guénaud, 1984.

Cobb, Matthew. *The Resistance.* New York: Simon and Schuster, 2009.

Cordier, Daniel. *Alias Caracalla.* Paris: Gallimard, 2009.

Frenay, Henri. *La Nuit finira.* Paris: Opera Mundi, 1973.

Fry, Varian. *Surrender on Demand.* New York: Random House, 1945.

Garcin, Jean. *Nous Étions des Terroristes.* Avignon: Barthélemy, 1996.

Gildea, Robert. *Fighters in the Shadows: A New History of the French Resistance.* Cambridge, MA: Harvard University Press, 2015.

Hardy, René. *Derniers mots: Mémoires.* Paris: Fayard, 1984.

Hogenhuis, Anne. *Des Savants dans la Résistance: Boris Vildé et le réseau du Musée de l'Homme.* Paris: Centre National de la Recherche Scientifique Editions, 2009.

Humbert, Agnés. *Notre Guerre: Souvenirs de résistance.* 1946. 2nd ed. Paris: Tallandier, 2006. Trans. Barbara Mellor as *Resistance.* London: Bloomsbury, 2009.

Isenberg, Sheila. *A Hero of Our Own: The Story of Varian Fry.* New York: Random House, 2001.

Kedward, H. R. *Resistance in Vichy France: A Study of Ideas and Motivations.* New York: Oxford University Press, 1978.

Michel, Henri. *Histoire de la Résistance en France, 1940–1944.* Paris: Presses Universitaires de France, 1987.

Ravanel, Serge. *L'Esprit de Résistance.* Paris: Seuil, 1995.

Sémelin, Jacques. *Unarmed against Hitler: Civilian Resistance in Europe 1939–1943.* Westport, CT: Praeger, 1993.

Sweets, John F. *Choices in Vichy, France: The French under Nazi Occupation.* New York: Oxford University Press, 1986.

———. *The Politics of Resistance in France.* DeKalb: Northern Illinois University Press, 1978.

Wieviorka, Olivier. *Histoire de la Résistance.* Paris: Perrin, 2013.

JEAN MOULIN

Assouline, Pierre. "Beneath the Scarf of Jean Moulin." Trans. Ruth Larson. *South Central Review* 25, no. 2 (2008).

Azéma, Jean-Pierre. *Jean Moulin: Le Politique, le Rebelle, le Résistant.* Paris: 2003.

Baynac, Jacques. *Les Secrets de l'affaire Jean Moulin.* Paris: Seuil, 1998.

Belot, Robert, and Gilbert Karpman. *L'Affaire Suisse—La Résistance a-t-elle trahi de Gaulle?* Paris: Armand Colin, 2009.

Benfredj, Charles. *L'Affaire Jean Moulin.* Paris: Albin Michel, 1990.

Clinton, Alan. *Jean Moulin, 1899–1943: The French Resistance and the Republic.* New York: Palgrave, 2002.

Cordier, Daniel. *Jean Moulin: La République des catacombes.* Paris: Gallimard, 1999.

———. *Jean Moulin: L'Inconnu du Panthéon.* 3 vols. Paris: Lattès, 1989–93.

Gelin, Jacques. *L'Affaire Jean Moulin: Trahison ou complot?* Paris: Gallimard, 2013.

Hardy, Rene. *Derniers mots: Mémoires.* Paris: Fayard, 1984.

Marnham, Patrick. *The Death of Jean Moulin: Biography of a Ghost.* London: Murray, 2000.

———. *Resistance and Betrayal: The Death and Life of the Greatest Hero of the French Resistance.* New York: Random House, 2002.

Moulin, Laure. *Jean Moulin.* Paris: Cité, 1982.

Péan, Pierre. *Vies et morts de Jean Moulin.* Paris: Fayard, 1998.

Storck-Cerruty, Marguerite. *J'étais la femme de Jean Moulin.* Paris: Desforges, 1977.

GERMAINE TILLION

Bromberger, Christian, and Tzvetan Todorov. *Germaine Tillion, une ethnographe dans le siecle.* Paris: Actes Sud, 2002.

Tillion, Germaine. *Combats de Guerre et de Paix.* Paris: Seuil, 2007.

———. *Ravensbrück: An Eyewitness Account of a Women's Concentration Camp.* New York: Anchor Books, 1973.

Todorov, Tzvetan. *Germaine Tillion: Fragments de vie.* Paris: Seuil, 2013.

HISTORY AND THEORY

Arendt, Hannah. *Between Past and Future.* New York: Viking, 1951.

———. *Crises of the Republic: Lying in Politics.* New York: Harcourt, 1972.

Cordier, Daniel, with Pierre Ismard. *De l'Histoire à l'histoire.* Paris: Gallimard, 2013.

WEB SITES

AERI (formerly the Association for Studies of the Resistance in the Interior). Online museum: www.aeri-resistance.com/html/musee_virtuel.php. Organization site: www.aeri-resistance.com/index.php

Center for History of the Resistance and of the Deportation (Lyon). www.chrd.lyon.fr/

Jean Garcin Museum. L'Appel de la Liberté, 1935–1945 (Fontaine de Vaucluse). www.vaucluse.fr/culture-et-patrimoine/les-musees-departementaux/le-musee-dhistoire-39–45/

Ministry of Defense Museum of the Resistance. www.cheminsdememoire.gouv.fr/fr/le-musee-de-la-resistance-en-ligne-1940-1945

Jean Moulin/General Leclerc Museum (Paris). museesleclercmoulin.paris.fr/

Resistance Foundation. Online museum: www.museedelaresistanceenligne.org/

INDEX